Also by Terri McGinnis

The Well Cat Book:
The Classic Comprehensive Handbook of Cat Care

Dr. Terri McGinnis's Dog & Cat Good Food Book

RANDOM HOUSE NEW YORK

THE
WELL DOG
BOOK

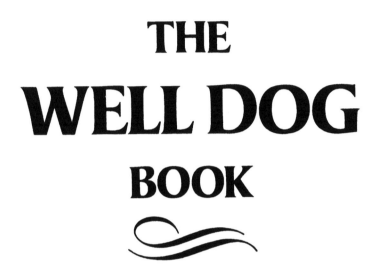

THE CLASSIC COMPREHENSIVE
HANDBOOK OF DOG CARE

Terri McGinnis, D.V.M.

ILLUSTRATED BY PAT STEWART

The information in this book, if followed carefully, will enable you to deal with a
wide range of dog care problems. However, this book is not designed to
substitute for care by a veterinarian, and if you have any questions about whether
the advice or procedures in this book are appropriate for your dog, consult your
veterinarian.

This work was originally published in hardcover by Random House, Inc., in 1991.
It is a revised edition of a work originally published by Random House, Inc., in
1974.

Grateful acknowledgment is made to National Academy Press for permission to
reprint two tables entitled "Minimum Nutrient Requirements of Dogs for Growth
and Maintenance" and "Required Minimum Concentrations of Available Nutrients
in Dog Food Formulated for Growth" from *Nutrient Requirements of Dogs,
Revised 1985* by the National Academy of Sciences; published by National
Academy Press, Washington, D.C. Reprinted by permission.

Library of Congress Cataloging-in-Publication Data
McGinnis, Terri.
The well dog book: the classic, comprehensive handbook of dog care/Terri
McGinnis; illustrated by Pat Stewart.—1st pbk. ed.
p. cm.
Includes indexes.
ISBN 0-679-77001-1
1. Dogs. 2. Dogs—Diseases. 3. Dogs—Health. I. Title.
[SF427.M473 1996]
636.7'0896024—dc20 95-39918

Manufactured in the United States of America

Book design by Lilly Langotsky

Dedication for the First Edition

TO WILDA,
WHO NEVER SAID
"LITTLE GIRLS DON'T GROW UP
TO BE VETERINARIANS."

Dedication for the Second Edition

TO DON GERRARD:
YOU BELIEVED IN YOUR IDEA, YOU BELIEVED IN ME,
AND YOU ALWAYS KEPT YOUR WORD. THANK YOU.

CONTENTS

PREFACE TO THE SECOND EDITION

In the many years since the *The Well Dog Book* was published, veterinary medicine has changed in extraordinary ways. Not only have new illnesses such as Lyme disease (see page 114) and parvovirus infection (see page 90) appeared, but medical procedures once restricted to the diagnosis and treatment of human maladies are now commonplace in veterinary practice. Blood tests, urinalysis, radiographs (X-ray pictures), electrocardiograms, computers, and the most modern anesthetics are used daily in animal hospitals around the world. Sophisticated medical equipment such as endoscopes, ultrasound machines, CAT scanners, and magnetic resonance imaging aid in the diagnosis and treatment of conditions as diverse as foreign objects eaten by puppies, heart ailments, and brain tumors. Veterinarians specializing in diseases of the eye or skin, internal medicine, surgery, neurology, emergency care, or dentistry can be found in most major cities. Nevertheless, the core of veterinary medicine remains the same. This new edition of *The Well Dog Book* reflects these changes in veterinary medicine while still addressing the common problems and concerns of every pet owner.

Although the ability to diagnose and treat disease in dogs is becoming ever more advanced, the dog has basically been unchanged for more than 10,000 years. Despite superficial differences in appearance and behavior between breeds, dogs resemble one another more than they differ, and this book is therefore useful for all types. By learning the basic information contained in this volume and by learning how to use this book as a quick reference, you will be able to be more self-reliant and confident that you are giving your dog the best daily care. The times you will need a veterinarian's help will be reduced, and those instances when a visit to a veterinary hospital is required will become less distressing and mysterious. Everyone should have the pleasure of living with a well dog!

ACKNOWLEDGMENTS

Nearly twenty years ago an astute client asked me about pet care books. Late one night he had found his pet injured, and wanting only to disturb his veterinarian if it was an emergency, he wished he had had a book to consult. Unfortunately, he had had none, and I could not suggest one since I was familiar only with the type of scientific books meant for veterinarians. Thus began the project to write *The Well Dog Book.*

The first edition would not have been published without the insight and support of Don Gerrard, the inquiring client, my editor, and the book's co-publisher. Thanks for help with the original manuscript also goes to George Ahlgren, Ian Dunbar, Nancy Ehrlich, Michael Floyd, the late Jay Fuller, Jim and Sandy Lane, Layton Smith, and Cindy Worland. Dr. Tom Reed was especially important as another veterinarian to consult, as a supportive friend, and as the original illustrator. His drawings, freely given, provide the basis for those found in the second edition.

Successful completion of the second edition rests as much on the shoulders of my excellent editor, Olga Tarnowski, as mine. Thank you very much. Thanks also go to the illustrator, Pat Stewart; the book's designer, Lilly Langotsky; the production editor, Nancy Inglis; the copy editor, Lynn Anderson; and all the other excellent members of the Random House book production staff who worked on *The Well Dog Book.* Dan Johnson, my original editor, thoughtfully and responsibly oversaw the book's initiation and transfer to Olga.

Finally special thanks go to the readers of the original edition, my clients and their pets, the staff, veterinarians, and owner of the Albany Veterinary Clinic, and my friends and family. Many thoughtful readers sent comments and suggestions that have been incorporated into the new edition. Loyal clients and their wonderful pets help keep me up-to-date, remind me what pet owners need, and sustain my practice. Without Dr. Michael Floyd, my original employer and owner of Albany Veterinary Clinic, my practice would be a lot different today and *The Well Dog Book* would never have been written. The clinic staff, and veterinarians take care of the myriad details necessary to provide good veterinary care and to nurture a busy solo veterinarian. If I had to do it all myself, I'd be completely crazy and I would have no time to write. Thank you all tremendously. My family and friends give me the best support of all—love. Thank you, Ted and Jake and everyone else; you know who you are.

INTRODUCING THE WELL DOG

This book is different from other books on dog care because it shows you how to understand the signs of illness or injury your dog may develop and how to evaluate those signs in order to begin proper treatment. In some cases you are advised to seek a veterinarian's help. In others you are advised how you can pursue home treatment. Think of this book as a kind of paramedic's manual for dogs that will enable you to recognize and treat many health problems on your own. It should help save you money that could be wasted on unnecessary veterinary visits.

This book will help you learn to use your veterinarian as a resource. It is intended not as a substitute for visits to the veterinarian, but rather as a supplement to them. Show this book to your veterinarian as a sign that you are interested in taking an active part in maintaining your dog's health.

This book will help you get to know your dog's body better—what about it is normal and what isn't. It will help you understand what your veterinarian is talking about when your dog's health is discussed, enable you to treat some illnesses at home and prevent others, and enable you truly to help your veterinarian get your dog well when the illness is too severe to be treated without professional skills. I've tried to include the basic things I as a dog owner most wanted to know before I became a veterinarian, and I've tried to answer the questions dog owners most often ask me about dog health care. I've tried not to oversimplify things, but in many cases technical information in which I thought the average dog owner would not be interested is not included. Only *common* problems are covered. If you are interested in details on certain subjects, go to some of the references mentioned or ask your veterinarian for titles of books that might help you.

You don't need any specialized equipment to use this book. Your eyes, hands, ears, and nose, as well as an understanding relationship with your dog, are your most important tools. Don't be afraid to use them. There are more similarities between dogs and people than many dog owners realize. As you read, you will probably find out that you know a lot more about "dog medicine" than you think you do.

The best way to use this book is to read it through once from beginning to end. In this way you will learn first what is normal and how to take care of a healthy dog, then the things that can indicate illness and what you should do about them. With this first reading you will find out which sections of the book you would like to read again and which sections you will need to refer to only if a specific problem arises. If you want to use this book to learn about a specific problem your dog may have now, look for the problem in the General Index and in the Index of Signs (To learn how to use these indexes, see page 125.)

Anatomy is the place to begin. With this chapter as a guide, you will become familiar with your dog's body. You may wish to refer back to this section when diagnosing signs as well.

Preventive Medicine is a general health care chapter covering important aspects of the daily life of your dog. It and the following chapter have been designed for easy reference by the frequent use of subheads.

Diagnostic Medicine is the heart of the book. Be sure to read enough of this chapter to understand how it is organized and how to use the Index of Signs. Then, when your dog shows a sign of illness or injury, use this section as a guide to your action.

Home Medical Care tells you the basics of home treatment. It includes general nursing procedures and advice on drugs. Since in most cases of illness or injury your dog will need to have some treatment at home, you may want to become familiar with the information in it before beginning to diagnose signs.

Breeding and Reproduction contains facts about the dog's reproductive cycle. Use it to learn how to prevent or plan pregnancy, how to care for a female before, during, and after birth, and how to care for newborn or orphan puppies.

You, Your Dog, and Your Veterinarian will help you if you don't yet have a veterinarian or are dissatisfied with your present one. Use it to learn what I think are characteristics of good veterinarians and what qualities I think most veterinarians like to see in their clients.

The body always tries to heal itself. This important fact will help your treatment when your dog is sick. In many cases you will not need veterinary aid. Remember, though, that by electing to treat your dog at home, you are taking responsibility for the results. Learn to recognize when the body is losing the battle to heal itself. If you can't be *sure* you are really helping your dog, discuss the problem with a doctor of veterinary medicine. Another caution: Medicine is not always black or white. There are often several equally good ways to approach most health problems. I've recommended the approach that works for me; your veterinarian may disagree and get equal success with other methods. Trust your veterinarian and your own common sense.

THE WELL DOG BOOK

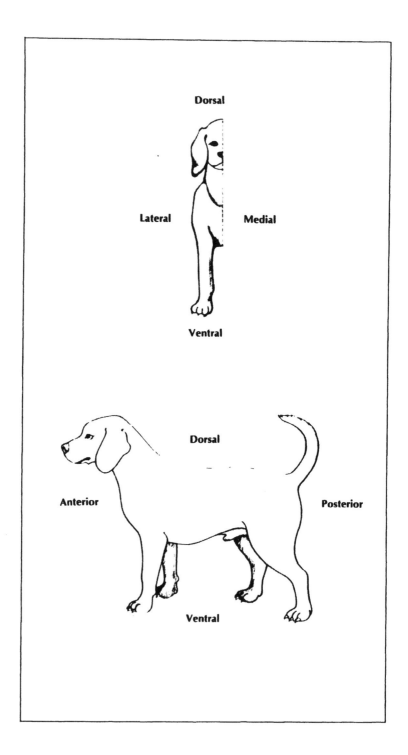

PHYSICAL EXAMINATION

Physical examination consists of applying a knowledge of anatomy in a routine and thorough inspection of all or part of your dog's body. Each person (including every veterinarian) develops his or her own method of giving a physical examination. The best routine to develop is one that prevents you from forgetting to examine any part and one with which you feel most comfortable.

> Example: Examine your dog by systems as set out in this chapter (muscle and bone, digestive system, etc.). Then return to examine miscellaneous items such as eyes, ears, and lymph nodes. Then take the dog's temperature.
> Example: Take the dog's temperature (see page 221). Proceed with examination, starting with the head and working toward the tail. In addition to examining special structures in each area, such as the ears, eyes, mouth, and nose for the head, the toenails and pads for the limbs, don't forget to examine the skin in each area and to look for the lymph nodes associated with each area. Follow up by watching your dog in motion.

Special tools needed for physical examination: A rectal thermometer is the only special tool necessary for performing a routine physical examination of your dog at home. Your other tools are your five senses, particularly the senses of touch, sight, and smell.

Special terms used in physical examination: Except for the anatomical names of body parts, which are mentioned and illustrated in this chapter, there are a few special terms you need to learn to help you with a physical examination. Refer to this page if any of the following words in the text are confusing:

Palpate—to examine with your hand. This is one of your most important methods of physical examination, which is why you are asked to palpate, or feel, parts of your dog's body so frequently throughout this book.

Terms that indicate direction in reference to the body are illustrated on the opposite page.

1

ANATOMY:

Getting to Know Your Dog's Body

**MUSCLE AND BONE
(MUSCULOSKELETAL SYSTEM)**

SKIN (INTEGUMENTARY SYSTEM)

EYES

EARS

**DIGESTIVE SYSTEM
(GASTROINTESTINAL SYSTEM)**

**REPRODUCTIVE AND URINARY ORGANS
(GENITOURINARY SYSTEM)**

RESPIRATORY SYSTEM

**HEART AND BLOOD
(CIRCULATORY SYSTEM)**

LYMPHATIC AND IMMUNE SYSTEMS

NERVOUS AND ENDOCRINE SYSTEMS

Yyou can't do a good job of giving your dog health care at home without some basic knowledge of anatomy and physiology. *Anatomy* is the structure of your dog's body and the relationships among its parts; for example, knowing the location of your dog's eyes and ears and their normal appearance is knowing anatomy. Knowledge of how the parts of your dog's eyes and ears function to enable your dog to see and hear is an example of understanding *physiology*. Although you will be able to examine and understand anatomy, physiology is much more difficult. Brief descriptions of how your dog's various parts work are given here, but it takes intensive study such as your veterinarian has had to understand animal physiology really well.

You will be most concerned with the external anatomy of your dog, but some internal anatomy is included as well since an introduction to it will help you understand your veterinarian more easily when you discuss any health problems your dog may have. The easiest and fastest way for you to become familiar with what you need to know is to get together with your dog and the following pages. Handle your dog as you read the descriptions and look at the drawings. If you have a puppy, you should examine the dog several times as he or she grows. You will see many changes over several months, and the physical contact will bring you closer to each other.

Looking carefully at your dog's anatomy and making your dog sit quietly during an examination are extremely important in preparing yourself and your dog for times when you will have to give health care at home. Also, the maneuvers you go through in examining your dog at home are the same ones your veterinarian uses when giving your dog a physical exam. A dog who has become accustomed to such handling at home is more relaxed and cooperative at the veterinarian's office.

If your dog squirms as you try to carry out an examination, say "No!" sharply and firmly. Be reassuring, and once he or she is still, begin again. Every time the dog wiggles, correct him or her, and every time the dog cooperates, be sure to give a reward of praise and petting. *Do not* give up if your dog squirms away, but don't forceably hold your dog down. It is not too much to ask a dog to stand, sit, or lie calmly to be examined. Gentle but firm restraint, repetitive praise, and correction will achieve the desired cooperation. (Puppies under four or five months of age have shorter attention spans, so limit your exams of them to five minutes or so.) If your dog is very uncooperative or very small, you may find that placing him or her on a smooth-surfaced table will enable you to give a physical exam more easily.

MUSCLE AND BONE
(MUSCULOSKELETAL SYSTEM)

Muscle tissue is composed of contractile units that provide the power for voluntary movement, breathing, blood circulation, digestion, glandular secretion, and excretion of body wastes, as well as many other more minor functions. There are three types of muscle tissue in your dog's body. *Smooth* or *unstriated* is involved in a host of primarily involuntary body functions, such as the peristaltic (wave-like) movements of the digestive tract. *Cardiac* (heart) muscle, which is capable of independent rhythmic contraction, is found *only* in the

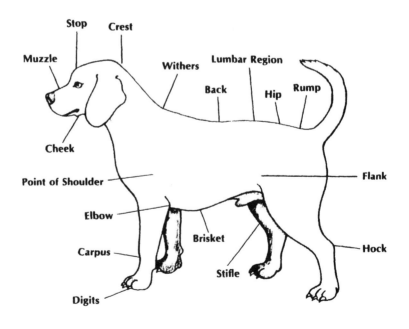

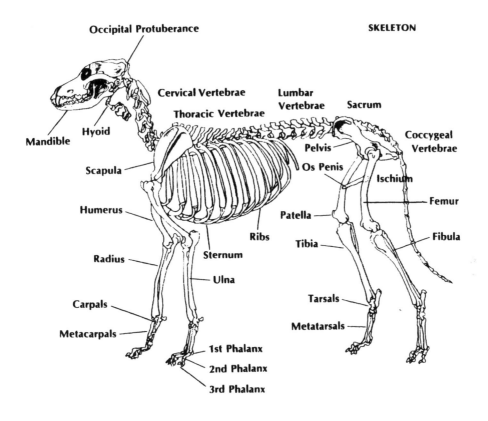

Occipital Protuberance

Cervical Vertebrae

Lumbar Vertebrae

Sacrum

Thoracic Vertebrae

Coccygeal Vertebrae

Mandible

Hyoid

Pelvis

Os Penis

Ischium

Scapula

Femur

Humerus

Patella

Ribs

Tibia

Fibula

Radius

Sternum

Ulna

Carpals

Tarsals

Metatarsals

Metacarpals

1st Phalanx

2nd Phalanx

3rd Phalanx

heart, the pump of the circulatory system. *Skeletal* or *striated* muscle makes up the rest of the muscles in the body, including the diaphragm and certain trunk muscles responsible for breathing. An illustration of the muscles in your dog's body and their names is not included in this book because such knowledge is not important for dog health care at home.

The bone of a living animal is a continually changing and actively metabolizing tissue. It is composed primarily of the minerals calcium and phosphorus in an organic connective tissue framework that is made up mainly of protein. The outstanding physical functions of bone are to form the *skeleton,* which supports and protects the *soft tissues* (organs, muscle, fat) of the body, and to provide levers against which the various skeletal muscles move. The bones have other functions as well: Mineral storage is provided in the hard bone, while fat storage and the formation of blood cells and antibodies (see page 83) take place in the marrow present inside the bones.

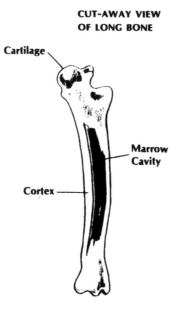

Cartilage

Marrow
Cavity

Cortex

The "average" dog has 321 bones in his or her skeletal structure. Names of bones that might be important to you in understanding your veterinarian are marked on the drawing of the skeleton. See if you can locate each of them with your hands.

Start with the *skull* (head). Thick and thin layers of muscle and connective tissue overlie the bones of the skull. You can feel the thick, paired *temporal* muscles covering the top of the head. Feel the bony area between these muscles and trace it back to its end behind the ears. This hard bump at the end is called the *occipital protuberance* and is a normal part of every dog's skull. It is more prominent in some breeds (e.g., Irish setters) than in others. The *masseter* muscles are another set of easily felt muscles on your dog's head. They form the cheeks and with the temporal and other smaller muscles help close the mouth. The rest of the skull feels very bony; in fact, in very small breeds of dogs you may have difficulty feeling any muscles at all. The *mandible* is the dog's lower jaw. Move this bone by opening and closing your dog's mouth (see page 25).

The skull is attached to the rest of the skeleton by the *cervical vertebrae.* Try to feel these neck bones by moving your fingers firmly over the sides and top of the neck. You will find it difficult to feel the bony structures because of the well-developed muscles that cover the neck. The cervical vertebrae along with the other vertebrae form your dog's *spinal column* (backbone).

The *thoracic vertebrae* start in the area between the edges of the shoulder blades. You can feel the curved upper edge of each *scapula* (shoulder blade) near the middle of the back at the *withers.* Each scapula and the muscles that cover it can be seen and felt to move freely when your dog walks or runs. Unless your dog is fat, you will be able to feel the spines (vertical projections) of the thoracic vertebrae between the shoulder blades. Use your fingers to trace these bones down the center of your dog's back. They become the spines of the *lumbar vertebrae* in the area behind the last rib and disappear near the hip, where several vertebrae are joined to form the *sacrum.* You can feel only the spines of the vertebral bones and not the rest of them because a heavy group of muscles lies on each side of the spinal column. Feel these *epaxial* muscles by running your fingers along each side of the bony spines. If your dog has a tail, you may be able to feel each *coccygeal* (tail) vertebra under its covering muscles.

Now examine each leg, starting with the feet. The "standard dog" has five *digits* (toes) on each front foot. The first is rudimentary and does not touch the ground. It is often removed a few days after birth to meet breed standards, and in working dogs in particular, to avoid tearing caused by snags. On each hind foot, your dog may or may not have a first digit, but it is commonly present in larger breeds. In fact, some, like Great Pyrenees, have two. This variably developed hindpaw digit is called the *dewclaw,* a term that is often inaccurately applied to the forepaw's first digit, which is normally present at birth.

Feel each toe carefully. You will see that it consists of three bones *(phalanges).* These correspond to the bones in your fingers and toes. Each toe is attached to a long bone, which corresponds to the bones that form the palm of your hand and the sole of your foot. These bones are called *metacarpals* in the front feet and *metatarsals* in the rear.

The front foot *(forepaw)* attaches to the *foreleg* (front leg) at the *carpus* (wrist). Flex and extend this joint. If you *palpate* (examine with your hands) carefully, you may be able to feel the individual bones that form this joint. Above the carpus are the long bones of the *foreleg,* the *radius* and *ulna.* These bones are well covered by muscles on the outside *(lateral)* surface except in the region of the elbow. On the *medial* (inside) surface you can feel the radius bone near the wrist. Cup the palm of one hand over the elbow. (For a small dog, place the fingers of one hand over it.) Grasp the foreleg with your other hand and flex and extend the elbow joint. A normal joint moves smoothly, causing no grating or grinding vibrations in your palm. The *humerus* is the bone that forms the foreleg above the elbow. It is well covered with muscles that correspond to those in your upper arm. The humerus is easy to feel at the point of the shoulder; in other areas you will be able to feel it only as a firm structure underlying the muscles.

In the *hindlimb* (rear leg), the foot attaches to the leg at the *hock.* This joint corresponds to your ankle. Flex and extend this joint to learn its normal movement. The fibrous band that attaches prominently on the posterior surface of the hock is the *Achilles tendon.* It is part of a mechanism that causes the hock to flex or extend whenever the *stifle* (knee) is flexed or extended, and vice versa. The *tibia* and *fibula* are the bones that lie between the knee and the

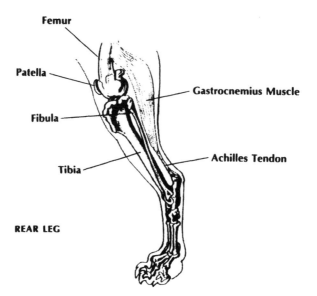

Femur

Patella

Fibula

Tibia

Gastrocnemius Muscle

Achilles Tendon

REAR LEG

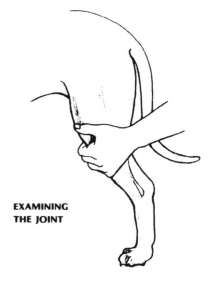

**EXAMINING
THE JOINT**

hock. Muscles cover the lateral surface of these bones, but you can easily feel the tibia on the inside surface of the leg in this area. These bones join with the *femur* to form the stifle joint. The *patella* (kneecap) is also an important part of this joint. Cup the palm of one hand over the patella (for a small dog, place the fingers of one hand over it) and flex and extend the knee joint.

You should be able to feel the patella move freely and smoothly as you manipulate the joint. Now move up the leg to the *thigh*. The femur is the long bone of the thigh. It is well covered by heavy muscles, so you will be unable to feel it except near the knee. Palpate the muscles of the thigh and try to feel the femur under them. The femur *articulates* (forms a joint) with the *pelvis* at the hip. To test this joint, place the palm of your hand against the hip and flex and extend the joint. You can do this with your dog either standing on three legs or lying on one side.

Complete your examination of the musculoskeletal system by running your fingers over the sides of your dog's chest. You should be able to feel each rib easily under a freely movable coat of skin, fat, and muscle. If you can't easily feel the ribs, your dog is too fat. Pick a rib and follow it with your fingers down the side of the *thorax* (chest) to its end. If you have chosen one of the first nine ribs, you will find that it attaches to a bone forming the *ventral* (bottom) surface of the chest. This is the *sternum*. The last four ribs do not attach directly to the sternum.

If you have a male dog, another bone to notice is the *os penis*. This bone is present inside the penis of the male dog. The urethra passes through it. An equivalent structure is not usually present in the clitoris of the female dog.

After you have examined the major parts of your dog's musculoskeletal system (or before, if you like), stand back and look at your dog as a whole. Are the legs straight? Are the wrist joints erect? Are there any unusual lumps or bumps? Some breeds, such as basset hounds and bulldogs, have certain essentially abnormal types of *conformation* (bony and muscular structure) bred into them and seem to function reasonably well in spite of anatomy that would be considered abnormal in other dogs. Most normal dogs, however, are similar in structure to the drawings in this book.

Now watch your dog move. All motion should be free and effortless. Do you see any signs of lameness? If you have any questions about your dog's conformation or gait, be sure to discuss them with your veterinarian.

SKIN (INTEGUMENTARY SYSTEM)

The *integumentary system* consists of the skin and its specialized modifications, the hair, the footpads, claws, and anal sacs. Dogs' skin protects their bodies against environmental changes, trauma, and germs. In the skin, vitamin D is synthesized; below the skin (in the *subcutaneous* tissues), fat is stored. The skin is both an organ of sensation and an organ (via certain skin glands) for waste excretion. Unlike in humans, however, the dog's body skin plays only a minor role in heat regulation. Skin disease is a common problem in dogs, and the condition of your dog's skin can sometimes tell you a great deal about his or her body's general state of health.

If your dog is healthy, his or her skin should be smooth, pliable, and free of large amounts of scales (dandruff), scabs, odorous secretions, and parasites (see page 104). Normal skin color ranges from pale pink through shades of brown to black. Spotted skin is completely normal and may be seen in dogs without spotted coats. The skin (and hair) color comes from a dark-colored pigment called *melanin,* which is produced and stored in special cells in the bottom layers of the *epidermis* (outer skin layer).

Examine your dog's skin carefully. To do this for a long-haired dog, part the fur in several places and look carefully at the skin itself. For a short-haired dog, run the thumb of one hand against the growth direction of the hair to expose the skin. Be sure to examine the skin in several places on the body, on the legs, under the neck, and on the head. Any buglike creatures you see attached to your dog's skin or hair or that quickly move away as you part the hair are *external parasites* and should not be there. They are likely to be ticks (see page 114), lice (see page 115), or fleas (see page 104). Any small salt-and pepperlike black-and-white granules present may be flea eggs and flea feces.

Roll your dog on his or her back to see where the skin forms the nipples of the *mammary glands* (breasts). The mammary glands are skin glands that have become modified for the production of milk. Male as well as female dogs normally have five nipples on each side, although the number may vary from four to six. The prominence of the nipples and mammary glands in the female varies with age and stage of the estrous cycle (see page 241). Examine your dog's mammary glands by feeling the areas between the nipples and a wide area around them. In a normal male or anestrous female (see page 241) you should not be able to feel any lumps or bumps. If you find *any,* discuss their importance with your veterinarian.

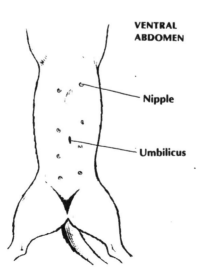

VENTRAL
ABDOMEN

Nipple

Umbilicus

While you are examining the breasts, you may notice a scarlike area of skin on the midline near the area where the chest meets the *abdomen* (belly). This is your dog's *umbilicus* (belly button). If you see a lump in this area, it may be an *umbilical hernia* (see page 267, and decide whether or not you need a veterinarian's help).

The skin over the nose is modified so that its superficial layers are thick and tough. This skin has no glands but is usually moist from nasal secretions and as a result feels cool. A cool moist nose or a warm dry one, however, is not an accurate gauge of your dog's body temperature; use a thermometer! Most dogs' noses are darkly pigmented, but brown to pink or spotted nose color is normal for some dogs.

The skin is also modified to be thick and tough over the footpads. The deepest layer of the footpads is very fatty and acts as a cushion to absorb shock. The middle layer *(dermis)* contains *eccrine* (sweat) *glands;* the only skin glands in the dog equivalent to humans' heat-regulating sweat glands. On warm days you may see your dog leave steamy footprints on the pavements from the watery eccrine gland secretion.

The footpads are named according to which bones they overlie—*digital, meta-carpal* (*metatarsal* on the rear feet), and *carpal* (none on the rear feet). Examine your dog's footpads and learn their names. Knowing the names may help you de-scribe the location of a prob-lem to your veterinarian.

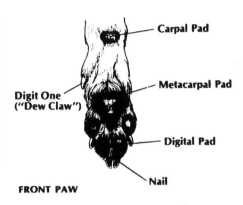

Carpal Pad

Metacarpal Pad

Digit One
("Dew Claw")

Digital Pad

Nail

FRONT PAW

Two unusual modifications of skin are the *anal sacs.* The anal sacs are located internally under the external sphincter muscles of the anus at about the four o'clock and eight o'clock positions. The duct of each sac empties just inside the anus. With some practice, you can feel the full sacs by placing your thumb externally on one side of the anus and your index finger on the other side, then gently moving your fingers up and down. When full, each sac varies from about the size of a pea in very small dogs to the size of a Concord grape in large dogs. The anal sac glands produce a sour to rancid-smelling, watery brownish secretion that may serve to mark your dog's stool like an identification tag. The sacs are often emptied explosively in stressful or frightening situations. Occasionally a dog's anal sacs don't empty properly on their own; then you or your veterinarian must empty them (see page 171).

Claws (toenails) are epidermis specialized for digging and traction. The outer layer of the claw is horny and may be pigmented, partially pigmented, or unpigmented. The inner layer is the *dermis* (quick), which contains many blood vessels and is contiguous with the connective tissue covering the third phalanx. If your dog has light-colored nails, you can see the dermis as a pink area inside the claw when it is held in front of a light. Normal claws just touch the ground, allowing the foot to stand compactly. Excessively long nails cause the foot to *splay* (spread out abnormally) and make walking uncomfortable and the gait unnatural. If some dogs' nails are neglected too long, they grow out, around, and into the digital pads, causing pain and sometimes infection. Be sure to check your dog's toenails now and repeat the examinations frequently to prevent them from becoming too long. (To learn how to cut your dog's toenails properly, see page 57.)

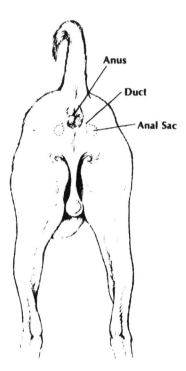

Anus
Duct
Anal Sac

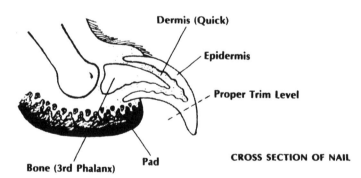

Dermis (Quick)

Epidermis

Proper Trim Level

Bone (3rd Phalanx)   Pad

CROSS SECTION OF NAIL

Dogs have three basic types of hair: guard hairs (primary hairs), fine hairs (secondary hairs), and tactile hairs. *Tactile hairs* (whiskers) grow out of very large sensory hair follicles on the muzzle and chin, at the sides of the face, and over the eyes. Their sensory function may

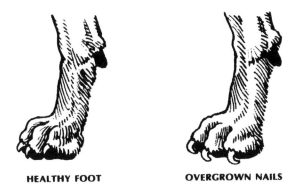

HEALTHY FOOT　　　　**OVERGROWN NAILS**

be of particular importance in helping dogs orient themselves in poor light. Wild *canids,* such as wolves, and domestic dogs with wild-type coats, such as German shepherds, have both guard hairs and fine hairs covering their bodies. *Guard hairs* are the longer, coarser hairs. *Fine hairs* make up the undercoat. They are arranged in bundles that typically contain a group of fine hairs and a single longer coarse hair. In other breeds, one or the other type of hair usually predominates. For example, the boxer has a coat of fine, short secondary hairs. The rottweiler has a coarse coat made up mainly of relatively stiff, short guard hairs. The poodle, on the other hand, has a coarse (woolly), long coat in which extremely modified secondary hairs predominate. Other classifications of hair types in dogs have been made but are unimportant for our purposes. Try to determine which kind of hair your dog has.

All dogs replace their coats continuously. At any one time some hairs are falling out, some are in a resting phase, and others are growing in. You may notice a particular increase in the number of hairs your dog sheds in the spring and again in the fall, but there is no reason to consider that your dog is shedding excessively unless you begin to see bare skin areas developing. Your dog's coat should appear glossy and unbroken. Dark-colored coats usually seem to have more natural sheen, so take this into consideration before judging your dog's coat, especially if it is a light-colored one. After clipping or shaving, the average dog's coat takes three to four months to grow in again completely. Long coats may take more than a year.

EYES

Your dog's eyes are similar in structure and function to your own, although dogs' eyes are more sensitive to movement and less able to perceive detail than those of humans. Light entering the eye passes through the cornea, anterior chamber, pupil, lens, and vitreous body before striking the retina. Specialized cells in the retina (the rods and cones) convert light striking them into nervous signals that pass to the brain via the optic nerve. In dogs these impulses result in an image thought to be perceived primarily in various shades of gray and degrees of brightness. Limited color vision may allow dogs to detect the color blue but prevent discrimination among green, red, yellow, and orange. Located behind the retina is an area of tissue called the *tapetum lucidum*. Its function is to reflect light that has already passed through the rods and cones back to them again, which increases visual acuity in dim light (a selective advantage for animals whose ancestors and relatives hunted at dawn and dusk). It is the structure that causes dogs' eyes to appear to "glow in the dark" when struck by a light in an otherwise dark environment.

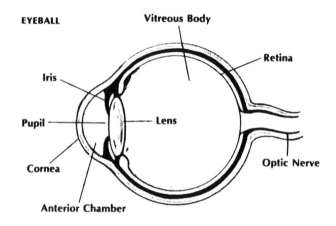

EYEBALL

As you examine your dog's eyes, you will see that each is surrounded by two modified skin folds, the eyelids. The edges of the lids should be smooth, even, and not rolled in *(entropion)* or out *(ectropion)*.

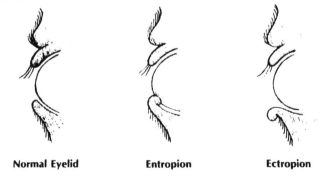

Normal Eyelid   Entropion   Ectropion

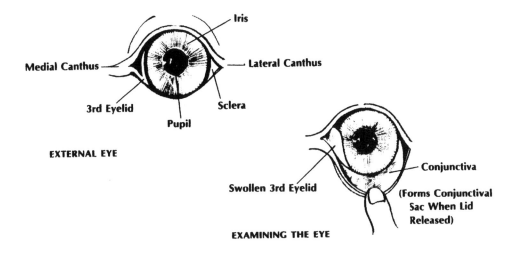

Iris
Medial Canthus
Lateral Canthus
3rd Eyelid
Sclera
Pupil

EXTERNAL EYE

Conjunctiva
Swollen 3rd Eyelid
(Forms Conjunctival
Sac When Lid
Released)

EXAMINING THE EYE

The margin of the upper lid has well-developed eyelashes. Look carefully for lashes that grow abnormally so that they rub against the eye, and look for fine lashes, which may form an abnormal extra row. Such lashes can be very irritating and must often be removed. Between the lids at the *medial canthus* (edge of the eye near the nose) you can see the third eyelid *(nictitating membrane)*. This may be pale pink or pigmented, and its normal position over the eye varies from dog to dog. Roll back the upper or lower eyelid by placing your thumb near its edge and gently pulling upward or downward. This allows you to view the inner lining of the lids, a pale pink mucous membrane called the *conjunctiva*.

The visible part of the eyeball consists of the cornea, bulbar conjunctiva, anterior chamber, iris, and pupil. The *bulbar conjunctiva* is a continuation of the lining of the eyelids. If it contains pigment, the area may look spotted or dark. In unpigmented areas the bulbar conjunctiva is transparent, allowing the eye's white fibrous coat *(sclera)* and the fine blood vessels that traverse it to be seen through it. The cornea should be completely transparent. Through it you can see the anterior chamber, iris and pupil. In most dogs the iris is colored dark to golden brown; however, in some breeds (e.g., Old English sheepdog) it is light blue or spotted. The iris controls the size and shape of the pupil. Along with the eyelids, the pupil controls the amount of light allowed to enter the eye. The pupils should constrict simultaneously in bright light and dilate in dim light. When only one eye is exposed to light or darkness, the pupil of the remaining eye should constrict or dilate when the exposed one does. The pupils of dogs' eyes are normally round in shape; see if your dog's are when you test their response to light.

19

EARS

Whether your dog's ears stand up, partially flop over, or hang completely down, their anatomy is basically the same. The external part of the ear, which you can see when casually looking at your dog, is called the *pinna*. The pinna receives air vibrations and transmits them via the ear canal to the eardrum. If your dog has nonerect ears, you can make them correspond to the illustration by grasping the tip of the pinna and lifting it straight up.

ANATOMY OF THE EAR

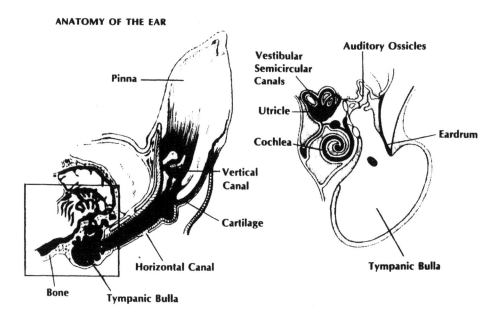

The outside of the pinna is covered with haired skin like that covering the rest of your dog's body. The inside is also partially haired, although the hair here is usually more sparse than that on the outside. Any visible unpigmented skin lining the inside of the pinna and ear canal should be pale pink in color. Bright pink or red is abnormal. All visible parts of the ear should be fairly clean. Normal accumulations consist of a very small amount of clear or brownish to black waxy material. Large amounts of this material, waxy orange material, or sticky, foul-smelling secretions are abnormal. If your dog's ears look normal to you, or if your veterinarian tells you that your dog's ears are normal, smell them. This odor is the smell of a healthy ear. Deviations from this smell may indicate ear trouble even if you can't see any external indication of it.

Notice on the drawing that the ear canal is vertical for a distance, then becomes horizontal before it reaches the eardrum. This makes it impossible for you or your veterinarian to see very deeply into the ear canal without a special instrument called an otoscope. An advantage of this type of ear canal structure is that it allows you to clean quite deeply into the ear canal without fear of damaging the eardrum as long as you clean vertically (see page 55).

The structure and function of your dog's middle and inner ear are very similar to your own. Vibrations reaching the eardrum are transmitted through the middle ear by small bones, the *auditory ossicles,* to the vestibular window. From the vestibular window the vibrations enter the inner ear, where the *cochlea* converts these mechanical stimuli to nervous impulses that travel to the brain via the auditory nerve. In addition to the cochlea, the *semicircular canals* and *utricle* occupy the inner ear. These organs are important in maintaining the dog's sense of balance.

Hearing is present in dogs when the ear canals open at twelve to fourteen days of age. Their hearing range is 67 Hz–45 kHz, which allows them to hear sounds in the upper ranges, which are inaudible to humans, whose hearing range is 64 Hz–23 kHz.

DIGESTIVE SYSTEM (GASTROINTESTINAL SYSTEM)

The digestive system consists of the digestive tube (mouth, pharynx, esophagus, stomach, small and large intestines, and anus) and the associated salivary glands, liver, gall bladder, and pancreas. Few foods necessary for growth, life, and work enter the body in a form that can be absorbed directly by the intestines and put straight to use by the body. Therefore it is the digestive system's function to convert foods to absorbable nutrients, using mechanical and chemical means.

Anatomically you will primarily be concerned with the beginning and end of the gastrointestinal tract—the mouth and the anus. The locations of the other structures are indicated on the drawing of internal anatomy. In most dogs it is difficult to feel the abdominal organs because they tense (contract) their abdominal muscles as you begin to feel for the organs. When your dog's stomach is very full, you may be able to feel its edge as a doughy mass against the left *anterior* (toward the head) part of the abdomen just behind the last rib. Try to feel it, but don't be disappointed if it's not obvious. You may be able to feel your dog's intestines by grasping your dog's

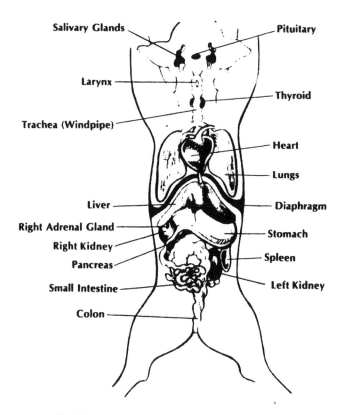

Salivary Glands — Pituitary

Larynx — Thyroid

Trachea (Windpipe) — Heart

— Lungs

Liver — Diaphragm

Right Adrenal Gland — Stomach

Right Kidney —

Pancreas — Spleen

Small Intestine — Left Kidney

Colon —

(urinary bladder not shown)

abdomen between your two hands, pressing your fingers toward one another gently, then moving them downward. The intestines will slip through your fingers like strands of wet spaghetti. If the colon contains feces, you may be able to feel it as an irregularly shaped tube located high in the *posterior* (toward the tail) abdomen parallel to the spine.

MOUTH

Many dogs, especially puppies, are reluctant to have their mouths examined for the first time. Don't give up if your dog squirms or pulls away as you start your examination. Make your intentions clear; be firm yet reassuring. Begin the examination by lifting each upper lip individually with the jaws closed. Use one hand to steady your dog's head, if necessary, while examining with the other. This allows you to examine the *buccal* (outer) surfaces of the teeth and gums.

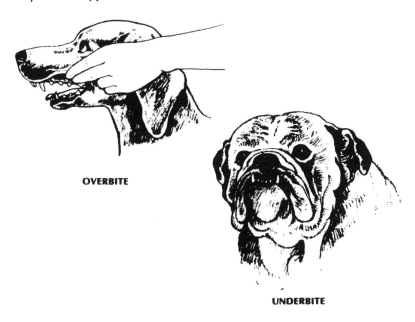

HEALTHY GUMS　　　　　**SEVERE GUM DISEASE**

Healthy gums feel firm and have edges so closely applied to the teeth that they actually look attached to the teeth. They fill the spaces between the teeth, forming a "V" you can see between each upper front tooth and its neighbor and an inverted "V" between each lower tooth and its neighbor. In unpigmented areas, healthy gums are pink. Red gum tissue or a red line along the lower edge (next to the tooth) of pink gums is abnormal, as are very pale pink, yellowish, or white gums. Many normal dogs have black or black-spotted gums.

Dogs' teeth are designed for grasping, tearing, and shredding. In a normal mouth, the upper front teeth (incisors) just overlap the lower ones ("scissors bite"). An excessive overlap (overbite) is abnormal, as is a mouth structure in which the lower front teeth extend beyond the upper ones (underbite).

OVERBITE

UNDERBITE

A mild overbite or underbite doesn't seem to cause functional problems, and an underbite is considered desirable (although it *is* abnormal) for certain breeds such as the bulldog and boxer. Be sure to check your dog's bite. Also check the surface of each tooth. Abnormal tooth placement in young dogs can affect jaw development and the later placement of adult teeth, so any problems you find should be immediately brought to your veterinarian's attention. The tooth surface is white in young dogs and gets yellower as the dog ages. A fingernail scraped along tooth surfaces should pick up little debris. Try it. Any mushy white stuff you may scrape off is called *plaque,* a combination of saliva, bacteria, their by-products, and food debris. This can easily be removed by "brushing" your dog's teeth (see page 58). Hard white, yellow, or brown material is *tartar* or *calculus* (mineralized plaque) and must usually be removed by your veterinarian. Teeth are categorized into four types: incisors (I), canines or cuspids (C), premolars (P), and molars (M).

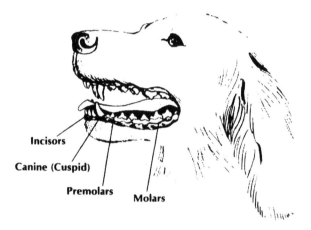

Incisors

Canine (Cuspid)

Premolars   Molars

The average puppy has twenty-eight *deciduous* (baby) teeth arranged in the following manner: Starting at the middle of the front teeth (incisors)

$$\frac{\text{Upper teeth of } \frac{1}{2} \text{ mouth}}{\text{Lower teeth of } \frac{1}{2} \text{ mouth}} = 2(i\frac{3}{3} \quad c\frac{1}{1} \quad p\frac{3}{3}) = 28$$

A puppy has no molars. The appearance of these baby teeth and their replacement by the permanent ones is a convenient way to estimate the age of a young dog (see table, page 27).

The average adult dog has forty-two permanent teeth:

$$\frac{\text{Upper teeth of } \frac{1}{2} \text{ mouth}}{\text{Lower teeth of } \frac{1}{2} \text{ mouth}} = 2(I\frac{3}{3} \quad C\frac{1}{1} \quad P\frac{4}{4} \quad M\frac{2}{3}) = 42$$

Dogs with short faces (*brachycephalic* dogs) often have fewer and/or crowded teeth due to the shortening of their jaws. They get along fine, though, with the teeth they have although they usually require more attention to dental hygiene. Once a dog's permanent teeth have erupted, it is more difficult to use them as a guide to age.

Now examine the inner *(lingual)* surfaces of the teeth, the tongue, and the posterior part of the mouth. To open your dog's mouth, place one hand around the upper part of his or her muzzle and push inward on the upper lips with your fingers and thumb as if you were trying to push them between the teeth. As your dog's mouth starts to open, use the fingers of your other hand to pull open the lower jaw by pushing downward on the lower incisor teeth.

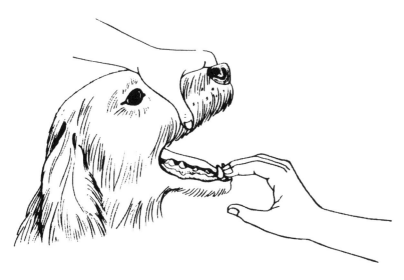

OPENING THE MOUTH

Look inside. You will see the tongue below, the hard palate above, and the inner teeth surfaces. You can use your fingers to push the tongue to one side or the other to look under it. Using the fingers of the same hand you used to open the lower jaw, press down on the posterior half of the tongue. As you press down, try to move the tongue slightly forward. If you do this properly, you will mimic your doctor's use of a tongue depressor on you, allowing you to see the soft palate as a continuation of the hard palate and the palatine tonsils. Dogs' tonsils reside in a pocket (the *tonsilar fossa* or *sinus*), so they aren't easily seen unless they are enlarged. Be very careful when examining the back of a dog's mouth. If there is any significant resistance, withdraw your hand immediately to avoid injury.

PHARYNX

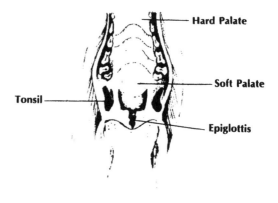

Hard Palate

Soft Palate

Tonsil

Epiglottis

LYMPH NODES

Tonsils are a type of specialized *lymphoid* tissue (containing many special cells called *lymphocytes;* see page 83) similar to your lymph nodes and to lymph nodes located in other parts of your dog's body.

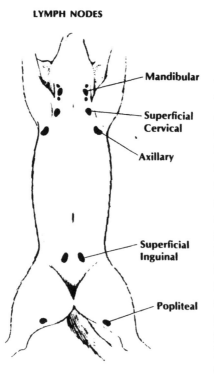

LYMPH NODES

Mandibular

Superficial Cervical

Axillary

Superficial Inguinal

Popliteal

You can feel some lymph nodes of your dog's head in the area below your dog's ear and behind the cheek where the head attaches to the neck. They are small, firm, smooth-surfaced lumps associated with a similar larger lump. The larger lump is one of the dog's several salivary glands, and the only one you will be able to feel. After you feel the normal salivary gland and its associated lymph nodes and become familiar with them, try to feel the other lymph nodes indicated on the drawing. (You may need your veterinarian's help with this.) When you find one, learn its normal size and shape. Lymph node changes (most commonly enlargement) should alert you to have your dog examined by a veterinarian since they are often a sign of serious infection or other illness.

TEETH AS A GUIDE TO YOUR DOG'S AGE

AGE	TEETH PRESENT
Birth	None
3–4 weeks	Deciduous teeth coming in
6 weeks	All deciduous teeth are in
3–5 months	Permanent incisors coming in
5–6 months	Permanent canines start to erupt and by end of 6 months are in
6–7 months	Last molar in lower jaw (M3) is in

Overall health and nutrition, sex, breed, and season of birth affect tooth eruption time. Females' teeth often erupt before those of males, and pups whelped in summer have teeth that erupt before those born in winter. All other factors being equal, teeth of large breeds of dogs tend to erupt more rapidly than those of small breeds. Some dogs, particularly those of small breeds, tend to retain their baby teeth as the adult ones erupt. These teeth have to be removed by a veterinarian when they prevent proper adult tooth placement.

After one year of age, chewing habits, mouth health, and mouth structure make it much more difficult to judge a dog's age by his or her teeth. As a guide:

1½ years	Cusp worn off lower middle incisor
2½ years	Cusp worn off lower incisor next to middle
3½ years	Cusp worn off upper middle incisor
4½ years	Cusp worn off upper incisor next to middle
5½ years	Wear on last incisors
6 years	Canines becoming blunt

YOUNG DOG'S TEETH

Cusp

ANUS

Just about everyone knows that the anus is the specialized terminal portion of the digestive tract through which undigestible material and waste products pass as stool. But some people have questions regarding what constitutes a normal bowel movement. Others are unaware of the anal sacs located in this area.

Most adult dogs have one or two bowel movements daily. The number of bowel movements and the volume of stool passed, however, are very dependent on the amount of undigestible material in the diet. Dogs eating dry food will tend to pass more feces than dogs eating a highly digestible muscle meat, egg, and milk products diet, due to the higher fiber content of dry dog food. Normal stools are well formed and generally colored brown, although some diet ingredients may make them darker (charcoal, liver) or lighter (bones). It takes about two days for ingested food to be completely passed as stool. Extremely large volumes of stool or unformed, particularly odorous or unusually colored stools may indicate digestive tract disease. Be sure to observe your dog's stools several times a week.

Anal sacs have already been discussed (see page 15). If you have not yet examined them, do it now while learning the normal appearance of your dog's anus. You may also want to learn to take your dog's temperature at this time since it should be a routine part of any physical examination and is usually taken rectally in dogs (see page 221).

REPRODUCTIVE AND URINARY ORGANS (GENITOURINARY SYSTEM)

Major portions of the male dog's reproductive system are located externally, where they are fairly easy to examine. The *testes* (organs that produce sperm) are located in the abdomen at birth and should be easy to feel in the *scrotum* (skin pouch) by six weeks of age. Normally there are two testicles present, each of which feels firm, smooth, and relatively oval. If your dog has one or no testicles in his scrotum (unilateral or bilateral *cryptorchidism*), the condition may need veterinary attention (see page 249). If you palpate carefully, you can feel a small lump protruding off the posterior end of each testicle. This is the tail of the *epididymis,* which stores sperm.

There are two ways to examine your dog's penis. First place your fingers on the outside of the *sheath* (skin covering the penis) and feel the penis through it. Near the posterior end you will be able to feel

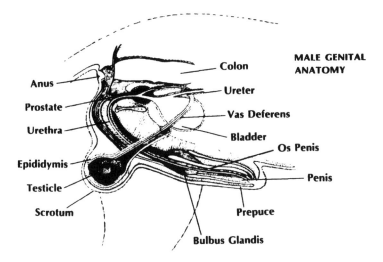

MALE GENITAL ANATOMY

Colon

Anus

Ureter

Prostate

Vas Deferens

Urethra

Bladder

Os Penis

Epididymis

Penis

Testicle

Scrotum

Prepuce

Bulbus Glandis

a slight enlargement. This is the *bulbus glandis*. It becomes engorged with blood during copulation, helping to produce the phenomenon known as the "tie" (see page 252). To examine the surface of the penis itself, grasp the penis firmly through the sheath near the testes and gently push it forward as you use your other hand to push the

HOW TO EXPOSE THE PENIS

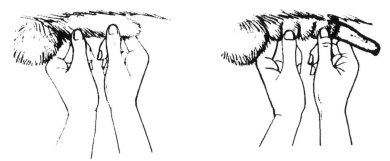

prepuce (sheath) back from the anterior portion of the penis. You can maintain the penis in its fully extruded position by placing your index finger between the penis and the abdominal wall with the folds of the prepuce held behind it. The surface of the penis and the inside of the prepuce are normally pink and relatively smooth. In young dogs any secretions present should be clear. In mature males a small amount of cloudy, yellowish discharge is not unusual.

Sperm are produced in the seminiferous tubules of the testicles. From the testis the sperm travels to the epididymis for storage and maturation. During ejaculation sperm travel through the vas deferens into the urethra, where they are mixed with secretions from the prostate gland before exiting the penis. The prostate is located within the abdomen and can be examined only by rectal palpation. If you would like to try to examine your dog's prostate gland, gently insert your gloved and lubricated index finger into the rectum and move it from side to side. As you pass over the prostate, you will feel two lumps joined together. Learn their normal size for your dog because the prostate size varies between dogs and changes with age.

The vulva and clitoris are the only genitals of the female dog that can be seen externally. The internal portions of the female reproductive tract—uterus, cervix, ovaries, and fallopian tubes—are illustrated here.

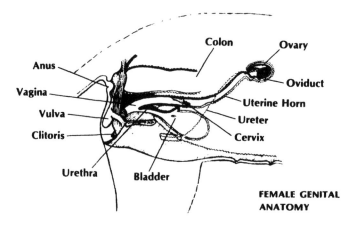

FEMALE GENITAL ANATOMY

The urethra empties into the vagina anterior to a point you can see without special instruments. You can see the clitoris in its fossa by gently pulling the tip of the vulva downward with one hand while spreading the vulvar lips with the other. This also allows you to see some of the lining of the vulva and vagina. These mucous membranes should be pink in color; any secretions present are normally clear unless the female is in heat.

You can find additional information on reproduction in Chapter 5, *Breeding and Reproduction.*

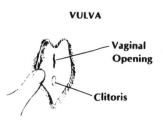

VULVA

The urinary system of both male and female dogs consists of two kidneys, two ureters, the bladder, and the urethra. Look for these organs on the illustrations. *Nephrons* (units of specialized cells) in the kidneys filter the blood to remove toxic metabolic wastes and

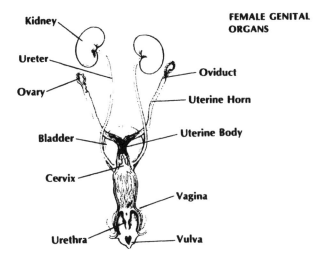

Kidney

Ureter

Ovary

Bladder

Cervix

Urethra

FEMALE GENITAL
ORGANS

Oviduct

Uterine Horn

Uterine Body

Vagina

Vulva

are also important in maintaining the body's proper electrolyte and water balance. Urine formed in the kidneys passes through the ureters to the bladder, where it is stored until it is eliminated through the urethra during urination. If your dog's bladder is full or partially full, you may be able to palpate it through the body wall. Feel for a structure similar to a water-filled balloon in the posterior abdomen. Normal urine is yellow and clear. The intensity of the yellow color generally increases as the amount of water excreted decreases and vice versa. If your dog is small and lean and has a relaxed abdomen, you may be able to feel the kidneys by deep palpation in the lumbar region, but they are more difficult to find than the bladder, so don't be disappointed if you aren't successful.

RESPIRATORY SYSTEM

The dog's respiratory system consists of two lungs, the air passages leading to them (nasal cavity, mouth, pharynx, larynx, trachea, bronchi), the diaphragm, and the muscles of the thorax. The system's main function, as in humans, is to supply oxygen to the body and to remove excess carbon dioxide produced by metabolism. In conjunction with the tongue and the mucous membranes of the mouth, the respiratory system has a secondary, but extremely important, function of heat regulation in the dog, since the dog has no highly developed mechanism for sweating. The nostrils and nasal passages are also important to the dog's well-known sense of smell. For some scents dog's have been shown to be a million times more sensitive at odor detection than humans.

The only parts of your dog's respiratory system you can see are the nostrils and mouth. Special instruments are needed to look into the nasal cavity, and most dogs will not let this area be examined without anesthesia. Look at your dog's nostrils. Any secretions from them should be clear and watery; sticky cloudy, yellowish or greenish, or blood-tinged nasal discharges are abnormal.

You can feel your dog's *larynx* (Adam's apple) by grasping the neck on the undersurface where it meets the head. The larynx feels like a hard, fairly inflexible mass. It helps control the flow of air through the trachea and lungs and is the location of the vocal cords responsible for your dog's bark, whine, or howl.

Notice the character of your dog's respirations at rest and after exercise. A normal dog at rest breathes about ten to thirty times per minute. The movements of the chest are smooth and unstrained. After exercise, of course, the rate is much faster and panting may occur. Changes in the rate and character of a dog's respiration may indicate disease. Be sure to become familiar with your dog's normal breathing at rest, on cool and warm days, and during and after exercise so you can tell when changes have occurred.

HEART AND BLOOD (CIRCULATORY SYSTEM)

Your dog's circulatory system is similar to your own. It consists of a four-chambered heart that serves as a blood pump, arteries that carry blood away from the heart to the capillaries where molecular exchange occurs, and veins that return blood to the heart. There are no direct methods you can use to examine this system. A stethoscope could aid your examination, but one is not necessary to deal with the everyday health problems you may encounter.

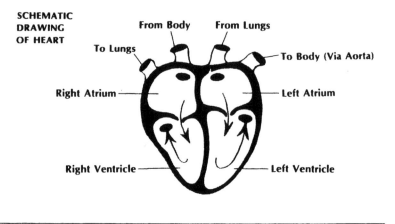

SCHEMATIC DRAWING OF HEART

From Body   From Lungs

To Lungs   To Body (Via Aorta)

Right Atrium   Left Atrium

Right Ventricle   Left Ventricle

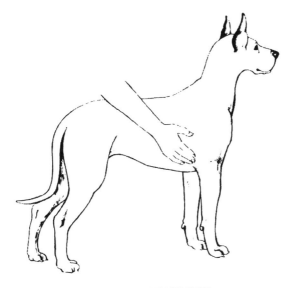

FEELING THE HEART BEAT

In the *resting* dog, the normal heart beats about 80 to 120 times a minute. Small dogs tend to have a more rapid heart rate than large ones. You can feel the heartbeat by placing your fingertips or the palm of your hand against your dog's chest just behind the point of the elbow. Many dogs are small enough for you to place your hand completely around the lower part of the chest with your fingers on one side and your thumb on the other. If your dog is very fat, you may not be able to feel the heartbeat. You can usually hear it, though, by placing your ear (or stethoscope) against the chest over the heart. Each heartbeat consists of a strong, low-pitched thud followed by a less intense, higher-pitched thud, followed by a pause—*lub-dup . . . lub-dup . . . lub-dup.*

To take your dog's pulse, place your fingers at the middle of the inside surface of the rear leg near the point where the leg meets the body. This is the area where the femoral artery passes near the skin, allowing you to feel the pulse. The heart rate and pulse rate should, of course, be the same. You may notice that they go faster and slower as your dog breathes in and out. This normal variation in rate is called *sinus arrhythmia*. It is easiest to count for fifteen seconds, then multiply by four to calculate the rate per minute.

A measure of capillary circulation is *capillary refilling time*. To determine this, press one finger firmly against your dog's gums. When you lift it away, you will see a pale area that should refill with blood almost instantaneously. This measure of circulation can be helpful in evaluating shock (see page 182).

Blood is the fluid transported by the circulatory system. Blood consists of plasma, platelets, red blood cells, and white blood cells. The composition of the liquid portion of the blood, *plasma,* is very complex. It carries nutrients throughout the body, removes wastes, including carbon dioxide, and provides a means of transport for the hormones produced by the endocrine glands, as well as transporting the particulate blood constituents. *Platelets* are produced primarily in the bone marrow of the adult dog. These small bodies help prevent hemorrhage when a blood vessel is injured by aggregating together to form a physical barrier to blood flow and by stimulating clot formation. *Red blood cells* carry oxygen to the tissues and to a much lesser degree transport carbon dioxide away. They give blood its red color. They also determine the dog's *blood group* (type). At least fifteen different blood factors have been identified on dog red blood cells, but only three are important enough to cause problems if incompatible blood is transfused. Ideally, the blood group of both donor and recipient should be known prior to blood transfusions. A veterinarian can have your dog's blood typed in anticipation of an emergency requiring blood transfusion or donation. There are several kinds of *white blood cells,* and each type has a particular function. As a group the white cells are most important in preventing and fighting infection. The red cells and white cells often change in number and in type when a dog becomes sick. The measurement of these cells by means of a *complete blood count* (CBC) is frequently necessary for correct diagnosis and treatment of health problems.

The *spleen* is an abdominal organ that, although not necessary for life, has many functions related to the blood. In the adult it is a site for the production of some white cells and for antibodies, and in times of need it can produce red cells as well. It is a blood reservoir that can supply large numbers of red cells rapidly when the body needs oxygen. The spleen also removes old and abnormal red blood cells from circulation and stores some red cell components, such as iron.

LYMPHATIC AND IMMUNE SYSTEMS

The lymphatic system consists of lymph nodes and a network of thin-walled, permeable lymph channels and collecting ducts distributed throughout the body and associated with localized lymph nodes (see page 26). The lymph nodes filter the tissue fluids (which constantly bathe all body cells), removing foreign particulate matter and returning the fluids and blood cells they may contain to the general circulation via lymphatic channels that eventually empty into the great veins associated with the heart. Through its immune functions the lymphatic system also provides a way for the body to detect, identify, and destroy foreign material that invades it.

Simply put, the immune system processes foreign materials such as viruses, bacteria, other microbes, and environmental proteins through specialized white blood cells. *Neutrophils,* produced in the bone marrow and normally suspended in blood, can migrate quickly to the site of an infection to destroy and engulf some foreign materials and microbes. *Macrophages* can engulf invaders not destroyed by neutrophils and signal other cells in the immune system to respond. Two types of *lymphocytes, T cells* and *B cells,* play central roles in the immune process. These cells are distributed throughout the body but are found aggregated in the lymph nodes, bone marrow, and spleen.

T cells arise in the fetal bone marrow and must be processed in the thymus gland to become functional. They play a major role in the body's ability to recognize itself and are, therefore, important in eliminating cancer cells and infectious agents. They also play a major role in graft rejection and in certain allergic responses. T cells elaborate complex protein substances that act on other cells in the immune process in a wide range of biological activities.

B lymphocytes mature in the bone marrow, which serves as a continuing source of this kind of cell throughout life. B cells are activated to produce proteins called *antibodies* that are very specific for the *antigens* (proteins identified as foreign) that provoke them. They can produce their antibodies only with the aid of specific T cells (called *helper* T cells) acting together with specific stimulated macrophages that present the antigen to both the T and B lymphocytes. As time passes, the immunostimulated B lymphocytes differentiate into *plasma cells,* which are short-lived but capable of producing large quantities of antibodies, and long-lived *memory* B cells. These memory cells retain the ability to respond rapidly with antibody production specific for the same invader should reexposure occur.

Although you will not be able to detect most parts of the immune system during your physical exam, its normal daily functioning is vital to your dog's daily health. (For information on how the immune system affects preventive vaccination of your pet, see page 82.)

NERVOUS AND ENDOCRINE SYSTEMS

The integration of the functions of the various parts of the body is the function of the nervous system and endocrine system. You cannot normally see or feel any of the components of these systems when you examine your dog. Nonetheless, if one system or the other is functioning abnormally, some striking change will usually occur in your animal before long. In general, the *nervous system* (brain, spinal cord, and peripheral nerves) is responsible for rapid body adjustments to environmental and internal stimuli. The *endocrine system,* for the most part, is responsible for more gradual responses that are mediated by chemical substances *(hormones)* secreted by endocrine glands into the bloodstream, tissue fluids, and lymph system in response to other stimuli.

Complete neurological and endocrine examinations are not a routine part of your veterinarian's physical exam. (A brief outline of the function of the various endocrine glands can be found below.)

ENDOCRINE GLAND	FUNCTION
Adrenal glands	*Cortex:* Influences fat, carbohydrate, protein, and electrolyte metabolism. Affects water excretion and blood pressure; stimulates stomach-acid secretion; inhibits inflammation and the immune system. *Medulla:* Secretes adrenaline and noradrenaline, which raise blood sugar and help adaptation to stress.
Enteroendocrine cells of digestive tract	Secrete various hormones that regulate digestive tract motility and secretion of digestive enzymes. Some control over insulin secretion and the regulation of satiety.

ENDOCRINE GLAND	FUNCTION
Heart	*Atrial natriuretic peptide:* affects sodium and water balance
Islet cells of pancreas	Secrete insulin, amylin, and glucagon, which affect blood sugar level, fat and protein metabolism. Insulin also stimulates the appetite at the brain hypothalamus level.
Kidney	*Renin:* Affects blood pressure and sodium balance. *Erythropoietin:* Enhances red cell production.
Ovaries	Influence development of feminine characteristics; influence sexual behavior, estrus, and pregnancy.
Parathyroid glands	Influence calcium and phosphorus metabolism.
Pineal body	Affects sexual development and sexual cycles by sensing photoperiods.
Pituitary–hypothalamus	Regulates the activity of the ovaries, testes, thyroid, and adrenal cortex. Secretes growth hormone, which stimulates growth of body tissues. Controls milk secretion and milk letdown. Affects body water balance and thermoregulation. May modulate both short- and long-term memory.
Testes	Influence development of masculine characteristics; influence sex drive.
Thyroid	Controls metabolic rate and affects calcium and phosphorus metabolism.

Look at the drawings of the internal anatomy to see where these various glands are located. For detailed information about these glands and other parts of your dog's anatomy and physiology, you may want to consult the following books:

Cunningham, James G., *Textbook of Veterinary Physiology*, W. B. Saunders Company, Philadelphia, 1992.

Evans, H. E., and G. C. Christensen, *Miller's Anatomy of the Dog*, W. B. Saunders Company, Philadelphia, 1979.

Swenson, Melvin J., ed., *Duke's Physiology of Domestic Animals*, Cornell University Press, Ithaca, New York, 10th ed., 1984.

Don't be surprised if your first examination of your dog takes an hour or two. If you have a puppy, it may take a full day to complete the exam because you may have to divide it into several parts separated by rest periods to compensate for a puppy's short attention span. Repeat your physical examination at least once a week while you are learning what is normal for your dog. By doing this, you will train your dog to cooperate and you will soon find that you no longer need to refer to this book so often. The time it takes for you to perform the examination will shorten considerably as you practice. You should eventually be able to finish it in about fifteen minutes. Most veterinarians become so skilled at physical examination that, until you become aware of what they are doing by reading this book, you may not even realize a physical examination is being performed. Your veterinarian may easily perform a routine physical in five or ten minutes. Special examinations, of course, take much longer.

Once you are familiar with your dog's anatomy, how frequently you repeat certain parts of a physical examination will vary. You can get a good idea of your dog's general health and of the health of his or her muscles and bones daily by just being aware of his or her appetite and activity. Be sure to examine the ears, eyes, teeth, skin, and nails at least once every two weeks. And examine the mammary glands of females, in particular, on a monthly basis. If your dog lives outside, you will probably have to make more a conscious effort to do the examinations than if you live together inside. If you leave your dog before it is light and return after dark, be sure to set aside time several times a week to study your dog's general condition.

2

PREVENTIVE MEDICINE:

How to Care for a Healthy Dog

TRAINING

GROOMING

NUTRITION

TRAVELING WITH OR SHIPPING YOUR DOG

BOARDING YOUR DOG

PREVENTIVE VACCINATION PROCEDURES

INTERNAL AND EXTERNAL PARASITES

THE VALUE OF PREVENTIVE MEDICINE

PREVENTIVE MEDICINE CALENDAR

Daily: Feed a balanced diet (see page 60).
Groom dog as demanded by coat type and dog's habits (see page 53).
Observe dog's general external appearance, attitude, activity, and appetite. Any change may indicate a need for a complete physical examination.
Remove stool from yard or kennel, observe stool, and, if possible, also observe the urine.
Clean teeth, if necessary (see page 58).

Weekly: Examine for external parasites and treat as necessary (see pages 91–121).
Examine ears (see page 55).
Clean teeth if necessary (see page 58).
Bathe, if necessary (see page 52).

Every two weeks: Check toenail length and appearance and trim, if necessary (see page 56).
Examine teeth if weekly cleaning is not necessary (see page 22).
Bathe, if necessary (see page 52).

Monthly: Examine mammary glands (see page 14).
Bathe, if necessary (see page 52).
Weigh

Every six months: Perform a complete physical examination if one has not been indicated earlier.
Take a fecal sample to a veterinarian, particularly if there is an internal parasite problem in your area (see page 92).
Take your dog to a veterinarian for a heartworm check if you live in a problem area (see page 102).

Yearly: Take your dog to a veterinarian for a physical examination and booster vaccinations as necessary (see page 82).

Preventive medicine is the best kind of medicine. Veterinarians practice it when they vaccinate your dog for certain communicable diseases (see page 82). You practice it by giving your dog good regular care at home as discussed in this section. If you practice preventive medicine, the occasions when your dog will need the care of a veterinarian can often be limited to yearly physical examinations and booster vaccinations. In the long run, preventive medicine will save you money and result in fewer stresses on your dog's body.

TRAINING

Unless you want to mold your life around your dog's, you need to devote some time to training. There are dogs who only occasionally let their owners pick them up without attempting (often successfully) to bite. Many other dogs will not let their owners medicate or bathe them when necessary. These are examples of unhealthy dog-people relationships that can be avoided by acquiring some basic knowledge of dog behavior and obedience training. The illustrations and text that follow will give you some understanding of the ways dogs use body language to communicate.

The dog's mouth may be open or closed. A dog in this stance is just calmly observing things in the environment. **NEUTRAL POSTURE**

The dog's mouth may be open or closed depending upon his or her excitement level and the environmental temperature. Although the *hackles* (hair along the shoulders and back) are usually down, dogs may raise them slightly as they become alert without having an aggressive intent. A dog in the alert position has taken note of an object or creature of interest and is focusing his or her attention on it. **ALERT POSTURE**

OFFENSIVE THREAT POSTURE In dogs without hairy faces, a wrinkled nose may be seen as the dog bares his or her teeth in this posture. All the hackles are raised, growling may be heard, and the tail is always held upright although *it may be wagging.* A dog in this stance is ready to attack. Many people misinterpret this posture if the tail is wagging, and they are bitten when they approach the dog. The proper human response to this posture depends upon the situation. Avoid looking in this dog's eyes and/or stepping toward the dog unless you are willing to risk a severe attack. A show of dominance is needed when a pet exhibits this behavior to family members.

DEFENSIVE THREAT This posture is often misinterpreted as aggression. Although the dog may be growling and snarling, the ears are laid back (a sign of submission in normal dogs) and the tail is hanging down or is slightly tucked under the body. Dogs exhibiting this body language are frightened and need reassurance, but if they are approached without having a way to escape, they will often bite.

GREETING Greeting dogs have relaxed faces with open mouths and loosely pulled back ears, and they wag their tails on a relatively horizontal plane. Dogs exhibiting this body language say a friendly hello by jumping on and licking one another; they prefer to greet people this way as well. People sometimes misinterpret this exuberant body language as aggressive behavior. Rarely, dogs learn to greet people with a *smile,* when the upper lip is briefly pulled back exposing the incisor and canine teeth. This expression is never exhibited to other dogs as a friendly greeting and is often misinterpreted as aggression by people who are not attentive to the dog's accompanying body language.

PLAY INVITATION The lowering of the front part of the body while keeping the rear end raised (the play *bow*) is done only when a dog is inviting play. Although the dog may bark, he or she does not growl aggressively (some dogs learn a nonthreatening play growl). Running around may be interspersed with the bowing and barking.

SUBMISSION Submissive dogs get as low to the ground and as compact as possible. The ears are drawn back and the tail is tucked tightly under the body. The dog may lie completely flat on the ground or roll over to expose the vulnerable underside as he or she would to another more dominant dog. Submissive dogs draw the corners of their mouths back but keep their mouths closed so their teeth are not exposed. This is called a submissive *grin* and is exhibited to other more dominant individuals whether they are dogs or people. Some submissive dogs urinate (see page 50). Since only a small part of this book is devoted to understanding your dog's behavior, however, and modifying it when necessary, you may find the following books useful:

Dunbar, Ian, *Dog Behavior,* TFH Publications, Inc., Neptune, N.J., 1989.

Fox, Michael W., *Behavior of Wolves, Dogs and Related Canids,* Harper and Row, New York, 1971.

———*Superdog: Raising the Perfect Canine Companion,* Howell Book House, New York, 1990.

———*Understanding Your Dog,* St. Martin's Press, New York, 1992.

Hart, Benjamin, *Behavior of Domestic Animals,* W. H. Freeman, San Francisco, New York, 1985.

———*The Perfect Puppy: How to Choose Your Dog by Its Behavior,* W. H. Freeman, New York, San Francisco 1988.

Monks of New Skete, *The Art of Raising a Puppy,* Little, Brown, Boston, 1991.

NEUTRAL POSTURE

ALERT POSTURE

OFFENSIVE THREAT POSTURE

43

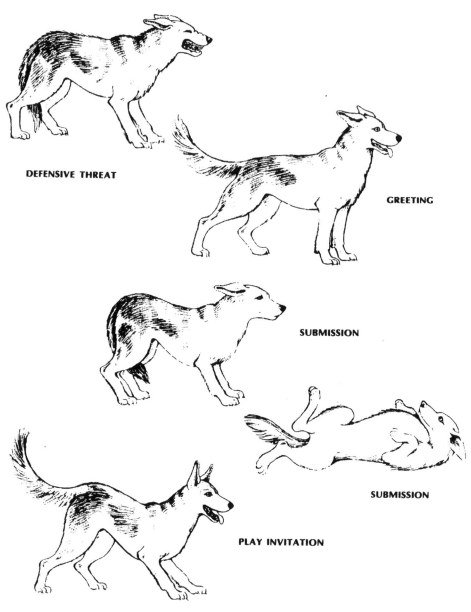

DEFENSIVE THREAT

GREETING

SUBMISSION

SUBMISSION

PLAY INVITATION

AGE TO GET A PUPPY

If you have a choice, the ideal time to bring home a new puppy is when it is between six and eight weeks of age. This is a dog's optimum period for socialization to people. If, before six weeks of age, a puppy is kept in an environment where there are no other dogs, he or she may not become properly socialized to other dogs. This can result in excessive fear of or aggression toward other dogs later in life, abnormal sexual behavior (e.g., inability to breed), or other dog-related behavioral problems. If a dog does not have close contact with people before eight to twelve weeks of age, he or she may never form a close bond with humans. Such dogs are often difficult to train and are also often the ones people find unsatisfying as companions. Of course, there are exceptions to these generalities, but if you have a choice, you might as well start out with the best possible base for a long-term relationship.

PUNISHMENT

Once you have your dog, you may more easily establish and maintain a good relationship if you remember that a domestic dog's behavior in many ways parallels that of wild pack canids such as wolves. Both form dominant-subordinate relationships easily. The dominant dog in a group (wolf in a pack) metes out fair punishment as necessary to maintain his position and the cohesiveness of the group. If you don't assert yourself as the dominant member of your dog-human "pack," your dog will.

In most cases *physical punishment is necessary to maintain your position only until your dog learns the meaning of the word "no."* Once learned, this word alone is usually sufficient correction. To teach your dog the meaning of "No!" voice the command firmly in a serious tone of voice each time you show him or her that certain behavior is unacceptable. Punishment can consist of picking your dog up by the scruff and giving a shake or holding the head or muzzle and pushing it to the ground.

These methods mimic the dominant behavior of some wild canids. It is not necessary or advisable to shout as it is important for the dog to learn to respond to corrections given at normal speaking volume. Corrective measures such as striking a dog with your hand or even a rolled-up newspaper are not recommended and, if used, often cause dogs to become hand shy.

OBEDIENCE TRAINING

A chain-link training collar (choke collar) is also an acceptable method of correction. A sharp jerk on the collar is administered at the time the word "no" is spoken, then the collar is immediately loosened. If used properly, a choke collar is a humane and invaluable aid to obedience training. Used improperly, it is ineffective and can be very confusing to the dog. Halter-type training muzzles have also been used successfully to help a dog learn basic obedience commands. If you have never obedience-trained a dog before, it is best for you and your dog to attend dog obedience classes together. In such classes, your dog is exposed to other dogs and other people, and you are shown how to train your dog properly. In some areas there are no such classes available; you may have to resort to books for information on obedience training. The following should be helpful:

Bohnenkamp, Gwen, *Manners for the Modern Dog,* Perfect Paws, P.O. Box 885214, San Francisco, CA 94188

Burnham, Patricia, *Playtraining Your Dog,* St. Martin's Press, New York, 1985.

Dunbar, Ian. *How to Teach an Old Dog New Tricks,* James and Kenneth Publishers, 2140 Shattuck Avenue, No. 2406, Berkeley, CA 94704.

Dunbar, Ian, and Gwen Bohnenkamp, Behavior Booklet Series, available from James and Kenneth Publishers, 2140 Shattuck Avenue, No. 2406, Berkeley, CA 94704. They include: *Preventing Aggression (Biting), Housetraining Supplement, Barking, Chewing, Digging, Shyness/Fearfulness toward People, Socialization with Dogs.* Also available from the same source is an excellent introductory puppy training video: *Sirius Puppy Training Video.*

Monks of New Skete, *How to Be Your Dog's Best Friend: A Training Manual for Dog Owners,* Little, Brown, Boston, 1978.

Strickland, Winifred, *Expert Obedience Training: Dog Obedience for Instructors,* 2nd ed., Macmillan, New York, 1987.

PICKING UP BY SCRUFF OF NECK

PUSHING NOSE DOWN FOR PUNISHMENT

IMPORTANCE OF PRAISE

Praise is even more important than punishment in helping a dog develop into a good friend. Every desirable behavior you observe in your dog should be rewarded *immediately* by praise administered in a warm, loving tone of voice. Physical praise in the form of stroking and petting is useful when coupled with the words "good dog" or other terms of approval. If punishment has been administered to stop a behavior, you must tell your dog how good he or she is *soon* after the undesirable act stops and a new, more desirable activity begins. Even better, try to motivate your dog as much as possible without punishment by consistently recognizing and praising appropriate behaviors. If you reward your dog in appropriate situations, he or she will be encouraged to behave in ways that consistently please you, and being a "good" dog will become second nature.

WHEN TO START TRAINING

The establishment of a workable relationship between you and your dog should begin as soon as you bring a dog home. Every dog-human interaction is a chance to mold the dog's character. *All* dogs have the potential to bite, bark inappropriately, eliminate indoors, and be destructive, as these are all normal dog behaviors. To guarantee that your dog will not engage in behaviors humans find undesirable, you must make a consistent effort. Training your dog to respond to simple commands such as "Sit!" and "Come" can begin as early as six weeks of age if you are not too severe, avoid confusion, and limit the training session to short periods (five or ten minutes) two or three times a day. Formal obedience classes should be avoided until your dog finishes his or her vaccinations. However, puppy training classes provide an excellent way to socialize young dogs to one another and to new people. They also provide a structured environment for dog owners to learn and practice their dog-training skills. Most veterinary clinics can provide dog owners with good information about quality puppy classes offered locally.

VALUE OF FOOD REWARDS

Food rewards are an acceptable way to encourage a dog to be attentive to his or her owner and a useful form of positive reinforcement. Food rewards are best used only as an immediate reinforcer for following a command rather than as a general form of praise for good behavior. Food rewards should always be linked with verbal praise and should never be used as a sole means of positive reinforcement since the final goal is to have a dog that responds to a command whether or not a food reward is available.

GIVE YOUR DOG A PLACE OF HIS OR HER OWN

If you don't want to share your bed with your dog, provide a place of his or her own the first night you have your dog home. An adult dog can be given an area indoors or, if he or she is used to being outside, a doghouse in the yard or in a run. If your dog is a puppy, barricade a corner of a room or get a large box or traveling crate (cage) and place your dog's bed in it. Cover the remaining area with a layer of clean newspapers. Puppies should be kept indoors and gradually acclimatized to the outdoors. Unless they have been raised outdoors since birth, most can't adjust easily to the temperature stresses encountered outdoors.

At bedtime, take your dog outside to urinate and defecate, then place him or her in the bed area. After you assure yourself that your dog is warm and comfortable, leave him or her in this area. The first time you do this, your dog will probably cry. When this happens, say "No!" seriously and firmly, be sure the dog is comfortable, and as soon as quiet reigns, give praise and leave the dog alone. This series of events may have to be repeated several times, and there is a point where you may just have to ignore the crying. *Don't give in.* Generally, after a few times the dog will fall asleep. Even if your dog cries frequently the first couple of nights, the lack of sleep and emotional stress of hearing your dog cry is worth it in the long run. It is a good idea to leave your dog in his or her special area any time you have to leave him or her alone, and also at other times when you are home but it is inconvenient to have a dog loose. If you are consistent, your dog will soon regard the area as a refuge or "den." This method is also useful to achieve early housebreaking. However, it is important for socialization, adjustment to the rest of the house, and normal physical development not to keep a dog confined most of the time. Confinement should never be used as a form of discipline or punishment if you want your dog to accept it willingly.

HOUSETRAINING

Housetraining (housebreaking) consists of repeatedly showing your dog the proper place to eliminate, giving praise when he or she uses it, and administering a reprimand when he or she doesn't. If at all possible, a puppy will not urinate or defecate in his or her bed. By restricting your dog's freedom at night and when you must leave the dog alone, you encourage retention of urine and feces as long as possible. If the dog has to go, elimination will be confined to the newspaper used to line the confinement area, making cleanup much easier. The learning process is probably easier for your dog if you housetrain directly to the outdoors, using papers only as an emergency measure during the night or when the dog must be left alone and unsupervised for several hours. (Dogs living in high-rise apartments can be trained to a particular newspaper-lined area or to a litter pan using the same principles as those for outdoor training.) With time your dog will progress from regarding only a small area as a den to regarding your whole house as a den and will then be inhibited from eliminating indoors. Fundamentals that make housetraining easier:

1. Take your puppy out when he or she awakens, not only first thing in the morning but after naps as well.

2. *Do not* send your puppy out alone. Go with the dog and stay out until he or she eliminates so you can give praise for the right behavior performed in the right place at the right time. *This is the single most important aspect of housetraining.*

3. Take the dog out about twenty minutes after eating. The *gastrocolic reflex* stimulates most dogs to defecate about this long after eating or playing. Until a dog is housetrained, a portion-controlled feeding method instead of free access to food will give you a better chance to predict when defecation will occur.

4. Give your puppy the last meal of the day early in the evening and take the dog out before bed. It is best to have water available at all times for your dog, but while you are housetraining, it may be removed at night.

5. Never leave an unhousetrained dog to roam free in the house. Opportunities to eliminate "behind your back" will seriously slow the housetraining process. Unsupervised pups should be confined to their dog crates or "den" areas.

6. Punish your dog only when you actually catch elimination in the wrong place. If possible, snatch the dog up in the middle of the act with a "No!" and get the pup to finish outdoors in the appropriate toilet area so you can then give praise. Punishment for elimination errors administered several hours after the act is not very effective.

Most dogs cannot be housebroken before about twelve weeks of age. No dog should be expected to remain continent for more than about eight hours (although many can), and many dogs are unable to pass a full night without elimination until they are five to six months old. If you can provide your dog access to an enclosed yard through a "dog door," you may solve the housetraining problem more quickly. However, failure to accompany the dog outside to the appropriate dog toilet area can easily result in a dog that eliminates indiscriminately outdoors in undesirable locations.

SUBMISSIVE URINATION

Submissive urination is often confused with failure of housetraining. This behavior occurs when a subordinate *normal* dog urinates in the presence of a more dominant individual. In certain pups the mere presence of the owner standing overhead elicits submissive urination, just as would the presence of an adult dog standing over the pup. This type of urination should *never* be punished, as this will only aggravate the situation. It is best to ignore the behavior and avoid situations that elicit it such as hearty greetings on arriving home. Kneeling to interact with a very submissive dog will also help avoid the standing-above posture that is a primary stimulus for submissive urination. With maturation most pups outgrow this type of urination providing it is not aggravated by inappropriate punishment.

CHEWING

Puppies investigate their environment by sight, smell, hearing, and *chewing.* It's reasonable to punish your dog for chewing on forbidden things, but unreasonable to expect no chewing at all. Provide your dog with acceptable things to chew on—rawhide toys, large hard rubber toys—and give lots of praise when the toys are used. Never give your dog objects that can easily be torn into pieces or are small enough to be swallowed (even with difficulty). I have seen several small rubber balls, pieces of carpeting, parts of a tennis shoe, and other objects removed from dogs' digestive tracts. One veterinarian has removed a large mechanical monkey from a relatively small dog's stomach, another pulled out an entire plastic troll doll, and one veterinary journal article described a dog that had swallowed a large carving knife whole! Avoid giving your dog objects such as old shoes or socks to chew on; they are too easily confused with possessions you don't want chewed.

BONES

Bones for chewing have their pros and cons. They satisfy a dog's chewing urge and help keep the teeth clean, but too much bone chewing can lead to excessively worn teeth and dogs sometimes break their teeth when chewing on bones. Bones that get eaten rather than just chewed on are a common cause of *gastritis* ("stomach-ache," see page 164) and constipation. If you choose to give your dog bones, they should be large enough and hard enough that they can't be eaten. Beef marrow bones or knucklebones are usually the best choices unless your dog is very small. It is best to parboil or roast these bones before allowing your dog to chew on them to avoid the transmission of parasites. Don't give poultry bones, pork bones, steak bones, or other bones that can be splintered. If you see that your dog is *eating* a bone, take it away. More than one dog has died from a gut perforation caused by a sharp bone splinter. Others have ended up with esophageal obstruction caused by swallowing a bone.

KNUCKLE BONE

MARROW BONE

ROAMING

Although dogs resemble wild canids in many ways, keep in mind that they are *domesticated* animals with very different needs than those of their wild counterparts. One of the outstanding characteristics of most dogs, particularly when they are young, is their adaptability. Some dogs have a greater need for activity than others, but no dog has an innate need to run free. If you let your dog run free while young, he or she will adapt to and expect this condition, but if you restrict roaming, he or she will adapt as readily to this situation. Most dogs' needs for activity can be met by taking them for short walks two or three times a day, through goal-directed play periods such as ball chasing, obedience lessons, or free access to an enclosed yard with a companion—you, another dog, or a cat. City dogs should not be allowed to run the streets unsupervised. Not only do most cities have laws prohibiting this, but roaming city dogs are among those who are injured or become ill most often. They are exposed to communicable diseases as they make their territorial rounds; they are hit by cars; they are poisoned; they get in dog fights much more often than dogs accompanied by their owners. You are doing a city dog a great disservice if you allow unsupervised roaming. If you live in a rural area away from automobile traffic, it may be safe to let your dog loose. However, if you live where there is livestock, be careful. Many dogs have been shot by disgruntled livestock owners. In other cases they have been poisoned by bait left out for wild predators.

GROOMING

Regular grooming makes a dog nicer to live with and to look at, and usually makes him or her feel more comfortable. It is important, as well, in maintaining a healthy coat and skin.

BATHING

How often you bathe your dog depends not only on how frequently he or she gets dirty, but on the type of skin and hair and the kind of cleanser you use. The average normal dog is usually said to have a slightly alkaline skin pH, as opposed to the acid environment of human skin. Actually, healthy dogs have a range of skin pH, and shampoos designed for dogs, like human shampoos, vary from acid to alkaline depending on the product.

SHAMPOO Unless your dog has a specific skin problem requiring medicated shampoo recommended by a veterinarian, use a good-quality dog shampoo or gentle human shampoo (e.g., baby shampoo) for bathing. Avoid bar soap and dishwashing detergents since they seem to be particularly drying or irritating to some dogs' skin and hair.

HOW OFTEN TO BATHE A clean dog is a pleasure to touch and should have no offensive odor. If you use a good-quality shampoo, most dogs can be bathed as frequently as once a week. Use your dog's appearance, feel, and odor as guides. Some dogs look and smell good when bathed only a few times a year. In general, more frequently bathed dogs have healthier skin and hair and many fewer flea problems than dogs bathed less often.

WHEN TO START BATHS Accustom your dog to bathing early in life so it won't be a problem later. You can bathe a puppy as young as six or eight weeks of age if you do it quickly and prevent chilling. Bathing itself does not cause illness, but the stress of being chilled can predispose any dog, particularly a young one, to disease.

HOW TO BATHE It is usually easiest for you and most comfortable for your dog if you use a sink or bathtub and warm water for bathing. If the weather is

warm, however, bathing can be done outside using water from a garden hose. This method is usually the easiest for very large dogs. Before the bath it is a good idea, but not absolutely necessary, to protect your dog's ear canals and eyes from the soap and water. This can be done by putting large wads of cotton firmly inside the ears and by placing a gentle opthalmic ointment, petrolatum, or a drop of mineral oil into each eye. Long-haired dogs should be combed out before bathing so grooming after the bath is easier.

If you accustom your dog to bathing at a young age, you should have no difficulty during baths. However, adult dogs who have never been bathed or allowed to swim when young may never adjust well to baths. If your dog seems very insecure in the tub, a rubber mat placed in the bottom of the bathtub will provide some traction and perhaps relieve some fears. A soft rope looped around the neck and tied to a fixture (*never* a hot-water faucet) will keep most uncooperative dogs in the tub. But *never* leave a dog alone when it is tied in this manner. Use the basic rules of training to get your dog to cooperate. Say "no" when he or she tried to get out of the tub. Praise when he or she stands quietly. As a last resort, your veterinarian can provide tranquilizers to use when bathing an extremely unmanageable dog.

To avoid a struggle, do not try to place your dog in a tub of water. Start the bath by placing the dog in an empty basin. Then wet the dog thoroughly, apply the shampoo, and suds it up. Two shampoo applications may be necessary if your dog is very dirty. Thorough rinsing is extremely important since any soap left on the skin can be very irritating. A human or dog creme rinse, used according to directions after the shampoo, makes the comb-out of long-haired dogs easier. Towel drying is usually sufficient, but if you accustom your dog to the sound, you can use a human hair dryer to speed the process. Be sure to prevent your dog from becoming chilled while drying.

GROOMING BETWEEN BATHS

The kind of grooming your dog's coat needs between baths depends on its length and character. Short-haired dogs usually need only an occasional rubdown with a hound mitt to remove loose hair and distribute oils. Dogs with longer hair need more specialized grooming. In addition to regular combing and brushing, many breeds need periodic clipping and/or plucking to keep their coats in manageable condition and the hair out of their eyes. Consult specific breed books for specialized grooming instructions for purebred dogs.

HAIR MATS Dogs of any breed with coats one inch or longer must have regular grooming to prevent mat formation. Severe mats cause painful pulling of the skin, and mats often provide a place for parasites such as fleas and maggots (see pages 104, 119) to hide.

Mats of hair often occur behind the ears and under the legs. These can be teased apart with a comb when they are small. If allowed to become large, such mats must be cut away with scissors or clippers.

FOXTAILS   In areas such as California where *foxtails* (wild barley) or other troublesome plant awns (seeds) grow, longer-haired dogs need to have their coats examined for awns daily in the late spring, summer, and fall. Particular attention should be paid to the areas between the toes, under the legs, and around the ears and genitals. Awns not discovered and removed can easily penetrate the skin and travel down the ear canals or up the genital tract, causing irritation and infection.

Foxtail

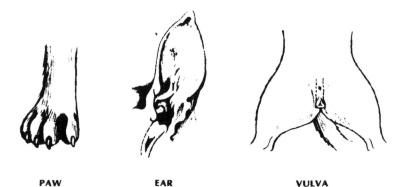

PAW   EAR   VULVA

SKUNK ODOR The traditional way to rid a dog of skunk odor is to give the pet a shampoo and water bath followed by a milk or tomato juice soak. The milk or juice is poured on undiluted and rinsed out in about ten minutes. A better remedy is to thoroughly wash the pet in a freshly made mixture of one quart 3% hydrogen peroxide, ¼ cup baking soda, and one teaspoonful liquid shampoo followed by copious tap

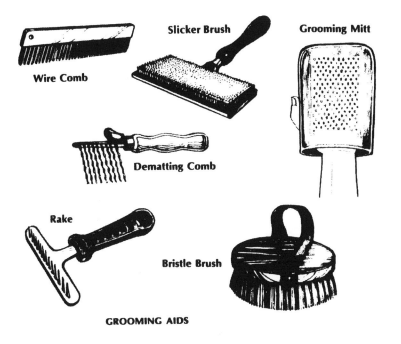

Wire Comb · **Slicker Brush** · **Grooming Mitt** · **Dematting Comb** · **Rake** · **Bristle Brush**

GROOMING AIDS

water rinsing. Commercial products for the removal of skunk odor are also available at pet stores.

Tar and paint are difficult substances to remove from the coat. *Do not* use gasoline, turpentine, kerosene, paint remover, or other similar substances in an attempt to remove them. Cut out small accumulations of tar or paint. Large amounts of tar can be removed without cutting by applying vegetable oil, mineral oil, or ointments containing the surface-active agent polyoxethylene sorbitan (polysorbate) for twenty-four hours (if the feet have tar on them, apply ointment or oil, then cover with a bandage), then washing with a mild detergent and water.

TAR AND PAINT

EARS

Most dogs need to have their ears cleaned about once a month. It is easy to do after bathing using a damp towel or soft cloth. Wrap the cloth over your index finger, then clean out the excess wax and dirt that has accumulated in the pinna and as far down the ear canal as your finger will reach. You cannot damage the eardrum in this way. Any folds or crevices you cannot reach into with your finger can be cleaned using a cotton-tipped swab moistened with water, mineral oil, or isopropyl alcohol. If your dog has an inflammation or

GENERAL CARE

infection of the ear *(otitis)*, special ear cleaning may be necessary (see page 226).

HAIRY EAR CANALS Some veterinarians feel that ear canals that have hair in them should have the hair removed periodically to prevent ear inflammations. Dogs such as poodles and poodle crosses, terriers and terrier crosses usually have hairy ear canals. If your dog's ears have so much hair inside that the ear canals are blocked and air cannot circulate, if large amounts of wax accumulate, or if there is irritation of the canals, pluck out the hair. Otherwise, plucking is probably not necessary.

To pluck ear canal hair, grasp protruding hair with your fingers or a pair of tweezers and give a quick jerk. Hair in the ear canal usually comes out easily, and the plucking process does not seem to be painful if done properly and if the ear canal is not inflamed. Be careful not to tug on the hair just outside the ear canal—that hurts. Hair not easily removed by plucking will need to be clipped out.

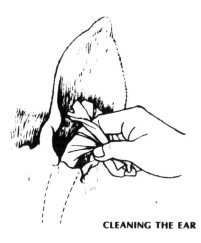

CLEANING THE EAR

TOENAILS

PROPER LENGTH Dogs' toenails should be no longer than just touching the ground, allowing the foot to remain compact and trim. Longer nails do not provide good traction, cause a dog to stand abnormally, and sometimes cause pain. Sometimes toenails will grow around in a complete circle, penetrating the pad. This is a particular problem with the nails on dewclaws, which do not touch the ground as they grow out.

Not all dogs need their nails trimmed. Large dogs that exercise outdoors a great deal usually keep their nails worn down to the proper length. However, small dogs and dogs that spend most of their time indoors usually do need their nails cut. Dogs with long hair on their feet are often allowed to grow nails to excessive lengths. If you have a long-haired dog, be sure to check the toenail length frequently.

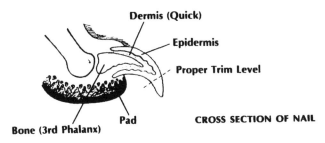

Dermis (Quick)

Epidermis

Proper Trim Level

Bone (3rd Phalanx)   Pad   CROSS SECTION OF NAIL

HOW TO TRIM TOENAILS

Light-colored nails are easiest to trim since the dermis (quick) can be seen when the nail is held up to the light. Cut the nail just beyond the point where you see the dermis end. If you cut into the dermis, it is painful and some bleeding will usually occur. The bleeding will stop, but the pain will make your dog reluctant to have a nail trim the next time. Black nails are harder to trim. The easiest rule to follow is to cut the nail just beyond the point where it starts to curve downward.

The dermis seems to get longer in nails that have been allowed to grow too long. Sometimes it can be driven back and the nails shortened to their proper length by frequent filing or running on a hard surface. The only other alternative is to have the nails trimmed short under anesthesia, then keep them the proper length.

RESCO NAIL TRIMMER

WHITE NAIL TRIMMER

There are two common types of nail clippers, White's and Resco's. I find the White's type the most maneuverable, and they are my preference for toenails that have become overgrown. Resco's works best for large, thick toenails. If you trim a nail into the quick and the bleeding doesn't seem to be stopping, you can apply a styptic pencil or cornstarch or a moistened and wrung-out black teabag to the area or bandage the foot firmly for about an hour (see page 228). One of these home remedies usually works to stop the bleeding. To treat bleeding problems at future nail-trimming sessions, purchase styptic powder or Monsel's solution from your local veterinarian, pet shop, or a pet-supply catalog.

TEETH

TARTAR

Almost all dogs, particularly small breeds, need special attention given to their teeth to preserve them and to minimize mouth odors. Most dogs, like most people, develop deposits called dental *tartar* or *calculus* on their teeth. When present it is most obvious on canine (cuspid) teeth and molars as a hard yellow-brown or grayish white deposit that cannot be removed by brushing or scraping with a fingernail. Its presence is *not* normal (see page 24). It causes gum disease, which is a common cause of halitosis (bad breath) and which can eventually lead to loss of teeth. *Periodontal* (gum) disease is the most frequently seen mouth disease in dogs. Most dogs do not develop cavities, but they can lose their teeth if their owners miss the early stages of gum disease.

TARTAR PREVENTION

Once tartar is present it can be removed properly only with special instruments—a tartar scraper (tooth scaler) or an ultrasonic tooth cleaner. Tartar is best removed by a veterinarian since anesthesia is usually necessary to do a really thorough cleaning job followed by polishing to provide a smooth surface that discourages new tartar formation. Tartar originates from a soft white to yellow-colored substance called *materia alba* or plaque. You can remove this and prevent tartar formation in the following ways:

1. Feed your dog dry food. Dogs that eat kibble or biscuit tend to have less tartar, possibly due to the abrasive action of this type of food. Feeding a hard-food diet will not absolutely prevent tartar in all dogs because its formation depends on the conditions in each dog's mouth, not only on diet. Some dogs, particularly small breeds, seem to form lots of plaque and tartar no matter what diet is fed.

2. Give your dog things to chew on—hard rubber toys, rawhide toys, bones big enough and hard enough to prevent swallowing them. These toys remove plaque by abrasion.

3. Clean your dog's teeth yourself once or twice a week. You can use a regular toothbrush or a finger toothbrush, but a gauze wound pad or a rough cloth wrapped around your finger can work very well. Moisten it with water, then scrub the teeth and gums vigorously. It's not absolutely necessary to do the inner tooth surfaces, because the movement of the tongue usually keeps the areas adjacent to it relatively free of plaque.

It is also not absolutely necessary to use a dentifrice, but many products are available that provide additional abrasion (pastes containing calcium or silicates), an oxygenating effect (to inhibit bacteria), or antimicrobials (to inhibit plaque-forming bacteria). *Chlorhexidine gluconate* or *acetate* (0.1%) is an easy-to-find liquid disinfectant that has been shown to inhibit plaque formation when brushed into the gum-tooth junction. The old-fashioned dentifrice of sodium bicarbonate mixed with a small amount of table salt and water is an adequate dentifrice for some dogs who are not on sodium-restricted diets; however, veterinary clinics sell more effective, better-tasting products. Avoid toothpastes designed for humans as they foam excessively.

If your dog's gums bleed even though they look healthy otherwise, it is not usually because you have scrubbed too hard but because they are in the early stages of disease. Good tooth care should cause an early problem to correct itself. If you see that the gums are red and pulling away from the teeth (receding), you will need the help of a veterinarian to clear up the condition. Loose teeth will have to be removed and dirty ones cleaned. Gum flap surgery may be necessary.

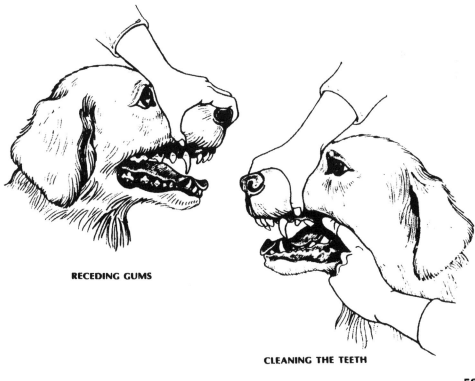

RECEDING GUMS

CLEANING THE TEETH

You can begin treatment at home with daily gum massage. Use your finger bare or wrapped in a cloth. Make gentle motions while pressing gently, but firmly, against the gums and teeth. This process will help a dog get used to the type of oral manipulation that will be necessary to restore a diseased mouth to health. Tooth brushing on a regular basis will be necessary to achieve a healthy mouth in any dog who has been allowed to develop periodontal disease.

NUTRITION

Most dog owners will face three distinct feeding situations: feeding the puppy; feeding the adult dog; feeding the old dog. The formulation of a diet to satisfy a dog's needs during each of these periods in life, and at times of special nutrient requirements, is difficult, time-consuming, and a task most dog owners cannot perform successfully without special training. If you think you would like to feed your dog from scratch, use a proven recipe such as those included on pages 77–78 or that your veterinarian may be able to supply. Before trying to formulate a diet yourself, and to find more information on nutrition than can be presented in this book, refer to the following technical publications.

Collins, D. R., *The Collins Guide to Dog Nutrition,* Howell Book House, Inc., New York, 1987.

Lewis, L. D., M. L. Morris, and M. S. Hand, *Small Animal Clinical Nutrition III,* Mark Morris Associates, Topeka, Kansas, 1987.

National Research Council, U.S. Subcommittee on Dog Nutrition, *Nutrient Requirements of Dogs,* National Academy Press, Washington, D.C., 1985.

Nutrition is a complicated subject with specialized terminology. To help you, here are some terms that are used in the following pages.

TERMS USED TO EXPRESS NUTRIENT CONTENT OF FOODS AND/OR NUTRIENT REQUIREMENTS

1. "As fed basis." This phrase refers to foods' nutrient and moisture contents expressed as percentages. Normally the percentages used refer to the amounts found in a pet food product as it comes directly from the can, bag, or box. However, the values for moisture will increase should water be added to the food, thereby diluting the other nutrients on an as fed basis. Since the moisture content of foods can vary considerably (from about 5% to about 80%) comparison of nutrients present to a nutritional chart or between products becomes difficult unless the differing moisture levels are taken into consideration (see term 2). However, when choosing among products of the same general moisture content (e.g., between canned foods) there will be no problems if they are compared with one another on an as fed basis. When adding foods or supplements to preformulated products, recommendations are often given on an as fed basis in order to facilitate addition of the item (e.g., one teaspoonful per pound dry food as fed).

2. "Dry-matter basis." This phrase refers to the nutrient content of food expressed as a percentage of the food after all water is removed. For example, a food containing 20% protein and 50% water (moisture) on an as fed basis will contain about 3 ounces (oz) (about 90 grams [g]) of protein in a pound (lb) (454 g). If all the water is removed, leaving ½ lb (227 g) dry matter, the amount of protein, 3 oz (90 g), per portion remains the same but the percentage expressed on a dry-matter basis increases to 40%. Expressing all nutrients on the same dry-matter basis (dry basis) makes comparison of different kinds of foods to one another and to charts of nutrient requirements easier. This is why requirements for certain vitamins, minerals, proteins, and fats are often expressed as a percentage of the dry matter of the food, i.e., on a dry basis (see chart, pages 70–71). (To convert an amount of nutrient from an as fed to a dry-matter basis, use the calculation on page 74.)

3. "As a percentage of calories." The biological availability of certain nutrients, especially protein, is affected by calorie intake. In instances where the amount of a nutrient needed will be affected by the energy (calories) provided by the diet, nutri-

ent content or requirements are often expressed as a percentage of calories provided by the diet. Although nutritionally correct, this concept is difficult for most people who are not professional nutritionists to apply, and information presented in this form is kept to a minimum in this book.

4. "Per pound (or kilogram) of body weight." The simplest, but sometimes less technically correct means to express the amount of any nutrient needed is to give the requirement as a unit per pound (or kilogram) of body weight. By convention, nutrients are expressed in various units such as international units (IU), milligrams (mg), or micrograms (μg).

TERMS USED TO DESCRIBE NUTRIENT AVAILABILITY

1. "Digestibility." This is the relationship between the amount of a nutrient or food eaten and the amount absorbed expressed as a percentage. For example, a dog consuming a pound (454 g) of a food that is 80% digestible has only 12.8 oz (384g) (16 oz [454g] × 80%) available to the body for actual use. The difference in the two amounts represents the waste matter that is excreted.

2. "Utilization." This term expresses the relationship between the quantity of a nutrient or food eaten and the actual amount retained by the body. Like digestibility, the ratio is expressed as a percentage. Food utilization is the best overall way to determine the actual nutritional value of a food. Scientific analysis of food disposition in the body can provide this information. However, since food utilization figures are often not readily available to pet owners, food digestibility is often substituted for it in discussions of nutrition.

3. "Metabolizable energy" (ME). This term represents the number of calories available to the body from food. It is conventional among nutritionists to specify nutrient concentration requirements for pet foods as quantities needed per each 1,000 calories of metabolizable energy (Kcal ME) provided by the food since some nutrient requirements change when the calories available from a given quantity of food increase or de-

crease. When comparing calories provided by food to calories required by the animal, it is important to be sure that both are expressed in the same energy units. Metabolizable energy units specify the actual energy available. Other units such as gross energy or digestible energy are less accurate measures of the actual calories provided by food.

Dogs meet their nutritional requirements by ingesting proteins, carbohydrates, fats, vitamins, and minerals just as humans do. Minimum requirements of each kind of nutrient, except carbohydrates, have been established for dogs (see tables, pages 68 and 69), and reputable dog food manufacturers formulate the *rations* (complete daily diets) they sell to meet these established requirements.

Proteins are essential for growth and repair. They cannot be synthe- **PROTEINS** sized in the body from dietary constituents other than protein. Therefore they are extremely important to nutrition. When protein is present in amounts that exceed the daily requirement, it can also be used for energy, supplying 3.5 calories for each gram consumed. It is best when properly balanced proteins supply 20%–30% of the diet's calories. Proteins are composed of amino acids and vary widely in the kind and proportion of amino acids present.

Essential amino acids cannot be synthesized in the dog's body and must be supplied by the diet in special proportions for optimum use. Proteins that supply the essential amino acids in nearly optimum quantities are given a high *biological value* because they are utilized efficiently by the body. Proteins with a high biological value are the best ones to feed and are the best bases for commercial dog foods. Examples of such proteins are eggs, milk, muscle meat, fish meal, and soybeans. In general, the higher the biological value, the lower the actual requirement for protein in the diet providing the diet as a whole provides enough calories that protein is not needed to supply energy. Protein deficiencies usually occur when dogs are fed diets based on high-carbohydrate, low-biological-value plant substances or diets that use poor-quality animal protein (e.g., tankage), deficient in essential amino acids as a protein source along with cereals, which are also deficient in amino acids.

Eggs are an excellent source of protein of high biological value (one egg = 7 g protein). If fed frequently, however, they should be cooked because raw egg white is not digested well. It also contains a substance called *avidin,* which binds *biotin* (an important B vitamin) and prevents its absorption from the gut, and a trypsin inhibitor that can induce diarrhea and weight loss in dogs. Raw eggs may also contain *salmonella* bacteria, which may infect dogs when eaten, causing illness and occasionally death.

Milk and milk products, such as cottage cheese or yogurt, are also good sources of protein as well as of calcium and phosphorus. Some dogs develop diarrhea when fed any milk products; others may develop diarrhea only when fed large amounts. Diarrhea associated with the ingestion of milk products occurs when the *lactose* (milk sugar) in them is not digested. Undigested lactose promotes bacterial fermentation and attracts water into the intestine, causing diarrhea. For this reason, it is often recommended that a dog's diet contain no more than 20% milk by volume. Dogs who cannot drink milk without developing diarrhea can often eat cottage cheese, which has a much lower lactose content.

CARBO-HYDRATES Carbohydrates (cellulose, starch, and sugars) are used by the dog as energy sources (3.5 calories per gram) and, under normal metabolic conditions, to maintain the blood glucose (sugar) level. Because carbohydrates are readily available as energy sources, they can be used to "spare" proteins, allowing proteins to be used for more important structural uses in the body instead. However, a diet adequate in protein can be entirely free of carbohydrates and still successfully sustain a dog's growth and reproduction. Cellulose, an indigestible carbohydrate, provides the necessary bulk for normal intestinal function.

Although a minimum carbohydrate requirement has not been established for dogs, they can readily digest large amounts of it (e.g., cereal grains, potatoes), particularly when cooked. And since carbohydrates are inexpensive nutrient sources, they are widely used as a basis for commercial dog diets. Authorities recommend that no more than 50%–65% of a dog's diet (on a dry-weight basis) be composed of carbohydrates, in order to allow for sufficient protein, fat, and minerals in the diet. Fiber should be less than 5% of the diet (dry-weight basis) unless the diet is specially designed to treat medical conditions such as constipation, *diabetes mellitus,* and obesity.

FATS Fats provide the most concentrated source of energy (9 calories per gram) of any of the necessary dietary components. They carry fat-soluble vitamins (D, E, A, K) and supply linoleic acid, an essential fatty acid that is important for healthy skin and hair. The fat requirement varies depending on the individual fat's degree of saturation and its essential fatty acid content. In general, fat should supply 5%–20% of the diet's calories. Linoleic acid should supply about 2.5% or more of the energy of the diet (about 1% by weight of a *dried ration*). This quantity is usually found in commercial dry food containing at least 7% fat on a dry-matter basis.

A deficiency of essential fatty acids can retard puppies' growth and produce coarse hair and dry, flaking skin. The idea that a young (or old) dog with scaly skin needs more dietary fat, however, is probably overworked, since most commercial diets provide sufficient levels of unsaturated fatty acids. Scaly skin and dry coat can also be caused by disease not related to diet, and good skin health depends on an interaction of various other nutrients as well as on fatty acids. **FAT'S EFFECT ON DRY SKIN**

If you think your dog has a fatty acid deficiency, you can supplement the diet with 1 teaspoon to 1½ tablespoons (no more) per pound of dry food of poultry drippings, lard, bacon fat, or vegetable oil (safflower, corn, soybean, or cottonseed oil are good). Canned foods containing 2%–3.5% fat (on an as fed basis) can have fat added at about 1 tablespoon per pound can. Soft-moist foods or canned foods containing more than 6% fat should not have fat added. Increasing the fat content of the diet so that fat supplies more than 40% of the daily caloric requirement may induce other nutritional deficiencies by lowering total food consumption, so beware. Skin improvement is usually seen one to two months after beginning supplementation if fat content is causing the problem. A better approach to treating unhealthy skin resulting from dietary deficiencies is to switch to a commercial diet that is known to be nutritionally adequate and to discuss the problem with your veterinarian if the condition does not improve.

Dogs require about 1 ounce (30 milliliters [ml]) water per pound of body weight ($\cong$ 65 ml per kg) daily. They obtain this water from the food they eat and the liquids they drink. Water is also a by-product of metabolism. A dog can go without food for days and lose 30%–40% of its normal body weight without dying, but a water loss of 10%–15% can be fatal. The actual amount of liquid a dog must drink daily is influenced by many factors (among them diet, exercise, environmental temperature, vomiting, or diarrhea). So the best solution to the problem of water intake is to be sure that your dog has access to·clean water at all times. Never provide water that would be considered unfit for human consumption. If you are unable to give your dog free water access, offer water at least three times a day, and let your dog drink until fully satisfied each time. **WATER**

CALCIUM, PHOSPHORUS, AND VITAMIN D

A description of the interrelationships between the minerals calcium and phosphorus and vitamin D demonstrates the importance of feeding a balanced diet and the importance of *not* using unnecessary dietary supplements in the form of unbalanced vitamin and mineral preparations.

Calcium and phosphorus should be present in the diet at a ratio of about 1.2 to 1. If an adequate amount of each of these minerals is present but the ratio is incorrect, abnormal mineralization of bone will occur in the growing puppy as well as in the adult dog. If adequate amounts of calcium and phosphorus in the proper ratio are provided, but without sufficient vitamin D, abnormalities of bone again result. Insufficient levels of vitamin D interfere with calcium absorption from the gut. Excessive amounts of vitamin D in the presence of adequate levels of calcium and phosphorus may result in excessive mineralization of bone, abnormal teeth, hypertension, and calcification of the soft tissues of the body. The delicacy of these relationships is remarkable.

SAY "NO!" TO ALL-MEAT DIETS

The calcium-phosphorus ratio found in raw beef, beef liver, and horsemeat is about 1 to 15. This fact alone makes it fairly obvious that feeding your dog an all-meat diet is not a good idea. In addition, the amount of raw beef sufficient to meet the caloric requirements of a 20-lb (9.9 kg) dog supplies inadequate amounts of the vitamins D, A, and E; inadequate iron, sodium, potassium, cobalt, copper, magnesium, and iodine; and an excessive amount of fat. All-meat diets are noted for their ability to produce diarrhea and flatulence in many dogs. They may also place an excessive metabolic load on an older dog with failing kidneys. Feed your dog a balanced canned, soft-moist, or dry food as a basic diet. All-meat products and other high-protein foods are not necessary as a protein supplement since good commercial rations already contain sufficient protein. They can be used as an expensive energy source and to improve flavor, if you add no more than 10%–20% by weight of the diet's total dry matter. For typical protein supplements such as meat, eggs, or cottage cheese, this is no more than 3 ounces (90 g) per pound (454 g) can or more than 8 ounces (227 g) per pound of dry food.

AVOID DIET SUPPLEMENTS

Many dog breeders and owners of large breeds of dogs have become believers in a practice that can easily do more harm than good for their dogs—routine supplementation of the diet with *unbalanced* vitamin and/or mineral substances (e.g., bone meal alone or cod-liver oil). Unbalanced supplements can result in abnormalities of structure and function every bit as severe as those you are trying to prevent. For example, an excess of vitamin D causes hypertension and secondary kidney damage. Calcium excess is suspected of aggravating bone deformities in growing dogs, and vitamin C may compound the situation. At best, excess nutrients such as calcium and phosphorus will be excreted unused.

Cod-liver oil should not be used as a routine daily supplement for dogs. One teaspoon of N.F. cod-liver oil (312 IU per teaspoon) provides more vitamin D than is required in a whole pound of diet (dry basis). Regular use, particularly with an already balanced diet, can lead to an excess of vitamin D.

The best procedure is to feed only a balanced diet. If you feel you must use supplementation to assure yourself that your dog is getting all the vitamins and minerals needed, use a *balanced* vitamin–mineral supplement that provides the substances in the proper proportions and follow your veterinarian's or the manufacturer's directions carefully to supply only the minimum daily requirement for each nutrient. Any improvement seen following supplementation of a diet means a switch to a new diet is needed as the original diet was inadequate and provided false savings.

CHOOSING A DOG FOOD

Commercial rations are sold as dry foods, semimoist foods, soft dry foods (a modification of semimoist foods), and canned foods. Each type of product can provide complete dog nutrition if it is formulated correctly.

In general, it is most economical to use dry food (10% moisture content) as a dog's basic diet; its crunchy texture, when fed alone, helps keep the dog's teeth clean. Semimoist foods (23%–40% moisture content) are considerably more expensive than dry foods if the additional water they contain compared to dry products is taken into consideration when calculating cost per feeding. Chemical humectants, corn syrup, salts, sugars, and acids are used to hold water in these products and keep them soft and free of spoilage. Soft moist products often contain artificial flavors and colors and are generally highly palatable to dogs. Some dogs develop digestive upsets and drink excessive amounts of water when fed soft-moist food, becoming uncomfortably bloated as a result. It is best to limit the use of such unnatural foods in a dog's diet.

Minimum Nutrient Requirements of Dogs for Growth and Maintenance (amounts per kilogram of body weight per day)[a]

NUTRIENT	UNIT	GROWTH[b]	ADULT MAINTENANCE[c]
Fat	g	2.7	1.0
Linoleic acid	mg	540	200
Protein[d]			
Arginine	mg	274	21
Histidine	mg	98	22
Isoleucine	mg	196	48
Leucine	mg	318	84
Lysine	mg	280	50
Methionine-cystine	mg	212	30
Phenylalanine-tyrosine	mg	390	86
Threonine	mg	254	44
Tryptophan	mg	82	13
Valine	mg	210	60
Dispensable amino acids	mg	3,414	1,266
Minerals			
Calcium	·mg	320	119
Phosphorus	mg	240	89
Potassium	mg	240	89
Sodium	mg	30	11
Chloride	mg	46	17
Magnesium	mg	22	8.2
Iron	mg	1.74	0.65
Copper	mg	0.16	0.06
Manganese	mg	0.28	0.10
Zinc	mg	1.94	0.72
Iodine	mg	0.032	0.012
Selenium	μg	6.0	2.2

NUTRIENT	UNIT	GROWTH[b]	ADULT MAINTENANCE[c]
Vitamins			
A	IU	202	75
D	IU	22	8
E[e]	IU	1.2	0.5
K[f]			
Thiamin	μg	54	20
Riboflavin	μg	100	50
Pantothenic acid	μg	400	200
Niacin	μg	450	225
Pyridoxine	μg	60	22
Folic acid	μg	8	4
Biotin[f]			
B$_{12}$	μg	1.0	0.5
Choline	mg	50	25

[a]Needs for other physiological states have not been determined.

[b]Average 3-kg growing beagle puppy consuming 600 kcal ME/day.

[c]Average 10-kg adult dog consuming 742 kcal ME/day.

[d]Quantity sufficient to supply minimum amounts of available indispensable and dispensable amino acids specified below.

[e]Requirement depends on intake of polyunsaturated fatty acid (PUFA) and other antioxidants. A fivefold increase may be required under conditions of high PUFA intake.

[f]Dogs have a metabolic requirement, but a dietary requirement was not demonstrated when foods made from natural ingredients were fed.

Charts reprinted with permission from National Academy of Sciences. National Research Council, *Nutrient Requirements of Dogs 1985.* Washington, DC, National Academy of Sciences, 1985.

SOURCE: National Research Council, U.S. Subcommittee on Dog Nutrition, *Nutrient Requirements of Dogs,* National Academy Press, Washington, D.C., 1985.

Required Minimum Concentrations of Available
Nutrients in Dog Food Formulated for Growth

NUTRIENT	PER 1,000 KCAL ME	DRY BASIS (3.67 KCAL ME.)
Protein[a]		
Indispensable amino acids		
Arginine	1.37 g	0.50%
Histidine	0.49 g	0.18%
Isoleucine	0.98 g	0.36%
Leucine	1.59 g	0.58%
Lysine	1.40 g	0.51%
Methionine-cystine	1.06 g	0.39%
Phenylalanine-tyrosine	1.95 g	0.72%
Threonine	1.27 g	0.47%
Tryptophan	0.41 g	0.15%
Valine	1.05 g	0.39%
Dispensable amino acids	17.07 g	6.26%
Fat	13.6 g	5.0%
Linoleic acid	2.7 g	1.0%
Minerals		
Calcium	1.6 g	0.59%
Phosphorus	1.2 g	0.44%
Potassium	1.2 g	0.44%
Sodium	0.15 g	0.06%
Chloride	0.23 g	0.09%
Magnesium	0.11 g	0.04%
Iron	8.7 mg	31.9 mg/kg
Copper	0.8 mg	2.9 mg/kg
Manganese	1.4 mg	5.1 mg/kg
Zinc[b]	9.7 mg	35.6 mg/kg
Iodine	0.16 mg	0.59 mg/kg
Selenium	0.03 mg	0.11 mg/kg

NUTRIENT	PER 1,000 KCAL ME	DRY BASIS (3.67 KCAL ME.)
Vitamins		
A	1,011 IU	3,710 IU/kg
D	110 IU	404 IU/kg
E[c]	6.1 IU	22 IU/kg
K[d]	—	—
Thiamin[c]	0.27 mg	1.0 mg/kg
Riboflavin	0.68 mg	2.5 mg/kg
Pantothenic acid	2.7 mg	9.9 mg/kg
Niacin	3 mg	11.0 mg/kg
Pyridoxine	0.3 mg	1.1 mg/kg
Folic acid	0.054 mg	0.2 mg/kg
Biotin[d]	—	—
Vitamin B_{12}	7 μg	26 μg/kg
Choline	340 mg	1.25 g/kg

[a]Quantities sufficient to supply the minimum amounts of available indispensable and dispensable amino acids as specified below. Compounding practical foods from natural ingredients (protein digestibility $\pm$ 70%) may require quantities representing an increase of 40% or greater than the sum of the amino acids listed below, depending upon ingredients used and processing procedures.

[b]In commercial foods with natural ingredients resulting in elevated calcium and phytate content, borderline deficiencies were reported from feeding foods with less than 90 mg zinc per kg.

[c]A fivefold increase may be required for foods of high PUFA content.

[d]Dogs have a metabolic requirement, but a dietary requirement was not demonstrated when foods made of natural ingredients were fed.

[e]Overages must be considered to cover losses in processing and storage.

Charts reprinted with permission from National Academy of Sciences. National Research Council, *Nutrient Requirements of Dogs 1985*. Washington, DC, National Academy of Sciences, 1985.

SOURCE: National Research Council, U.S. Subcommittee on Dog Nutrition, *Nutrient Requirements of Dogs*, National Academy Press, Washington, D.C., 1985.

Canned products tend to be the most expensive way to feed dogs as you pay for 65%–78% water. These products are also highly palatable to dogs, so they are often used as a mixer to encourage a reluctant eater to consume more dry food. Although a nutritionally complete canned diet can provide a dog with all of his or her dietary needs, dogs fed such foods exclusively generally need more attention to home tooth care and may become both obese and, paradoxically, very finicky eaters as well. For these reasons, experienced dog owners often prefer to use canned products only as flavor enhancers or as special treats in a diet based primarily on dry foods.

Federal law requires that all dog foods in interstate commerce carry a listing of ingredients in decreasing order of predominance by weight. Other regulations require a guaranteed analysis listing minimum or maximum levels of certain nutrients present on an *as fed* basis (i.e., not corrected for the amount of moisture present). Unfortunately, the required labels do not contain enough information to enable you to compare dog foods adequately with one another. The guaranteed analysis gives no indication of the *quality* of the nutrients present, nor does it give the exact quantities present. Companies are restricted from misrepresenting their products, however, and certain large manufacturers of dog foods have conducted extensive research and feeding trials in order to produce nutritious diets that need no supplementation. These foods carry labels that indicate their nutritional adequacy based on calculation, chemical analysis, or feeding trials (the best). The following rules of thumb will help you choose a dog food:

1. Look at the food. This is a fairly effective way of evaluating many canned foods. If you see pieces of bone, discolored meat, and poorly digestible items such as blood vessels and skin, it's a pretty good indicator of poor quality.

2. Consider the price. Cheap dog foods often contain cheap ingredients—poor-quality protein and poorly digestible nutrients that pass through your dog unused. "Gourmet"-type dog foods, on the other hand, may contain high-quality ingredients but are often overpriced as well.

3. Well-known manufacturers noted for their research generally produce good-quality dog foods you can trust.

4. See what kind of effect the food has when eaten. If your dog gets diarrhea or becomes flatulent on a food, it's not the diet you should continue to feed. Voluminous stools following feeding of certain brands of food often indicate excessive amounts of fiber or other undigestible substances. Good products are 75%–80% absorbed by the gut unless specifically formulated to be therapeutic high-fiber foods.

5. Read the label and choose only products that have label claims of *complete* nutrition. Those that indicate that they are adequate for *all life stages* based on *feeding* trials are the products that have stood up to the most rigorous testing. Calculation or chemical analysis cannot measure exactly how the product will be utilized by the dog.

6. Calculate the cost per feeding since the price per bag, can, or box may be misleading. Record the cost per package and the purchase date. When empty, divide the price by the number of days it took to finish the product. The most "expensive" foods per package are often less expensive to feed per day than the apparently cheaper brands as less volume is needed to provide proper nutrition.

7. Write or call the food manufacturer to obtain any additional information you might need. For example, the protein and dry-matter digestibility of good foods usually exceeds 80%. This information, however, is often not available on the food label. Reputable food manufacturers are happy to provide the customer with information and often provide toll-free numbers for this purpose.

PET FOOD LABELS

Pet food labels are legal documents that must include the following information unless they are intended to be used solely as treats or snacks and are labeled as such:

1. Name of product
2. Animal species for which it is to be used
3. Net weight of the product
4. Ingredient list in descending order of content of the ingredients by weight
5. Guaranteed analysis listing protein, fat (minimum), and fiber and moisture (maximum) content
6. Manufacturer's name and address
7. Nutritional adequacy claim

An example: *Complete* (contains adequate levels of all required nutrients) and *balanced* (contains the proper proportions of required nutrients) for *all life stages* (will support puppy growth, pregnancy, and nursing, in addition to maintaining adult dogs).

Nutritionally incomplete products not labeled as snacks or treats must carry a statement that the "product is intended for intermittent or supplemental feeding only."

To understand lists of ingredients fully, consult another reference since pet food manufacturers use a language of their own. For example: A beef-*flavored* product does not have to contain any actual beef muscle meat. The best reference is the *Manual of the Association of American Feed Control Officials* (AAFCO), which is published annually.

To compare foods adequately to one another, differences due to water content must be eliminated. To do this, first calculate the percentage of *dry matter:* 100% − moisture = % total dry matter.

To calculate the amount of nutrient present on a dry basis (e.g., % protein on a dry-matter basis):

$$\frac{Guaranteed \text{ \% of nutrient as fed}}{\text{\% dry matter}} \times 100$$

= % nutrient present on dry basis

FEEDING A PUPPY

Dogs under eight months of age require about twice as much protein and about 50% more calories per pound of body weight daily than adult dogs in order to meet their growth requirements. These special needs can most easily be filled by a diet based on a good-quality commercial puppy food. Adult dog food can be used if puppy foods are not available, but the protein and energy content must be increased by adding a good-quality supplement such as milk, eggs, or meat. Foods for puppies must provide *at least* 25% of their energy from *high-quality* protein.

CHANGING A PUPPY'S DIET   If your puppy has not already been started on a commercial diet, find out what he or she has been fed and continue feeding this diet for a few days, gradually switching over to a complete ration. Rapid changes in diet often cause gastrointestinal upsets in young dogs, which are characterized by diarrhea. (For information on feeding very young puppies and weaning, see pages 263 and 265.)

Self-feeding is the most convenient method for a young dog. Leave the food out where your dog has free access to it and change as necessary to keep it fresh. Most puppies will not overeat with this system, and it seems to prevent boredom in dogs who must be left alone. On the other hand, if the self-feeding method is not suitable, feed your puppy four times a day until about three months of age, three times a day until about six months of age, then twice daily until full grown. A combination of self-feeding and scheduled feeding (feeding by hand) can be used as well and can be especially helpful during the housetraining period. When feeding by hand allow about twenty minutes for a meal then pick up any remaining food.

HOW OFTEN TO FEED

As a rough guide, puppies need about 100 calories per pound of body weight per day. The information on the dog food package can also be used as a feeding guide. But remember that each dog is an individual and has individual caloric requirements. Individual dogs may need as much as 20% more or 20% less calories than the average requirement. If you are feeding a balanced diet, your best guide is your dog's appearance. Look at and feel your puppy. If the spine and ribs are prominent, you may not be feeding enough. Each meal should fill a puppy comfortably. If your dog's stomach is distended and taut following a meal, or if vomiting occurs shortly after eating, your dog may be eating too much at one time. More frequent, smaller meals may be necessary. A fat pup is being overfed and has a much greater chance of developmental bone defects (see pages 157 and 160). It is best to feed a puppy to encourage an *average* growth rate since feeding for maximal growth is not compatible with optimal skeletal development.

HOW MUCH TO FEED

Most dogs prefer canned meat or table scraps to a commercial dry or semimoist dog food. However, don't let this lead you into feeding your puppy an unbalanced diet. If you don't routinely feed large quantities of meat or other "goodies," they won't be demanded. If you feel the commercial food needs a flavor supplement, add chicken or beef broth, canned-meat dog food, cottage cheese, yogurt, milk, or eggs—*at not more than 10%–20% dry weight of the diet.* Use table scraps carefully; feed them only as a special treat, and avoid fatty or spicy foods that can upset your dog's digestion. Human foods that can be toxic include chocolate (see page 193), moldy cheese, and onions, if fed in large quantities. Avoid them! (Feeding more than 0.5% of the dog's body weight of onions can cause death from red blood cell breakdown; less is harmless.)

TABLE SCRAPS

FEEDING AN ADULT DOG

As your puppy becomes an adult, you can switch from a puppy ration to an adult dog food or decrease the protein supplements if you have been using an adult ration as a basic diet. Self-feeding can be continued and can be desirable as scientific studies have shown that dogs left to their own devices prefer to eat about four meals a day. If you notice your dog becoming overweight, you will have to switch to one or two individual meals per day and/or select a less palatable basic diet. (Normal dogs will stop eating once their daily calorie requirement is attained unless the food offered is too tasty.) Some dogs vomit clear or yellow-tinged stomach juices if fed only once every twenty-four hours. These dogs especially benefit by being fed two smaller meals (breakfast and dinner) daily.

An average-size dog (30 lb, 13.7 kg) requires about 30 calories per pound of body weight per day (14 calories/kg). Large breeds generally require less (about 20 calories per pound, 10 calories/kg) and small breeds (e.g., Chihuahuas) usually require more (about 40 calories per pound, 18 calories/kg). As with puppies, however, each individual has individual requirements. During cold weather, dogs kept outside whether in kennels or not need more calories. Hot weather also causes an increase in calories needed, but it is accompanied by a decrease in food intake (about 7.5% for each 10°F rise in ambient temperature). Therefore, the food offered must be more calorie dense to avoid weight loss caused by reduced volume consumed. Working dogs require more calories than sedentary ones and need to have snacks provided when active for several hours to avoid hypoglycemia and exhaustion. Pregnant and lactating females also have special requirements (see pages 254 and 260), and in the presence of some illnesses your veterinarian will suggest a special diet.

FEEDING AN OLD DOG

Dogs undergo aging changes just as humans do and often require special diets for maximum health and activity in old age. In general, older dogs require fewer calories per pound of body weight than when they were young; the amount of food given must usually be decreased in order to avoid obesity. Body changes can result in decreased utilization of nutrients; additionally, intestinal absorption of nutrients may be impaired. There is then a rationale for using balanced vitamin-mineral preparations to supplement the older dog's diet. Dietary fat should be kept at the minimum level necessary to fulfill essential fatty acid requirements since some older dogs seem to have greater difficulty digesting fats and since the excess fat's calories increase the likelihood of obesity. Certain diseases such as heart or kidney failure, which tend to occur more often in old dogs (see pages 215 and 216), require special diets. However, the presence of such conditions should be determined by a veterinarian before any special diet is used as restricted diets can cause nutrient depletion when fed to pets unnecessarily.

PREVENT TRICHINOSIS

Trichinosis is a roundworm infection disseminated primarily in pork. It occurs when the larval forms of *Trichinella spiralis,* which encyst in muscle tissue, are eaten and encyst in the consumer's muscle tissue. This disease affects humans, pigs, and other mammals including dogs and rats. The infection can cause severe muscular pain. Prevent trichinosis by feeding only well-cooked pork to your dog. This will also prevent *pseudorabies* infection (see page 86). You may want to avoid giving your dog any pork at all since some dogs get indigestion after eating it. Feeding raw salmon or trout can also cause disease (see page 94).

FEEDING YOUR DOG FROM SCRATCH

If you choose not to use commercial dog food and want to feed your dog from scratch, be advised that creating a nutritionally balanced diet is difficult and complex and will require research and consultation with your veterinarian. Below are two nutritionally balanced recipes you can try.*

HOMEMADE DIET FOR DOGS I*

½ cup (113 ml)	farina (commonly known as Cream of Wheat), cooked to make 2 cups (490 g)
1 ½ cups (340 g)	creamed cottage cheese
1 large (50 g)	whole egg, hard-cooked
2 tablespoons (25 g)	inactive brewer's yeast
3 tablespoons (45 g)	granulated sugar or 1 tablespoon (15 g) honey
1 tablespoon (15 g)	corn oil or lard
1 teaspoon (5 g)	potassium chloride
1 teaspoon (4.5 g)	dicalcium phosphate
1 teaspoon (5 g)	calcium carbonate
	Balanced supplement that fulfills the canine minimum daily requirement for all vitamins and trace minerals

Cook farina according to package directions. Cool. Add remaining ingredients and mix well. This recipe yields about 2.2 lb (1 kg) food containing approximately 485 calories per pound (220 calories/kg).

For growing dogs, add to the above:

2 large (50 g each)	whole eggs, hard-cooked
	or
2 ounces (56 g)	canned mackerel
	or
1 ¾ ounce (49 g)	cooked ground beef or lamb, or liver

HOMEMADE DIET FOR DOGS II*

Cook as a stew:

1 pound (454 g)	ground beef
1 pound (454 g)	can stewed tomatoes
6	large potatoes
2	large onions
1 cup (130 g)	macaroni
1 pound (454 g)	dry rice
Juice of 2-one-pound (454 g)	cans yellow beans
Juice of 2 one-pound (454 g)	cans green beans
Juice of 2 one-pound (454 g)	cans carrots

Balanced supplement that fulfills the canine minimum daily requirement for all vitamins and trace minerals Add green beans, yellow beans, and carrots and mix well. (To substitute fresh vegetables, use 3 cups. Add additional water only if needed.) This makes 10 quarts of food to be fed at the rate of about 1 quart per 40 pounds of body weight per day (about 1 liter/20 kg). (This is a restricted-protein diet and, as such, may not be suitable for growing puppies.)

A balanced homemade diet can be mixed with a commercial balanced dry diet to provide a feeding ration halfway between "home cooking" and "store-bought."

*Thanks to Dr. Mark Morris of Mark Morris Associates, Topeka, Kansas, for supplying the basic recipes for these diets.

TRAVELING WITH OR
SHIPPING YOUR DOG

ACCUSTOM YOUR DOG TO TRAVELING EARLY

Sooner or later, most dog owners have to make a decision about traveling with their dog. If you accustom your dog to riding in automobiles and to confinement when he or she is young, many travel problems are avoided. Take your dog for frequent short rides at first, then gradually lengthen them. Remember to enforce good behavior from the start. An adult dog that does not sit or lie quietly while traveling can be annoying and sometimes very dangerous. The safest arrangement is to confine your dog to a traveling crate that can sustain some impact should an accident occur. Restraint harnesses that attach to automobile seat belts are also available. Dogs should never be allowed to ride unrestrained in the open back of a pickup truck since they frequently fall or jump out. Again, crating is the best choice for safety, but crossties attached to a harness can be used if necessary. (See page 166 for information on motion sickness and page 206 for information on heat stress, which often occurs when dogs are confined improperly while traveling.)

The following items may help you when traveling with or shipping your dog on commercial carriers:

1. Most states require evidence of current rabies vaccination and a health certificate signed by an accredited veterinarian for entry. Airlines require these documents for shipping. Each foreign country has its own entry requirements for animals. Veterinarians can usually supply information regarding U.S. requirements; individual consulates are the best sources of current information for each foreign country.

2. Your veterinarian can prescribe safe tranquilizers for your dog if he or she is apprehensive about strange people and sounds. These are helpful for the average dog traveling in a baggage compartment. Seasoned travelers may not need them, however, and their use for dogs with special problems, such as the short-faced bulldog or aged animals, may not be recommended by your veterinarian. If your dog is small, special arrangements may be made for travel with you in the passenger area, which may eliminate the need for tranquilization.

3. A traveling crate should be strong and have enough room to enable your dog to stand up, turn around, and lie down comfortably. Federal regulations specify which crates are permissible for shipping with commercial carriers; as they may change from time to time, it is best to check with the shipper before purchasing a crate.

4. Attach an identification tag to *both* the crate *and* the dog stating the owner's name, dog's name, address, and destination, and the time and date when food and water were last given. (Dogs should wear I.D. tags at all times even if they are not being shipped.)

5. Exercise your dog before shipping.

6. Do not feed immediately prior to shipping.

7. Avoid giving water within about two hours of shipping unless it is absolutely necessary because of environmental conditions such as extreme heat or when shipping an aged pet.

8. Do not place food or water bowls loose in the crate. A *healthy adult* dog can go twenty-four hours without water, unless the environmental temperature is high, and much longer without food. If the trip is going to take longer than twenty-four hours, or if your pet is very young or very old, be *sure* special arrangements are made for feeding, watering, and exercise. Special water bottles that attach to crates are available, and dogs can easily be taught to drink from them in preparation for travel.

For more information about travel with your pet, consult:

American Society for the Prevention of Cruelty to Animals, *Traveling with Your Pet,* available for a fee from the ASPCA education department, 441 E. 92nd Street, New York, NY 10028.

Nicholas, Barbara, *The Portable Pet: How to Travel Anywhere With Your Dog or Cat,* Harvard Common Press, Boston, 1984.

Randolph, Mary, *Dog Law,* Nolo Press, Berkeley, California, 2nd ed., 1994 (good travel section, but also very useful for all general legal issues relating to dogs).

BOARDING YOUR DOG

Although many owners would prefer to travel with their dogs, regulations increasingly prevent even well-behaved pets from accompanying their owners away from home. It is wise to accustom your pet to being left without you while he or she is still young to prevent separation anxiety from developing later.

Dogs who are crate-trained (see page 48) while young adapt readily to confinement when they are adults. Likewise, young dogs who are left alone at home, a veterinary hospital, boarding kennel, or the groomer's for a few hours at a time learn to accept this situation as normal. Once a fully vaccinated (see page 82) dog can successfully spend a few hours away from his or her owner, it is time to arrange for an overnight without you. Many veterinarians are happy to provide this service, and it is a good way to help your pet learn that a night in the veterinary hospital need not be frightening. Should you anticipate frequent, long (five days or more) separations, be sure the veterinary hospital provides appropriate facilities for healthy, active pets separate from sick animals, or select a boarding kennel that will provide adequate supervision and exercise for long stays.

Avoid any boarding operation (including veterinary hospitals) whose proprietors will not allow you to visit the animals' quarters at an appropriate time. Unannounced visits are often disruptive to the kennel's schedule, but it is entirely reasonable to expect a request for a scheduled visit to be honored. Kennel employees should have a good rapport with the animals. Good kennels look clean, smell fresh, are regularly disinfected, and provide safe and secure individual housing that prevents nose-to-nose contact with other boarders. Proper housing is also adequately lighted, well-ventilated, heated or cooled to avoid temperature extremes, and designed to protect boarders from exposure to the elements.

Owners of reputable boarding kennels will require certificates of vaccination against infectious diseases. They should also inquire about the pet's usual diet and be willing to feed your pet familiar foods. Drinking water, of course, should be provided at all times. It is also customary to administer medications normally given at home. Kennel policy about toys and bedding varies, so inquire about it should your pet need some comfort items from home.

Another good kennel policy is inspection of your pet for fleas before admission and the requirement that flea-infested pets be de-fleaed before entry. This is an indication that the kennel makes every effort to keep the facility free from parasites.

Finally, the kennel operator should record your pet's veterinarian's name and telephone number, your instructions for care in case of an emergency, and where you or your legal representative can be reached should a problem arise.

Members of the American Boarding Kennels Association (ABKA), a non-profit trade organization, pledge to operate their kennels in a manner that meets high standards. If the kennel you select is not only a member but accredited as well, it has had to pass an inspection.

Professional pet-sitting services have developed in many areas as an alternative to boarding kennels. Also many veterinary clinics have staff members who pet-sit on a part-time basis. When the cost is not prohibitive, use of these services is an excellent way to leave a pet at home when you must be away. Even if well adapted to boarding, many pets are happier in the familiar surroundings of home. Also home stays avoid the ever-present danger of acquiring infection or parasites in a boarding kennel, even a well-run one. Ask your veterinarian for names of reputable pet-sitting services in your area.

PREVENTIVE VACCINATION PROCEDURES

There are several major infectious canine diseases for which safe and effective vaccines are available: rabies, canine distemper, hepatitis, leptospirosis, and parvovirus are among the most serious. Each of these diseases can easily cause death in an unprotected dog. We are very fortunate to be able to prevent such serious illnesses with a procedure as technically simple as vaccination.

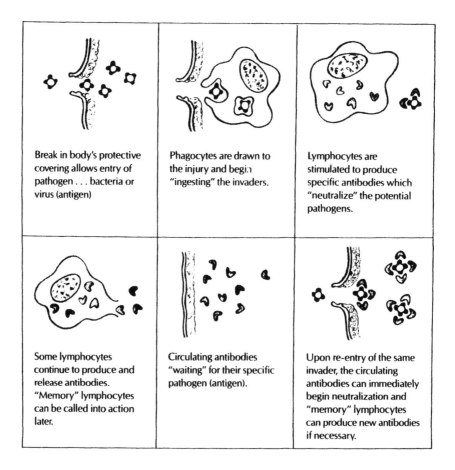

Break in body's protective covering allows entry of pathogen . . . bacteria or virus (antigen)	Phagocytes are drawn to the injury and begin "ingesting" the invaders.	Lymphocytes are stimulated to produce specific antibodies which "neutralize" the potential pathogens.
Some lymphocytes continue to produce and release antibodies. "Memory" lymphocytes can be called into action later.	Circulating antibodies "waiting" for their specific pathogen (antigen).	Upon re-entry of the same invader, the circulating antibodies can immediately begin neutralization and "memory" lymphocytes can produce new antibodies if necessary.

HOW VACCINES WORK

Antigens are molecules that have particular areas on their surfaces that are recognized as foreign to the body. *Antibodies* are protein substances produced in the body that are responsible for recognizing these antigens. They are produced by cells called *lymphocytes* that originate in the bone marrow and multiply in the thymus, spleen, and lymph nodes. When lymphocytes recognize that a foreign substance (antigen) such as a virus or bacterium has entered the body, they begin copious production of antibodies specific for the invader. Lymphocytes capable of antibody production against the invader multiply to produce progeny cells capable of producing the same antibodies. Some of these progeny cells immediately begin producing antibodies, while others become resting cells that serve as the body's "memory" of the invader. If the same (or a very similar) invader makes an appearance again at a later time, these cells are able to respond quickly to its presence.

Vaccination introduces a modified disease agent into the body. Common methods of altering an organism's ability to produce disease are by chemical killing and by "breeding" to an innocuous state. Biotechnology can also produce vaccines that consist of harmless immunity-inducing portions of agents that cause disease when they enter the body intact. Modified viruses or bacteria are able to induce lymphocytes to produce antibodies capable of protecting the body against disease without actually producing illness. Frequently the body produces a higher (usually more protective) level of antibodies that are more specific to a disease agent on the second exposure to a vaccine, but different vaccines vary in their ability to produce a protective antibody level on first exposure. The duration of the body's immunological memory for different viruses and bacteria also varies. These are two reasons why the number of original vaccinations necessary for protection and the frequency of booster vaccinations vary with each disease.

YOUNG ANIMALS ARE SPECIAL CASES

Additional factors influence the vaccination of a young animal. Dogs and cats receive a small amount of antibody across the *placenta* (the organ that communicates between mother and fetus before birth). They receive a much greater amount in the *colostrum* (first milk) and milk when they are nursing. Puppies are capable of absorbing some antibodies through their gut for several days following birth, but the first twenty-four hours are most important. The amount of antibody against each particular disease received is dependent on the level of circulating antibody in the mother. The circulating antibody serves

83

primarily to protect the puppy against disease for the first few~weeks of life. Even if the puppy nurses adequately, whether or not he or she receives a protective level of antibody depends on how recently the mother was exposed to the disease in question or how recently she was vaccinated. The antibody a puppy receives can be a disadvantage as well as being useful since it can interfere with vaccination by tying up the vaccination-introduced antigen before it can stimulate the puppy's immune system. The protection puppies receive early in life against canine distemper is an example.

Some puppies lose their protective immunity against distemper acquired in nursing as early as six weeks of age, others as late as four months after birth. Therefore, the ideal vaccination schedule is individualized for each pup and the last vaccination is given after sixteen weeks of age. There are tests for determining the level of antibody against distemper in each puppy, but in general, they are too expensive and time-consuming for routine use.

The techniques of vaccination are relatively simple. Knowledge of the proper handling of vaccines and of the physiology of the immune response is what makes it important to have your dog vaccinated by a veterinarian who is interested in each animal as an individual. Vaccination by a good veterinarian also assures that your dog gets a physical examination when he or she is young, and then also later, which may detect important changes you have missed. Regular visits during the initial puppy vaccination series also provide a time to discuss any behavior or training problems you may have and allows a young animal to become well adjusted to visits to an animal hospital. If a veterinarian vaccinates your dog without taking a thorough history or performing a thorough physical examination and discussing your pet with you, something is amiss!

RABIES

The rabies virus can infect any warm-blooded animal, including humans. It causes a disease of the nervous system often manifested by changes in behavior followed by paralysis and death. The principal reservoirs of rabies in the United States are skunks, raccoons, bats, and foxes. Bats and skunks may shed (secrete) rabies virus in their saliva without exhibiting behavior that would arouse suspicion of infection. Any wild animal that allows you to get close enough to handle it should certainly be suspected of rabies and left alone. Dogs should be supervised when outdoors to prevent exposure to rabid wildlife, especially during the night.

Rabies is usually spread when one rabid animal bites another, depositing virus from its saliva into the bite wound. However, rabies virus can enter the body through any break in the skin, through the mucous membranes of the mouth, and probably of the nose and eyes as well. After entering the body, rabies virus becomes "fixed" to nervous tissue, where it multiplies. Signs of rabies usually begin between about two to ten weeks following infection, but cases have developed after more than one year from contact.

HOW RABIES IS SPREAD

Rabid dogs usually first show changes in temperament. At this time rabies can be particularly difficult to diagnose because the signs are so variable. A dog may become restless, insecure, or apprehensive, overly affectionate, or shy. Some dogs snap at imaginary objects. Some dogs have a normal appetite; others have to be coaxed to eat. Some dogs are febrile and have dilated pupils. Following these early signs, a dog may become particularly restless, wandering long distances while biting and snapping at any moving object. This is often referred to as the *furious* form of rabies. These animals become insensible to pain and, if confined, may bite or slash at the bars of their cages. Partial paralysis of the vocal cords results in a change in the voice. Convulsions may be seen and may cause death.

THERE ARE TWO FORMS OF RABIES

The *dumb* form of rabies may follow the furious form or may be seen by itself. It is characterized mainly by paralysis. The dog's mouth often hangs open, and saliva drips from it. Since such dogs cannot ingest food or water, they become dehydrated. Eventually, total paralysis followed by death occurs.

Recovery from rabies is so extremely rare that animals suspected of being infected are usually euthanized and tested for infection after death. Protect your dog from rabies so you will never have to deal with the problem of owning a rabid animal. Dogs should first be vaccinated against rabies when they are three to four months of age. There are several types of vaccine available. The most commonly used types are inactivated virus. The vaccine is administered by *intramuscular* (in the muscle) injection into one of the hindlegs or *subcutaneously* (under the skin), usually near the shoulder blades. Protection against rabies is reached within one month after primary immunization. Vaccination against rabies is required by state law, and the same law regulates the frequency of booster vaccination as well. The current recommendations of the Centers for Disease Control vary with the type of vaccine administered. In general, a booster shot is given one year following the original vaccination, then booster

RABIES VACCINATION

doses are given every one to three years depending on the product used.

If you or your dog is exposed to a rabies suspect, that animal should be confined if possible and turned over to a public health officer for rabies quarantine or euthanasia. All bite wounds should be thoroughly washed with large quantities of soap and water and flushed with 70% ethyl alcohol, which kills rabies virus. Whether or not your dog will be quarantined following exposure to a rabies suspect will depend on state and local regulations. However, it is recommended that exposed, currently vaccinated dogs be revaccinated immediately and confined for observation for ninety days.

PSEUDORABIES MAY MIMIC RABIES *Pseudorabies,* a herpesvirus-induced disease of swine that is *fatal* when transmitted to dogs or cats, may be confused with rabies infection. Although aggressive behavior has not been reported, the fever, lack of appetite, restlessness, drooling, and self-mutilation that often accompany this disease can look similar to signs of rabies. Since no treatment is successful, the affected animals must be euthanized. Prevent this infection by not feeding your dog raw pork.

CANINE DISTEMPER

Canine distemper is an extremely common and often fatal viral disease occurring in dogs, other canids, and members of the Mustelidae (e.g., ferrets, minks, skunks) and Procyonidae (e.g., raccoons, pandas) families. It is seen most often in young, unvaccinated dogs but can occur in dogs of *any* age who have not been vaccinated or who have lost their immunity to distemper. The *incubation period* (time from exposure to signs of disease) for distemper is about four to nine days.

SIGNS OF DISTEMPER The first signs of distemper are often fever (103–105°F [39.4–40.5°C]), listlessness, lack of appetite, and vomiting. These signs may be followed by pneumonia and coughing, sticky yellowish discharges from the nose and eyes, diarrhea, thickening of the skin of the nose and footpads, muscle twitches, and convulsions. Any or all of the signs may be present at one time, and they may occur in almost any order. If the disease is not fatal, the dog is often left with incurable muscular tremors called *chorea* and discoloration of teeth forming at the time of infection. The distemper virus is shed in various bodily secretions and excretions and is an airborne infection that can be transmitted to a dog without bodily contact with the infected "carrier" dog.

The procedure for initial immunization against distemper varies with the immune status of your puppy and your ability to isolate your dog from exposure to the virus before vaccination is complete. Every effort should be made to keep your puppy away from dogs that might be shedding distemper virus and distemper-contaminated environments until vaccination is complete after fourteen to sixteen weeks of age. *Do not* allow your dog to play with strange dogs or go to parks or other areas frequented by large numbers of unsupervised dogs. While at your veterinarian's office keep your puppy in your lap and out of contact with possibly sick dogs.

Take your puppy to a veterinarian for a first distemper vaccination at six to eight weeks of age. A good veterinarian will perform a complete physical examination before administering the vaccine. (At this time he or she will also be able to answer any questions you may have about the care of your dog. Don't be afraid to ask questions; no question is "dumb," and you may learn something very important by asking.) The injection is usually given under the skin *(subcutaneously)* in the back area between the shoulder blades. It is usually pretty painless. If your puppy cries and wiggles when vaccinated, *don't* give a reward of hugging and praise, which may encourage uncooperative behavior later. Just remain calm and gently restrain your pet. If, like most dogs, your dog doesn't whimper, give lavish praise. Your veterinarian will advise bringing your dog back for a second vaccination in three weeks or more. In the meantime, be sure to keep your puppy well isolated from exposure to disease. In general, two or three vaccinations are given before immunity is complete. In some cases more vaccinations are necessary. The important thing to remember is that no matter how young a puppy is when vaccination is begun, the vaccinations should finish *after* fourteen to sixteen weeks of age. If you think the series is finished or have been told the series is finished before your dog is this age, go back to the veterinarian's for another injection.

If your dog contracts distemper, a large part of the responsibility for treatment may fall on you since many veterinarians will not hospitalize dogs with signs of distemper in order to avoid exposure of other dogs. It is important, however, to discuss the problem with a veterinarian and get intensive treatment started early. Treatment consists of appropriate antibiotics and vitamins and supportive care such as hand feeding, fluids, antidiarrheal medications, and anticonvulsant medication as necessary. Although distemper is often fatal, there is no reason to give up at the first signs of the disease. Many dogs have survived severe cases to live out normal lives. Premises contaminated with distemper virus should be thoroughly cleaned; disinfectants containing hypochlorite, phenol, or quaternary ammonium compounds are effective against distemper virus. Chlorine bleach mixed one part to thirty parts water is an effective hypochlorite disinfectant; phenol-containing disinfectants are available at drugstores. Your veterinarian may have to provide you with others. A susceptible dog may be introduced into a formerly distemper-contaminated environment about one month after cleaning as the virus (a morbillivirus) is quite susceptible to disinfectants, drying, and heat.

INFECTIOUS CANINE HEPATITIS

Infectious canine hepatitis is a viral disease caused by *canine adenovirus type I,* which may infect dogs, other canids, and bears. It is not a disease that affects humans. It should not be confused with human hepatitis, although the liver is involved in both diseases. In the early stages of canine hepatitis, the virus is shed in the feces and saliva of infected dogs. Later, the virus may be shed in the urine. Urine shedding may continue for several months following recovery. Infection may occur in dogs of any age when they come into contact with virus transmitted by urine, stool, or saliva.

SIGNS OF HEPATITIS — Canine infectious hepatitis may take several forms. Newborn puppies may die suddenly when infected, without previous signs of disease. Adult dogs with the *fulminating* form first run a high fever (as high as 106°F [41.1°C]), then develop bloody diarrhea and may vomit blood as well. These dogs often die within twenty-four to seventy-two hours. Such cases are often confused with cases of poisoning. In somewhat less severe cases there may be no blood in the stool, but signs of abdominal pain, loss of appetite, and an abnormal intolerance to light. Dogs with hepatitis usually require intensive veterinary care (hospitalization). Blood transfusions may be necessary if hemorrhaging is severe.

"BLUE EYE" — A mild form of hepatitis causing some depression and fever may be easily overlooked. It may be followed by the development of "blue eye," a corneal opacity (cloudiness) caused by damage to the corneal cells responsible for corneal fluid balance. This condition sometimes follows other forms of hepatitis and in the past occasionally followed vaccination against hepatitis. Newer vaccines do not have this side effect. It usually disappears spontaneously, but may be permanent. Your veterinarian may prescribe antibiotic ophthalmic medication for blue eye, but has no control over its occurrence and little over its permanence. In time most mild cases of viral hepatitis resolve with supportive care consisting of vitamins, special diets, and rest.

Vaccination against infectious hepatitis is usually initiated during the series of vaccinations for distemper. The vaccines are usually given together as one injection. Yearly booster injections should be given to maintain your dog's immunity.

HEPATITIS PREVENTION

LEPTOSPIROSIS

Leptospirosis is a disease caused by a type of bacterium called a *spirochete.* The organism is spread by contaminated urine, which recovered animals excrete for as long as a year. Rats and cattle, as well as other dogs, may shed species of *Leptospirae* that produce disease in dogs. Humans are susceptible to leptospirosis as well. The bacteria enter the body through breaks in the skin or mucous membranes, by ingestion, and occasionally during breeding. Disease occurs about seven to nineteen days after exposure.

Leptospirosis can affect many systems, but the primary signs of disease in dogs are those of kidney failure—loss of appetite, depression, vomiting, diarrhea, increased drinking and urination, dehydration, and weight loss. An infected dog may walk in a "hunched-up" posture due to muscular or kidney pain. Fever is present early in the disease. Dogs infected with leptospirosis can be left with chronic liver disease.

SIGNS OF LEPTOSPIROSIS

Leptospirosis is a serious disease requiring hospitalization. Supportive care, including intravenous fluid administration, is important. Refined techniques, such as *peritoneal dialysis* or *hemodialysis,* are sometimes necessary to save a dog with leptospirosis. In addition, the drugs of choice against this disease *(penicillin* and *dihydrostreptomycin)* must be administered by injection twice daily.

INTENSIVE CARE IS IMPORTANT

Vaccination against leptospirosis is usually done together with distemper and hepatitis vaccination. A series of two doses given two weeks apart is necessary for initial protection. The American Veterinary Medical Association currently recommends yearly booster shots. However, the immunity produced by *Leptospirae* vaccinations seems to be short-lived, and in high-risk areas booster doses every six months may be advisable. Ask your veterinarian whether twice-yearly injections for leptospirosis are necessary where you live.

LEPTOSPIROSIS PREVENTION

89

PARVOVIRUS

Parvovirus enteritis (inflammation of the bowel) is a highly contagious infectious viral disease of dogs that first appeared during the late 1970s. Canine parvovirus is closely related to feline panleukopenia virus (another parvovirus); however, neither virus causes disease in the other species.

SIGNS OF PARVOVIRUS

Parvovirus can infect a dog of any age not protected by maternal antibody or vaccination. However, the most severe illness is usually seen in dogs less than one year of age. The disease is usually acquired by ingestion of virus shed in the stools of infected dogs, and signs of illness usually start anywhere from three to ten days postinfection. Extremely young puppies (four to eight weeks of age) may die of sudden heart failure following infection of the heart muscle by canine parvovirus. More often, affected dogs develop fever (often 104–106°F [40–41.1°C]), loss of appetite, mental depression and lethargy, repetitive vomiting, and severe diarrhea, which may contain blood. If untreated, severely affected dogs become extremely dehydrated and soon die.

OTHER VIRUSES MAY MIMIC "PARVO" INFECTION

It is impossible to tell parvoviral infection from other viral *bowel* infections in dogs, such as canine *coronavirus,* on the basis of the pet's signs alone. However, the parvovirus replicates (reproduces itself) in many organs, and damage is most evident in tissues that have rapid cell proliferation such as the lymph nodes, intestine, and bone marrow. Therefore, a veterinarian may suspect parvovirus in a dog displaying typical signs of viral enteritis accompanied by a low white blood count (due to bone marrow infection) and then perform other blood or stool tests to confirm the diagnosis.

PARVOVIRUS TREATMENT

Treatment of any viral bowel infection must counteract the effects of diarrhea and/or vomiting *independent* of the cause (see pages 166 and 164). Any puppy sick more than a few hours with signs of possible viral enteritis should be examined by a veterinarian. Most very sick puppies will need hospitalization so fluids can be administered intravenously to maintain proper water equilibrium and to correct electrolyte imbalances. Injectable antibiotics are used to prevent secondary complications from bacterial infection, and antivomiting drugs may be needed.

"PARVO" PREVENTION

Protection against parvovirus infection is usually administered at the same time as other vaccinations against common infectious diseases.

Several different vaccines are usually combined into one product (a *multivalent* vaccine), so only one injection has to be given at each visit. As with other major infectious diseases of dogs, the first injection against parvovirus should be given between six and eight weeks of age and be followed by booster injections at two- to four-week intervals. Maternal-derived antibody interferes significantly with inoculation. There is often a period during which the passive protection afforded by maternal antibody is too low to protect a pup against disease but high enough to prevent a protective response to vaccination, leaving a dog in great danger of infection despite regular veterinary visits. In some dogs this effect is not overcome until sixteen to twenty weeks of age, when the last vaccination against parvovirus should be administered. Prior to this time, pet owners should be extremely cautious about exposing their puppy to other dogs and to environments that could have become contaminated with the virus. Puppies that have not finished their vaccination series should be kept on their owners' laps in veterinary waiting rooms, should only play with other healthy, vaccinated dogs in clean environments, and should not be placed in boarding kennels. Environments contaminated by parvovirus should be thoroughly cleaned and disinfected with chlorine bleach (one part bleach to thirty parts water) as this virus is resistant to many other common disinfectants and can survive for at least several weeks in an environment that has not been disinfected.

CORONAVIRUS

Although some veterinarians vaccinate against coronavirus, the disease it causes is usually relatively mild compared to parvovirus and it is unclear whether blood-borne antibody induced by vaccination can successfully protect the bowel against infection by the virus for any significant period of time.

CANINE RESPIRATORY DISEASE COMPLEX

For information on vaccines to prevent infectious causes of cough in dogs, see page 151.

INTERNAL AND EXTERNAL PARASITES

Parasites are creatures that at some point during their life cycle are dependent on a host (e.g., your dog). Not all parasites are harmful. In fact, in most well-cared-for small animals, owners overrate them as causes of illness. Under specific circumstances, certain parasites do cause disease; however, don't *assume* that because your dog is sick he or she has worms or that because he or she is scratching fleas must be present.

HOW TO USE THIS SECTION If you think your dog has a parasite problem, look for the signs in the Index of Signs. (Remember, though, not all animals with parasite infection show signs.) If you find the signs, turn to the appropriate pages and use the information there to help you decide whether or not you need to see a veterinarian. In most cases of internal parasite infection you will need professional help (see page 93). Many times you can correct an external parasite problem yourself.

If you don't think your dog has a parasite problem, it's a good idea to read or skim this section anyway to complete your knowledge of preventive medicine. The information is included here in the preventive medicine pages because the key to a successful fight against parasites is good prevention and control, which require good daily care. If you fail in your general daily care to take into account the life cycle of certain parasites, you may continue to have a problem even though you have administered treatment against the parasite to your dog. Learning about the different parasites discussed below will help you provide a healthy environment, thus preventing serious infection and reinfection of your dog as well as preventing human infection with certain parasites.

As with the diseases in the "Diagnostic Medicine" section, only the relatively common parasites of dogs are discussed here. They are:

> **Internal parasites:** Protozoans, flukes, tapeworms, and the following roundworms: ascarids, hookworms, whipworms, threadworms, stomach worms, eyeworms, lungworms, heartworms.
> **External parasites:** Fleas, ticks, lice, mites, flies.

INTERNAL PARASITES (ENDOPARASITES)

The *endoparasites* consist of *protozoa, trematodes* (flukes), *cestodes* (tapeworms), and *nematodes* (roundworms). For the most part, the adults of these parasites live in the intestines. *They may be present with or without causing illness, and you may or may not see them in your dog's stools.* Only if your dog is infected with one of the larger forms *may* you be able actually to see the parasites. If you think your dog has intestinal parasites but can't be sure because you have not seen them, or if you have a new puppy, take a fecal sample to your veterinarian. (A tablespoonful is plenty.) It should be as fresh as possible, in any case not more than twenty-four hours old even if kept under refrigeration. Veterinarians use special procedures to separate the parasites and/or their eggs from the stool and look for evidence of infection microscopically. A variety of drugs are used to treat internal parasites. Most can be administered orally by you at home. The products mentioned here are generally designated by their chemical generic name.

PROTOZOANS

There are few intestinal protozoans that cause illness in dogs. Signs of infection, if present, are variable but often include diarrhea not responsive to home treatment. There is no method to diagnose or treat these parasites at home, so you as an owner must rely on the help of a veterinarian who can diagnose their presence microscopically or with special lab tests and prescribe proper medication.

The most common intestinal protozoan infections of dogs are by *coccidia* or *Giardia* organisms, and most are self-limiting and asymptomatic. However, puppies that are raised in dirty kennels highly contaminated with parasites may become ill and develop diarrhea (sometimes bloody) when infected with coccidia.

NEOSPORUM CANINUM

An unusual protozoan parasite of dogs that resembles, but is distinct from, the *toxoplasmosis*-causing organism that may infect cats and sometimes causes serious illness in humans, was discovered in 1988. This parasite, *Neosporum caninum,* is suspected to be acquired by dogs consuming raw flesh of infected animals such as cattle, sheep, or mice and/or by direct contact with organisms shed in infected stool. Puppies may be infected before birth by transmission across the placenta. Dogs infected with this organism can have a wide variety of signs, such as hindlimb weakness or paralysis, swallowing difficulty, severe muscle atrophy, skin inflammation, and brain, heart, and eye abnormalities. Signs are ususally most severe in puppies, but infected dogs of any age may die. To prevent infection with this organism, avoid feeding dogs any raw meat and practice good hygiene on their premises by keeping stool picked up and rodents controlled.

FLUKES (TREMATODES)

Trematode parasites are also uncommon causes of disease in dogs. One fluke, *Paragonimus,* can cause cysts in the lungs of both cats and dogs, leading to a chronic cough and pneumonia. Infection can be prevented by keeping your pet from eating raw crayfish or from drinking water contaminated with infective stages of the fluke. Infection can be diagnosed by finding the microscopic fluke eggs in the stool or lung secretions. Treatment is with praziquantel or fenbendazole.

SALMON POISONING Another fluke of importance is *Nanophyetus salmincola*. This fluke is host to organisms *(rickettsia)* that cause a severe disease called salmon poisoning. Signs of this disease, including bloody diarrhea and lymph node enlargement, occur in dogs fed fluke-infected raw salmon and trout from the Pacific Northwest. Prevent this often fatal disease by not feeding your dog raw fish.

TAPEWORM LIFE CYCLE

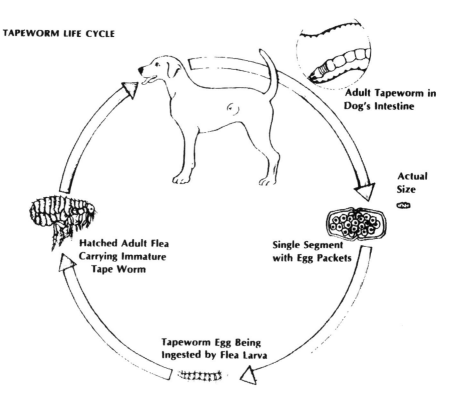

Adult Tapeworm in Dog's Intestine

Actual Size

Single Segment with Egg Packets

Hatched Adult Flea Carrying Immature Tape Worm

Tapeworm Egg Being Ingested by Flea Larva

TAPEWORMS (CESTODES)

Dogs acquire tapeworms by eating any of three types of infected material: (1) prey, offal (discarded animal parts), or uncooked meat, (2) raw freshwater fish, or (3) infected fleas or biting lice. The common tapeworms (*Taenia,* sp. *Dypylidium caninum*) are acquired by ingesting prey or infected fleas and have similar life cycles. The adult tapeworm has a head with hooks and suckers that attach to the intestinal wall and a body consisting of a series of reproductive segments. It obtains nourishment by absorbing nutrients in the digestive tract directly through the cuticle that covers each body segment of the worm. Eggs produced by the adult tapeworm pass out with the dog's feces and are eaten by an intermediate host (such as a rabbit, rodent, or flea), where they grow into an infective stage commonly called a "bladderworm." When the dog eats an intermediate host, this immature form completes the life cycle by becoming an adult tapeworm in the dog. The life cycle of tapeworms acquired from fish is more complex.

DIAGNOSING TAPEWORMS

Although heavy tapeworm infestations can cause poor growth or weight loss, coat changes, variable appetite, or gastrointestinal disturbances, in general you will have no reason to suspect infection until you see tapeworm segments clinging to the hair or skin around the anus or in a fresh bowel movement. Fresh tapeworm segments are opaque white or pinkish white, flat, and somewhat rectangular-shaped. They often move with a stretching-out and shrinking-back motion. When dry, the segments become yellow or off-white, translucent, and shaped somewhat like grains of rice. Tapeworm segments are not always present with tapeworm infection. When these are absent, diagnosis must be made through microscopic fecal examination.

REMEDIES FOR TAPEWORMS

In most cases it is easy to rid a dog of tapeworms. If you demonstrate that your dog has tapeworms, most veterinarians will supply you with safe, tapeworm-killing medication that can be administered at home without unpleasant side effects such as vomiting or diarrhea. Praziquantel or epsiprantel are common veterinary prescribed antitapeworm drugs. Sometimes, however, the deworming must be done in the veterinary hospital. Avoid using antitapeworm drugs available in pet stores. Most are ineffective, and effective over-the-counter drugs that contain *arecoline* cause purgation and can be dangerous. They may cause excessive vomiting, severe diarrhea, and sometimes convulsions. They should never be used for pregnant animals, and if used at all should always be administered by a veterinarian. After deworming, make an effort to prevent your dog from reexposure to sources of tapeworm infection. If you don't, deworming may have to be repeated several times a year.

Can people get tapeworms from their dogs? In general, the answer is no, but in certain cases dog tapeworms can pose a health hazard. Small children have sometimes gotten a tapeworm following accidental ingestion of a flea. The dog tapeworms *Echinococcus granulosus* and *Echinococcus multilocularis* can also pose health hazards. Dogs acquire *Echinococcus* infection by eating infected raw sheep, cow, horse, pig, deer, moose, or rodent meat, so these tapeworms are a problem mainly in rural areas. The tapeworms mature in infected dogs, and their eggs are passed out in the dogs' stool, where they contaminate the soil and infect intermediate hosts such as sheep or humans. Humans may be infected by direct contact with the eggs whether they are on the dog, in the stool or soil, or on unwashed vegetables contaminated with infective soil. When the "bladderworm" forms in human body tissues, severe disease can occur. If you live in a rural area, it is important to have your dog's stool examined periodically by a veterinarian, always avoid allowing dogs to scavenge raw meat or hunt, and practice good hygiene to prevent infection. Hands, utensils, or foods that may come into contact with infective eggs on the dog or in the soil should always be washed before contact with your mouth.

ASCARID LIFE CYCLE

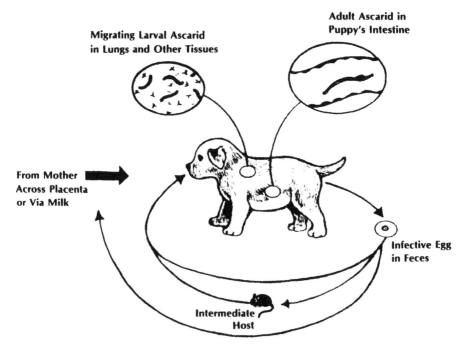

Migrating Larval Ascarid in Lungs and Other Tissues

Adult Ascarid in Puppy's Intestine

From Mother Across Placenta or Via Milk

Infective Egg in Feces

Intermediate Host

ROUNDWORMS (NEMATODES)

Roundworms seem to be the internal parasite most dog owners mean when they ask veterinarians about worms. Although most people are aware that roundworm infections occur in dogs, most are unaware that, like the other classes of internal parasites, there are several kinds of roundworms. Common ones are covered in the following pages.

ASCARIDS

Ascarids are the type of roundworms commonly seen in the stool of puppies. They are white, cylindrical, and pointed at both ends. They may be relatively small and threadlike in appearance, or as long as four to seven inches (10–18 cm), somewhat resembling white earthworms. Adult ascarids live in the small intestine and get their nourishment by absorbing nutrients in the digestive juices through their cuticle. Mature ascarids produce eggs that pass out in the dog's stool. After about one to four weeks, depending on environmental conditions, the eggs become infective and contain larval worms. If the infective eggs are ingested by an appropriate host, they complete their life cycle, eventually becoming adult worms in the intestine. Adult worms may begin passing eggs into an infected dog's stool as early as four weeks after infection. If they are eaten by an inappropriate host, such as a rodent, the larval worms encyst in the tissues of this host, where they remain unless a dog or other animal eats the host and releases the larvae.

When many dogs over one month and most dogs over one year of age ingest an infective egg of the common ascarid, *Toxocara canis,* the larvae do not complete their life cycle but become encysted in body tissues. When a female dog with such encysted stages becomes pregnant, the larvae are mobilized and penetrate the uterus to infect the unborn puppies. Therefore, puppies can be born with ascarid infection. **PUPPIES CAN HAVE ASCARIDS AT BIRTH**

Larval *Toxocara canis* ascarids are also shed in infected mother's milk and can infect nursing puppies after birth via this route. Benzimadole carbamate drugs are available that can reduce or eliminate the activated larvae if administered in the last trimester of pregnancy and during the first two weeks after birth. A common strategy is the administration of fenbendazole at 25 milligrams per pound of body weight (55 mg/kg) from the fortieth day of pregnancy to fourteen days after the pups' birth. To avoid drug administration during pregnancy, newborn puppies expected to be heavily infected with ascarid larvae can be treated daily for the first three days after birth and again two to three weeks later. Nursing mothers should be treated at the same time as their pups.

Ascarids do not usually cause obvious disease in adult dogs. Heavy prenatal infection with *Toxocara canis* in puppies can, however, lead to death. This roundworm migrates through the lungs en route to the intestine and can cause a cough or even pneumonia. More commonly, vomiting (of worms, sometimes), diarrhea, and progressive weakness are seen. Severely infected puppies may have dull coats and potbellies on a thin frame, and some develop bowel obstruction or rupture from impaction with ascarid roundworms.

ASCARID
TREATMENT
AND
ELIMINATION
FROM
PREMISES The drugs *piperazine* (at a dose of 50 mg/lb base, 110 mg/kg base) and *pyrantel pamoate* (2.27 mg/lb, 5 mg/kg) are used to remove adult ascarids from the intestines. Both are very safe and effective drugs that you can obtain from your veterinarian or a pet shop and that can be administered at home. There is no need to make your dog fast before administering the dewormers, and they do not usually cause vomiting or diarrhea. Avoid over-the-counter products containing dichlorophene and/or toluene since they have been associated with toxicity. Other drugs used to kill ascarids may be available only on a prescription from a veterinarian. These include products such as ivermectins, milbemycins, and benzimadole carbamates (e.g., mebendazole, fenbendazole). Puppies can be dewormed as early as two weeks after birth in order to remove ascarids before they start shedding eggs into the stool, resulting in environmental contamination. Public health authorities strongly recommend this procedure. Deworming should be repeated *at least* once two to four weeks later to remove any adult worms that were immature and not killed at the first dosing. For extremely heavy infections, deworming may have to be repeated several times before all worms present are killed. Therefore, it is common to deworm puppies every two to three weeks until they are three months of age.

Ascarid eggs are very resistant to environmental stresses. They can remain alive and infective for months or years once they have contaminated soil. These factors make it very important to practice good sanitation to prevent reinfection of your own dogs, as well as infection of other dogs and humans. Roundworm eggs cannot survive on surfaces that dry completely and that are exposed to sunlight on a regular basis. Therefore, stools should be removed at least weekly (preferably daily), and kennels should be built with impervious surfaces (e.g., concrete), exposed to sunlight as much as possible. They should be thoroughly cleaned with iodine-based disinfectants containing 120 parts per million free iodine. A 1% sodium hypochlorite solution (3 cups liquid chlorine bleach to 1 gallon water) will damage, but not kill, roundworm eggs as an aid to removal. Rodents and cockroaches, which may serve as intermediate hosts for the worms, should be controlled.

Although canine ascarids do not live in human intestines, their larvae can cause *visceral larval migrans,* a rare condition in which the larvae migrate in the body. *Visceral larval migrans* may cause anything from no signs of illness to severe signs, including blindness. It occurs most often among young children who play in egg-infested soil and put their contaminated hands into their mouths. Although complete recovery is the rule, the possibility of human infection is a significant reason for good ascarid control and good general hygiene.

ASCARIDS ARE A HUMAN HEALTH HAZARD

HOOKWORMS

Hookworms are small internal parasites (about ¼–½ [6–12.5mm] inch long) that attach to the wall of the small intestine and suck blood. Dogs may become infected by ingesting infective larval worms off the ground or by penetration of the skin by infective larvae. Puppies may become infected before birth by larvae migrating in the mother's body tissues and/or shortly after birth via larvae passed in the colostrum. (Antihookworm treatment identical to that described for females infected with ascarids can prevent these infections.) Prenatal hookworms can be treated with ivermectin.

Migration of hookworm larvae through the skin can cause itching reflected by scratching. Hookworms living in the intestine can cause diarrhea, severe anemia, weakness, and emaciation leading to death. Infection of puppies before birth sometimes causes anemia and death even before hookworm eggs are detectable in the stool. Puppies suspected to have these early infections should be dewormed with pyrantel pamoate (2.27 mg/lb., 5 mg/kg) every one to two weeks until twelve weeks of age.

POSSIBLE SIGNS OF HOOKWORMS

Hookworms cannot be diagnosed and treated effectively without the aid of a veterinarian, who will examine a stool sample for parasite eggs. Hookworms are small enough to be overlooked even when they are passed in the stool. The signs of illness caused by hookworm infection can be caused by other diseases as well. The safest and most effective compounds for treatment are available primarily through veterinarians. If your dog has to be treated for hookworms,

DIAGNOSIS AND TREATMENT

your veterinarian will probably use pyrantel pamoate or milbemycin oxime (not effective against *Uncinaria* hookworms), which you may be able to administer at home. Other kinds of effective drugs include febantel, disophenol, dichlorvos, butamisole hydrochloride, styrl-pyridinium chloride, ivermectin, and benzimadole carbamate drugs such as oxibendazole, fenbendazole, and mebendazole.

HOW TO
PREVENT
HOOKWORM
INFECTION

HOW TO PREVENT HOOKWORM INFECTION Hookworms are a problem only in areas that provide an environment suitable for the development of infective larvae. The preinfective stages require moderate temperatures (about 73–86°F [22.8°–30°C]) and moisture for development. If you live in a problem area, several prescription drugs (e.g., styrlpyridinium chloride, oxibendazole) can routinely be administered to your dog alone or with a heartworm prevention program (see page 103) to prevent hookworm infection. Prevent reinfection by and spread of hookworms by removing stool in a yard *at least* weekly, keeping lawns clipped short, and watering infrequently. (To kill larvae, grass must be kept dry for three weeks.) Paved runs should be hosed down daily, exposed to sunlight, and allowed to dry thoroughly. If you keep your dog on gravel, dirt, sand, or bark, concentrated sodium chloride solution (irritating to dogs' feet) or sodium borate (borax, 10 lb/100 ft², broadcast dry, raked lightly, and moistened) must be applied to kill the larvae. Repeat the application monthly.

HOOKWORMS ARE A HUMAN HEALTH HAZARD Rarely do people acquire intestinal infection with one of the dog hookworms *(Ancyclostoma caninum).* Visceral larval migrans (see page 99) may also occur. A more common problem in hookworm-infested areas is a condition called *cutaneous larval migrans.* It occurs when the skin is penetrated by larval hookworms, causing small bumps, red tracks, and itching. The condition is acquired not directly from an infected dog, but from contaminated ground.

WHIPWORMS

Whipworms (*Trichuris vulpis*) are intestinal parasites that live in the dog's large bowel and cecum (part of the large intestine), feeding on blood, tissue fluids, and intestinal cells, and that sometimes cause diarrhea, mucus and/or blood in the stool, and weight loss. Dogs acquire the parasite directly by ingesting infective larvae from contaminated soil. Humans are rarely infected. Diagnosis must usually be made by a veterinarian since the infection is often symptomless, although occasionally a dog may die from infection. Ask your veterinarian if you live in an area where whipworms are found. If you do, consider having a stool sample examined semiannually for evidence of infection. Infected dogs can be treated with several different drugs including dichlorvos, butamisole hydrochloride, milbemycin oxime, ivermectin, and benzimadole carbamates. Repeated treatments at monthly intervals are often necessary for dogs not removed from infected environments.

THREADWORMS (STRONGYLOIDES)

The threadworm, *Strongyloides stercoralis,* is a roundworm parasite of dogs, cats, and humans. Infection is most commonly acquired when infective larvae penetrate the skin. This can cause red lumps, crusts, and scratching. Dogs can also become infected by ingestion of infective larvae, and they may develop pneumonia as these larvae migrate through the lung. *Strongyloides* are very small worms and will not be seen in the stool. When diagnosis is established by a veterinarian, thiabendazole, diethylcarbamazine citrate, ivermectin, or pyrantel pamoate is often used for treatment. Prevent *Strongyloides* infection by providing your dog with a clean, dry environment.

STOMACH WORMS

Stomach worms infect both dogs and cats and occur mainly in the southeastern United States. They frequently cause vomiting, which cannot be differentiated from other causes of vomiting without examination of a fecal sample and the aid of a veterinarian. You can prevent infection of your dog by preventing the ingestion of cockroaches, crickets, and beetles, which serve as intermediate hosts for the development of one type of stomach worm *(Physoloptera),* as well as the ingestion of vomitus from other infected animals, which may carry a worm called *Ollulanus tricuspis.* Piperazine salts, dichlorvos, or fenbendazole is used for treatment.

EYEWORMS

Eyeworms are small roundworms (less than about ½ inch [≈1.25 cm] long) that live in the conjunctival sac of the infected dog. They cause reddening and irritation of the conjunctiva, discharge from the eye, and sometimes damage to the eyeball itself. They occur in North America (especially the western United States) and Asia and are transmitted through the mouth parts of flies that feed on secretions from the eye. You can eliminate infection with these worms if you find them by removing them with a pair of fine forceps or tweezers.

LUNGWORMS

Several species of worms that live in the respiratory system of dogs are commonly referred to as lungworms. They include *Capillaria aerophyla, Oslerus osleri,* and *Filaroides hirthi* among others. Depending on the species of worm that is causing the infection, signs may range from none to a mild cough to severe respiratory tract problems including repeated coughing and retching and severe difficulty breathing due to pneumonia. Lungworm infection cannot be diagnosed or treated at home. Therefore, any dog showing chronic respiratory signs should be examined by a veterinarian. As with other parasites, lungworms may be prevented by keeping premises clean and free from dog stool and by preventing dogs from eating potential intermediate hosts of lungworms such as snails and earthworms.

HEARTWORMS

Heartworm infection in dogs can be a serious and life-threatening problem. Adult heartworms *(Dirofilaria immitis),* which range from about 6 to 12 inches (15 to 30 cm) long, live mainly in the right atrium and ventricle, the pulmonary arteries, and the vena cavae. Mature worms produce *microfilaria* (larvae), which circulate in the blood. Mosquitoes feeding on an infected dog take up microfilaria with the blood meal. After about two weeks in the mosquito the microfilaria become infective larvae that can be passed on when another dog is bitten. These young forms become mature worms in the heart in about three months, and after an additional three months they can produce microfilaria, thus perpetuating the heartworm life cycle. Heartworms may occasionally infect cats and very rarely lodge in human lung tissue. There are areas all over the world where heartworm infection may occur. In the United States, infection is particularly common along the Atlantic and Gulf coasts, in the Mississippi Valley, and in Hawaii. However, it is also found in the Midwest, Pacific Far West, and Alaska.

HEARTWORM SIGNS AND DIAGNOSIS Dogs with heartworm disease may tire easily, cough, have difficulty breathing, and be *unthrifty* (lose weight in spite of a good appetite). Signs of liver disease or heart failure may also occur (see page 215). Dogs harboring only a few worms in their hearts, however, may show no signs of disease. (Some of these dogs react adversely when other medications such as deworming drugs are given.) Therefore, it is *extremely* important to have your dog checked every six months for heartworm infection if you live in an endemic area and once a year in less heavily infected areas. The test consists of a veterinarian drawing a blood sample, which can be examined by various techniques for the presence of microfilaria or heartworm antigen or antibody.

HEARTWORM LIFE CYCLE

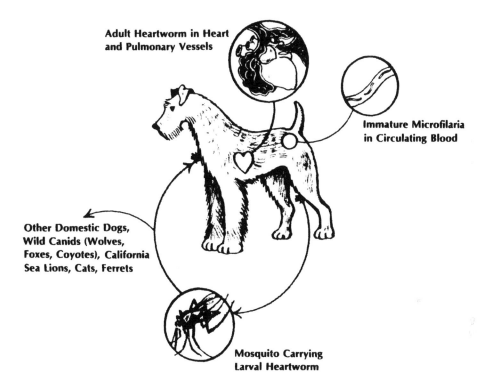

Adult Heartworm in Heart and Pulmonary Vessels

Immature Microfilaria in Circulating Blood

Other Domestic Dogs, Wild Canids (Wolves, Foxes, Coyotes), California Sea Lions, Cats, Ferrets

Mosquito Carrying Larval Heartworm

VETERINARIANS MUST TREAT HEARTWORMS

If your dog shows evidence of heartworm infection, your veterinarian will want to take a chest X-ray and perform blood tests for kidney and liver function before beginning treatment. Treatment consists of *intravenous* (into-a-vein) injections of a drug called *thiacetarsamide*. Reactions to the drug do occur, so treatment should be performed only by a veterinarian and only while your dog is hospitalized. Six weeks after the elimination of adult heartworms, a treatment to clear the bloodstream of microfilaria must be given.

YOU CAN PREVENT HEARTWORMS

Susceptibility to heartworm infection is not affected by breed, sex, or hair length. Scientific studies have proven, however, that dogs kept indoors during mosquito-active times have a lower incidence of

103

heartworm infection than dogs in the same geographic area kept outdoors. Fortunately, drugs provide easier means of control. Products available on a veterinarian's prescription may be given once a month (milbemycin oxime, ivermectin) or once a day (diethylcarbamazine citrate). The pros and cons of each preventive strategy should be discussed with your veterinarian for each dog on an individual basis. Be sure your dog is heartworm-free, however, before using any preventive medication. Puppies under six months of age should also be tested for microfilaria before taking a heartworm preventive, as *Dirofilaria immitis* larvae in an infected pregnant dog may cross the placenta into the unborn pups.

PINWORMS

In answer to a common question: Dogs do not get or spread pinworms. The human pinworm, *Enterobius vermicularis,* occurs only in humans and higher primates such as chimpanzees.

EXTERNAL PARASITES

External parasites of dogs are *arthropods* (hard-coated insects and insectlike animals) that live on dog skin, feeding off the blood, tissue fluid, or skin itself.

FLEAS

Fleas are probably the most prevalent external parasite of dogs. They are wingless, small dark brown insects capable of jumping great distances relative to their body size. They obtain nourishment by sucking blood. Fleas are not very host-specific. In spite of the fact that there are several flea species, cat fleas *(Ctenocephalides felis)* can be found on dogs, dog fleas *(Ctenocephalides canis)* can be found on cats, and cat and dog fleas will feed from humans. Human fleas *(Pulex irritans)* also feed on dogs and occasionally on cats. The important thing is not the kind of flea present, but that a dog should not have fleas at all. A *single* flea on a pet is a cause for concern. Flea infestation should not be considered a normal or natural condition, and just a few fleas can sometimes be responsible for serious disease. Large numbers of fleas can be responsible for significant loss of blood in puppies, old animals, or any weakened dog. This blood loss *(anemia)* can result in death, particularly in young puppies. Fleas are carriers of disease, including the organism that causes human plague and also tapeworms (see page 94). Allergic dermatitis is also commonly caused by fleas (see page 129).

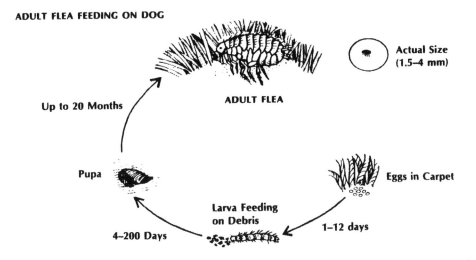

ADULT FLEA FEEDING ON DOG

Actual Size
(1.5–4 mm)

ADULT FLEA

Up to 20 Months

Pupa

Eggs in Carpet

Larva Feeding
on Debris

4–200 Days

1–12 days

Optimum Environmental Conditions for Development 65–85°F (18–27°C) 75–85% Humidity

Female fleas lay their eggs only after consuming a blood meal. They may lay them directly on the host, but because the eggs aren't sticky, they usually drop off. Flea eggs are white and about the size of a small grain of salt. If a dog is heavily infested with fleas, eggs may be found in the coat mixed with flea feces (partially digested blood), which are about the same size but colored black. (Moistening suspected flea excreta should produce a blood-red spot.) The eggs hatch into larvae anytime from two days to two weeks after being laid. Mature flea larvae resemble very small fly maggots. They are about ¼ inch ($\approx$6 mm) long and white to creamy yellow in color. They are usually found in cracks in floors, under carpets, in dog bedding, and other similar places. The larvae feed only a little, eating adult flea excreta or other organic debris in the environment. Then they spin cocoons in which they develop into adult fleas. Depending on environmental conditions, larvae may take from about ten days to several months to become adult fleas. They are very sensitive to drying; therefore, they prefer an environment that is uniformly moist but not wet, a condition that is often found in sandy areas outdoors. Once larval fleas enter their cocoons, they are called *pupae*. Pupae are extremely resistant to any chemical or physical means of destruction and may survive for up to twenty months before emerging as adult fleas. After hatching, adult fleas can live up to twelve months without feeding, just waiting to jump on your pet.

Since a major part of the flea life cycle takes place off the dog, flea control on a single host is not sufficient to get rid of fleas completely. Fastidious housekeeping is essential, and flea control must be prac-

FLEA LIFE CYCLE IMPORTANT IN CONTROL

ticed on all pets living in a single house. Existing fleas must be removed from the premises (including from vehicles in which flea-infested pets have been transported) so that the pet can be used as a sentinel to alert you to any potential reinfestation.

Washing or burning infested bedding and thorough vacuuming can be sufficient to get rid of small numbers of fleas providing that the cleaning routine is kept up weekly year-round and providing that all pets in the household are kept scrupulously clean. In the case of a moderate to heavy infestation, houses, yards, and kennels must be sprayed or fumigated with commercial insecticides, or the services of professional exterminators must be obtained.

HOW TO DETECT FLEAS AT HOME

Two ways to detect fleas in your environment are the white handkerchief and white sock techniques. In the first, a white linen handkerchief is inserted between the end of the vacuum cleaner hose and its coupling to the power source. After vacuuming the pet's sleeping area, the carpet, and other areas (even the dog), remove the handkerchief and place it quickly and carefully into a plastic bag. Then seal it. With a magnifying glass, it is easy to detect flea eggs, larvae, pupae, and even adult fleas trapped in the handkerchief.

The white sock technique detects adult fleas in a suspected area. Put on a pair of white knee socks and walk briskly around the suspected area for five minutes. Fleas respond to vibrations in the environment, body heat, and exhaled carbon dioxide and often jump onto the socks, where they can be seen. *Any* flea observed is significant, as one adult female flea can lay up to forty eggs per day and a breeding pair of fleas can easily produce 600 offspring in a month!

HOW TO SELECT FLEA CONTROL PRODUCTS

Products for treating premises against fleas include a variety of insecticides, insect growth regulators, and a few noninsecticidal products. Insecticides for treatment of premises are available as liquids to be sprayed in or outdoors or as indoor foggers (antiflea "bombs") that release a fine mist into the air when activated. Any good veterinary clinic should be able to help you select a product, but be sure to read the labels of any products you choose and ask any questions that may come to mind. It is very important to select insecticidal products that have the lowest possible toxicity to species other than the flea and that are *nonpersistent* in the environment (see chart, pages 111–113). Most products that meet these requirements need *repeated application* to the infested area (usually every two weeks for at least three or four applications) to eliminate adult fleas, which will continue to emerge from the pesticide-resistant cocoon stage as the previously applied pesticide degrades.

Insect growth regulators (e.g., methoprene, pyriproxyfen, fenoxycarb) are biochemicals that mimic the insect hormone necessary for proper flea development, thus disrupting the early flea life stages and causing them to die. These products can provide about two to five months of persistent flea control when applied to areas harboring only flea eggs and larvae. They cannot kill pupae or adult fleas. Although these relatively environmentally safe chemicals cannot by themselves provide full flea control, they can lessen the amount of pesticide that has to be applied to the environment over time in order to kill adult fleas by eliminating fleas in the earlier life stages. Insect growth regulators are included in various premise sprays, foggers, and pet sprays in combination with a variety of insecticides. Nematodes that disrupt the flea life cycle by killing the larvae and pupae are the basis for some other products used for flea control on premises. Read the labels and, if necessary, ask your veterinarian for advice to find the best product for your circumstances, as more than 300 products are available for the control of fleas on pets and on premises.

Nonchemical methods of flea control are important to the success of any program using chemicals and for continuing good flea control once fleas are eliminated from the premises. Before using flea control products, thorough cleaning of washable floor surfaces and vacuuming of carpets and furniture is critical. Special attention should be given to baseboards, sheltered areas under furniture, and the spaces around and under furniture cushions. Burn the vacuum cleaner bags after use. Pieces of flea collars or flea powders placed in vacuum cleaner bags will also kill emerging adult fleas. However, they may also result in additional aerosol environmental contamination by pesticides, and this is not an approved use of insecticides by the Environmental Protection Agency. Also avoid using napthalene moth crystals (moth balls) in vacuum cleaner bags to kill fleas since they can generate explosive gas. Area rugs should be washed on a regular basis, and steam cleaning of wall-to-wall carpets will kill all flea life stages if done properly. Various insecticides and larvacidal products can be applied in carpet-washing solutions if necessary, and drying products that kill fleas by dessication can be sprinkled on carpets. However, the major key to good flea control is absolute cleanliness in the environment and on the pet.

If your dog has fleas, the first thing to do is to give him or her a good bath. You can use any gentle shampoo or a commercial dog shampoo containing insecticide to kill fleas. If you use a regular shampoo, remember that you are only removing fleas mechanically. If you don't rinse your dog's coat well, fleas stunned by the water will wake up as the coat dries and still be around to cause trouble. Insecticidal

START PET FLEA CONTROL WITH A BATH

shampoos have no significant residual action, but they do help kill fleas during the bath. A bath once a week followed by a cream rinse can be sufficient for flea control in low-flea-density areas. (Certain bath oils and creme rinses designed for people seem to have flea-repelling effects. Ask your veterinarian for instructions for using a specific product on your dog.) Once your dog is clean, use any of the following for continued flea control.

FLEA DIPS Dips are insecticides that are applied to the dog's coat as a liquid and allowed to dry. It is easiest to sponge on a dip while the dog is still wet following a bath. It is not necessary to immerse a dog physically in the dipping liquid. Avoid applying insecticides around the eyes, nose, and mouth (even if directed to do so by the label). Dips containing pyrethrins or synthetic pyrethrins (see chart, pages 111–113) are generally less toxic and less environmentally persistent than those containing other insecticides, and they can provide very effective flea control if applied regularly. Some dips contain insect growth regulators. In areas with a major flea problem, it is desirable to switch between product categories periodically to avoid the possible emergence of a strain of flea resistant to any single insecticide group.

FLEA SPRAYS, Flea sprays, roll-ons, spot-ons, and powders (dusts) are made from
ROLL-ONS, a large variety of insecticides, insecticide potentiators, and some-
SPOT-ONS AND times insect-growth inhibitors in an alcohol or water carrier (sprays,
POWDERS roll-ons), proprietary carrier (spot-ons) or a diatomaceous earth or silica carrier (powders). The same considerations about toxicity, environmental persistence, and flea resistance apply to the selection of these products as to a dip. In general, powders, sprays, and roll-ons must be applied frequently—often daily—to provide good flea control. Many animals and owners object to this process. It is important to apply most powders and sprays moderately and regularly rather than infrequently and heavily if good flea control is to be achieved. The legs, back, tail, and rump are the most important areas to cover, and it is essential to apply these products near the skin by pushing the hair against its direction of growth and rubbing the product in. It is often helpful to apply sprays or powders just before a pet is allowed outdoors or is taken for a walk. This allows any fleas that jump on during outdoor activity to be killed immediately (and not brought back indoors!), as well as allowing sprays to dry and excess powder to fall out of the fur.

    The introduction of highly effective, relatively safe spot-on products designed to remain in the surface oils of the pet's skin has simplified flea control for thousands of owners. These spot-ons have been developed to limit deposition of the insecticide in the environment while providing flea control for a month or longer even with exposure to water. Ask your veterinarian which product is best for your dog. All of them spread spontaneously over the body after direct application to small areas of the skin. Some will control ticks.

Avoid applying any topical insecticide to irritated or raw skin. Insecticides are more readily absorbed systemically from areas where the skin has been broken. Alcohol can be irritating to sensitive skin, and the drying action of the carriers in flea powders—which itself helps kill fleas—can also be irritating to both normal and abnormal skin.

FLEA COLLARS Many flea collars contain organophosphate or carbamate insecticides incorporated into a plastic base that allows their slow release. These chemicals kill fleas by direct contact. Some collars contain growth regulators that prevent flea eggs laid on the pet from hatching. A false sense of security may arise when a pet wears a flea collar, resulting in infested premises if early evidence of collar failure is not noticed. Collars should be replaced on a regular schedule *well before the stated expiration date on the package.* Pets wearing flea collars should be bathed frequently and examined often for fleas. Any evidence of fleas on a pet who is wearing a flea collar is grounds for reevaluation of the full flea control program with special attention to the premises.

Always follow package directions for the use of flea collars. Apply them so they can move freely on the pet's neck, and avoid wetting them to prevent premature loss of the antiflea effect. Other insecticides should not be applied in the presence of a flea collar unless advised by a veterinarian.

FLEA COLLARS CAN CAUSE CONTACT DERMATITIS A few dogs are sensitive to insecticides and develop *contact dermatitis* when a flea collar is applied. The dermatitis often first appears as hair loss and reddening of the neck skin under the flea collar. If the collar is removed at this time, the condition usually clears up with no other treatment. If the collar is not removed, the skin condition can progress to large raw areas, sometimes secondarily infected with bacteria, which can be difficult to clear up and need the attention of a veterinarian. Flea collar dermatitis can sometimes be prevented by airing the collar for two or three days before putting it on the dog. Dogs that cannot wear flea collars should not have similar insecticides applied to their skin in the form of dips, sprays, or powders.

MANUAL FLEA REMOVAL Removal of fleas by hand or with a flea comb is an extremely inefficient method of flea control. To ensure a flea-free animal, the

entire coat must be flea-combed by hand for at least forty-five minutes daily, a process few people will routinely undertake. Of course,
if you see a flea, you should remove it, but don't rely on this as a
means of routine control if other methods can be used. If they cannot
be, be sure to combine flea-combing with regular bathing and extremely fastidious housekeeping. And consider purchasing a flea-
comb unit that can attach to your vacuum cleaner. Suction increases
the effectiveness of the combing process.

HOME
REMEDIES
Scientific experiments have been unable to substantiate the effectiveness of home remedies against fleas such as applying ultrasonic
or eucalyptus bud–or pennyroyal oil–impregnated collars or feeding
brewer's yeast. Flea traps that consist of a light source suspended
over a sticky paper have been shown by scientific experiment to
catch no more than 2% of fleas released into a controlled environment. If you want to stick to such remedies, examine your dog
thoroughly and *frequently* for evidence of fleas. If *any* are present,
immediately reevaluate your means of flea control.

SYSTEMIC FLEA
CONTROL
Organophosphate insecticides have been developed that are designed to kill fleas only after they have taken a blood meal from the
dog. One drug, *cythionate,* is given orally; another, *fenthion,* is
applied to the dog's skin, from which it is systemically absorbed.
Both these drugs have a potent ability to lower the dog's blood level
of *cholinesterase,* an enzyme that is important to normal nervous
system function and either can result in significant drug interactions
when other drugs with similar effects are administered in the course
of anesthesia or disease treatment. Accidental overdose can result in
vomiting, muscle tremors, hyperexcitability, drooling, diarrhea, and
death. Systemic flea control drugs can also cause serious illness and
death if a treated dog is exposed simultaneously to other flea control
products or insecticides used to eliminate fleas from the house or
yard. Such drugs cannot be given to puppies, old dogs, dogs with
liver disease, or dogs with any kind of debilitating illness. Dogs with
flea bite allergies (see page 129) are not helped by these antiflea
treatments as the fleas must bite the dog before they are killed. These
drugs also have no effect whatsoever on flea life stages off the dog.
The only justification for their use may be when an owner is so fearful
of personal exposure to any other product that he or she is willing
to subject his or her dog to a *subclinical* (not visible on physical
exam) level of toxin exposure in order to kill fleas.

Lufenuron, an orally administered insect growth regulator, prevents eggs from fleas that have fed on treated dogs from hatching.

Although it is a relatively safe drug, it is best used only with a full understanding of your dog's flea control needs.

The sticktight flea, *Echinophaga gallinacea,* is mainly a parasite of poultry, but it can attack dogs. You can recognize sticktight fleas easily because the adults stick tightly to the dog's skin and don't run off when approached. They are voracious blood suckers and, if found, should be removed by the use of a topical insecticide followed by routine means of environmental flea control.

STICKTIGHT FLEAS

In the Middle Ages it was common for both humans and dogs to be infested with fleas. Modern standards of cleanliness have made human infestation with fleas rare and unacceptable in normal, clean environments. This state is maintained without antiflea dips, sprays, and powders as part of one's daily toilette. A similar state exists for dogs who are kept clean and who live in clean households surrounded by neighbors who set the same high standards for their pets. Flea infestation could be a thing of the past for pets if all dogs and cats had owners who gave them good care.

DOG OWNERS CAN ELIMINATE FLEA INFESTATION

TYPICAL INSECTICIDES

CHEMICAL CLASSIFICATION	INSECTICIDE	ADVANTAGES/ DISADVANTAGES
Botanicals	d-limonene† linalool† pyrethrin (Sectrol*)† rotenone	Rapid kill; usually safe; degrade rapidly after application; short residual action
Carbamates	aldicarb (Temik*) bendiocarb (Ficam*) carbaryl (Sevin*)† carbofuran (Furandan*) methiocarb (Mesurol*) methomyl (Lannate*) propoxur (Baygon*)†	Slow environmental degradation; more potentially toxic than pyrethroids, less so than organophosphates; longer residual activity; flea resistance reported in certain geographic areas

CHEMICAL CLASSIFICATION	INSECTICIDE	ADVANTAGES/ DISADVANTAGES
Growth regulators/ development inhibitors	fenoxycarb (Tenocide*, Torus*)† lufenuron (Program*)† methoprene (Precor*, Siphotrol*)† pyriproxifen	Usually very safe; target immature insect stages; do not kill adult fleas; not species specific
Nitromethylenes	imidocloprid (Advantage*)†	Rapid kill; usually safe; degrades in the environment and on the animal; not species specific
Organochlorides	aldrin chlordane chlordecone (Kepone*) DDT dieldrin endosulfan (Thiodan*) endrin lindane methoxychlor toxaphene	Good residual action; persist in the environment; toxic to wildlife therefore many now banned
Organophosphates	chlorpyrifos (Dursban*)† coumaphos (Co-ral*) cythionate (Proban*)† diazinon† dichlorvos (DDVP*, Vapona*, Task*)† dimethoate (Cygon*) disulfoton (Di-Syston*)	Potent nerve toxins (cholinesterase inhibitors) with high potential for acute toxicity, suspected chronic toxicity for some products; good residual activity; broad spectrum of external and internal parasite- and "pest"-killing activity

CHEMICAL CLASSIFICATION	INSECTICIDE	ADVANTAGES/ DISADVANTAGES
	famphur (Warbex*)	
	fenthion	
	fonofos (Dyfonate*)	
	malathion†	
	naled (Dibrom*)	
	parathion (Baldan*)	
	phorate (Thimet*)	
	phosmet (Paramite*, Kemolate*, Imidan*)	
	propetamphos (Safrotin*)	
	ronnel (Korlan*, Nankor*, Ectoral*, Etrolene*, Trolene*),	
	temephos, (Abate*)	
	tetrachlorvinphos (Rabon*)	
	trichlorfon (Neguvon*)	
Phenylpyrazoles	Fipronil (Frontline*)†	Rapid kill; degrades slowly on the animal; not species specific
Pyrethroids (Synthetic pyrethrins)	allethrin (Pynamin*) d-trans allethrin cypermethrin fenvalerate (Ectrin*) permethrin† d-phenothrin resmethrin tetramethrin	Rapid kill; usually safe; moderately rapid degradation in environment and on animal; longer residual activity than botanicals

*Trade name
†Common ingredient in flea control products

TICKS

Adult female ticks look different before and after they have taken a blood meal from a dog. Males, however, don't eat blood meals and swell so they will be small if found on your pet. Dogs are most likely to pick up ticks in wooded or rural areas. The worst thing ticks usually do to dogs is to cause an area of skin inflammation at the site of attachment. Ticks can, however, cause serious disease—anemia due to blood loss, tick paralysis—and in some geographical areas they carry organisms that cause disease in dogs. So their presence should never be ignored. *Babesia,* a parasite of dog red blood cells, is spread by ticks. Rickettsial organisms, which cause Rocky Mountain spotted fever (a disease that affects humans as well as dogs) and ehrlichiosis, another blood disease of dogs, are also transmitted by ticks. *Borrelia burgdorferi,* the bacterium responsible for Lyme disease,* can be transmitted by ticks to both humans and dogs.

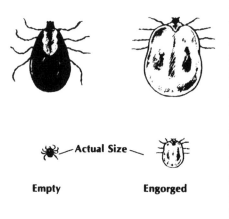

FEMALE TICKS

—Actual Size—

Empty   **Engorged**

HOW TO REMOVE TICKS

The average dog usually has so few ticks that the easiest method of removal is by hand. Using forceps, tweezers, or your thumb and first finger protected by a tissue or disposable gloves, grasp the tick as close as possible to where its mouthparts insert into the dog's skin. Then exert a firm but gentle, constant pull. (There's no need to twist.) If you've pulled just right and gotten the tick at the optimum time after attachment, the entire tick will detach. If the mouthparts are left embedded, don't worry. The tick never grows back, the mouthparts fall out naturally, and only rarely does a tick bite become infected. The site of the tick bite usually becomes red and thickened in reaction to a substance secreted in the tick's saliva, but it usually heals in about two weeks. *Do not* try to burn off ticks with a match or apply kerosene, gasoline, or other similar petroleum products. Numerous effective commercial tick extractors are now available, eliminating the need to kill an individual tick in order to remove it. Always avoid contact with the body fluids of ticks to avoid infection of yourself by disease-causing organisms (the Lyme disease spirochete bacteria can penetrate skin directly) and always wash your hands with soap and water after removing a tick.

If your dog gets many ticks or if you live in a particularly tick-infested area, use a commercial dip, spray, or spot-on to remove them and act against further infestation. There is no effective method to prevent ticks from getting onto a dog; however, products containing the synthetic pyrethrin *permethrin* have been found to repel them and will kill ticks in a few days. Special anti-tick collars are also available. Use them only if other methods are unsuitable. Inspect your dog for ticks daily in order to keep your pet healthy and comfortable and to prevent infestation of the premises with ticks.* **CONTROL TICKS WITH DIPS**

To learn about ear ticks, see *otitis externa,* page 145. **EAR TICKS**

LICE

In well-cared-for dogs, lice are much less common than fleas or ticks. Adult lice are pale-colored and about 1/10 (≈2.5 mm) inch or less in length. They spend their entire life on one host and attach their tiny white eggs (nits) to the hair. Some lice require blood or body fluids to live; others eat skin scales. They can cause intense signs of itching and can carry certain tapeworm larvae. Kill lice with a thorough bath followed by a dip effective against ticks and fleas.

LOUSE

Actual Size

*The first reported case of Lyme disease in a dog was published in 1984. Apparently many dogs exposed to *Borrelia burgdorferi* do not come down with the disease, as positive blood tests for the Lyme spirochete (spiral bacterium) are sometimes found in up to 50% of symptom-free dogs in a community. Therefore the diagnosis of Lyme disease is based on the dog's clinical signs, which may include fever, swollen lymph nodes, heart conditions, neurological abnormalities, eye inflammation, arthritis, and/or kidney inflammation. After other diseases are ruled out, a dog with suspected infection can be treated with appropriate antibiotics (usually a penicillin- or tetracycline-family drug). As the efficacy of any vaccine against Lyme disease is unclear, the best prevention is to keep your dog away from brushy areas, which may be tick infested, apply tick-killing insecticides to the dog's fur frequently, and/or remove ticks daily since *infection does not occur until the tick has been attached and feeding for some time.*

115

EAR MITES

Ear mites, *Otodectes cynotis,* live primarily in the ear canal of dogs and cats and feed on skin debris and tissue fluids. They cause the formation of large amounts of dark reddish brown to black wax in the ear and usually vigorous head shaking and ear scratching.

HOW TO DIAGNOSE EAR MITES

If you think your dog has ear mites, remove some of the discharge from the ear canal with a cotton swab. You may be able to see the mites by examining the waxy material in a bright light or by putting it on a piece of black paper. (A magnifying glass may help you.) Live ear mites look like moving white specks about the size of a pinpoint.

TREATMENT OF EAR MITES

If you have seen mites and there is not much of a discharge, you may be able to treat the condition at home. *Do not* attempt home treatment unless you have seen the mites. Other ear problems can cause similar discharges and may be complicated by the use of an ear mite preparation. Treatment consists of cleaning out the ears and instilling insecticidal liquid with an eyedropper or dropper bottle. How often this must be done depends on the product used. However, no matter which topical product is selected, the full treatment period must extend over a total of thirty days' time in order to kill all stages in the life cycle. It is also advisable to clean the premises thoroughly and to bathe the dog and apply topical insecticides to the dog's coat as ear mites are occasionally found in the fur or in the environment, where they may survive for months. Whether or not you will need to see a veterinarian to obtain an effective ear mite preparation depends on the area in which you live, as some states control over-the-counter sale of insecticides more closely than others. Effective preparations often contain one or more of the following: *rotenone, pyrethrins, piperonyl butoxide, thiabendazole, dichlorophen, methoxychlor polyhydroxidine.* If your dog's ears are very dirty or very inflamed, it is best to have them thoroughly cleaned by a veterinarian before treatment is begun. Veterinarians may also administer some injectable drugs to kill the mites.

SARCOPTIC MANGE MITES

Sarcoptes scabiei (var. *canis*) is a microscopic mite that infests dogs and that can transiently infest human beings. These mites burrow beneath the outer, nonliving layers of the skin, causing intense signs of itching followed by hair loss. They seem to prefer the skin of the ears, elbows, legs, and face, so early hair loss and crusts are often seen in these areas. Untreated cases can spread until the whole body is involved. *Sarcoptes* infestation *(scabies)* is easily spread from dog to dog.

SARCOPTES MITE

If your dog scratches intensely and you find small, itchy, red bumps on yourself (particularly on the abdomen), you may suspect the presence of sarcoptic mange. Infection can be confirmed only by microscopic examination of a skin scraping, and often several scrapings must be taken by a veterinarian before mites are found. It is advisable to have your dog examined by a veterinarian before beginning treatment for sarcoptic mange. Not only can a veterinarian confirm the presence of mites and give you detailed information on the use of a proper insecticide, he or she can also administer a *corticosteroid* (see page 235) to help relieve the itching until the mites are completely gone and antibiotics in cases of secondary bacterial infection. In some cases, veterinarians may treat scabies with antimite injections.

SIGNS OF SARCOPTIC MANGE

If you live in an area in which you cannot obtain the services of a veterinarian and choose to begin treatment yourself, be sure to follow the directions on the insecticide container carefully and avoid contact with your own skin. Treatment consists of clipping the affected areas (of long-haired dogs), bathing, and applying a dip that kills *Sarcoptes* once every two weeks for a total of three dips. Among the insecticides effective against *Sarcoptes* are *gamma isomer of BHC (lindane), ronnel, malathion,* and *dichlorvos.* Lime sulfur dips (2%–3% orchard spray solution) may also successfully be used.

SCABIES TREATMENT

DEMODECTIC MANGE MITES

Demodex canis is a mite that is present in small numbers in the hair follicles of almost all dogs. This mite can be present without causing disease, and all the factors involved in the production of skin disease by this mite have not yet been determined. It has been shown that puppies acquire *Demodex* mites from their mother early in the nursing period, long before signs of infestation occur. When demodectic mange does occur, it may take several forms.

117

The *localized (squamous)* form of demodectic mange usually occurs in dogs under one year of age. It causes relatively small (about 1-inch-diameter [2.5 cm]) areas of hair loss, exposing healthy-looking patches of skin that do not usually seem to itch.

Occasionally the affected areas may look red and/or scaly. These patches often occur on the face or forelegs. This form may also be seen as hair loss around the eyes. Hair loss appears gradually, and after the patches have reached their maximum size, hair usually begins to regrow in about a month. Most cases of localized *Demodex* heal spontaneously. If hair loss isn't progressing, it is usually safe to watch and wait. Be cautious, however; localized *Demodex* and ringworm (see page 132) may be confused, and some cases of local *Demodex* progress to the generalized form.

In *pododemodicosis,* the mites may be limited to the feet, where

DEMODEX MITE they cause hair loss and redness. Secondary infection with bacteria may result in swelling and drainage accompanied by pain.

Generalized cases of demodectic mange may occur in dogs of any age. Hair loss progresses from many small patches to large areas, and exposed skin often becomes secondarily infected with bacteria, resulting in crusts (scabs) and oozing. It is often extremely difficult to treat and can have a fatal course if it does not respond to therapy. Older dogs affected by generalized demodectic mange often have other underlying illness or develop other serious diseases or cancer later. Professional veterinary help is needed if you think your dog might have this type of demodectic mange or if the localized form seems to be spreading. Diagnosis requires expression of the hair follicles followed by a skin scraping and examination of the material obtained under a microscope. Some cases may require a skin *biopsy* for diagnosis. Treatment requires antibiotics and antimite medications available only on a veterinarian's prescription.

It is strongly recommended that dogs affected with generalized demodicosis be neutered and not be used for breeding even if visibly cured. The tendency to develop this disease is clearly inherited, and its incidence can be lowered by strict breeding programs.

CHEYLETIELLA DERMATITIS

Cheyletiella are off-white or yellowish large mites that most commonly infest young puppies brought up in dirty environments. They cause a dandrufflike condition and mild signs of itching. This mite can be seen with the naked eye if an infested dog is carefully examined. Control is easily achieved by cleansing with insecticidal shampoo or using insecticidal dips, sprays, or powders (e.g., pyrethrins, carbaryl, lime sulfur) once a week for three weeks on *all* animals on the premises. Cheyletiella mites are capable of infesting cats, foxes, rabbits, and humans as well as dogs. Infection of people with the common "walking dandruff" mite of dogs *(Cheyletiella yasquri)* is usually only transient and, if necessary, can be treated with insecticidal shampoos. Premises should be treated with insecticides (see flea control, pages 106–107) as a few female mites may live off the host for as long as ten days. If topical treatment is not possible, some veterinarians may administer antimite drugs by injection.

TROMBICULID MITES (CHIGGERS)

Trombiculid mites (chiggers, harvest mites) are red, orange, or yellowish mites that have larvae that are parasitic on dogs and other mammals. (The nymphs and adults feed on plants or invertebrates.) The larvae are often found on the head and neck, particularly in and around the ears, but can infest any part of the body, causing scratching that is sometimes very severe. Look for red, orange, or yellowish specks about the size of the point of a dressmaker's pin in affected areas. Use a magnifying glass if necessary. If you cannot find the mites, diagnosis may have to be made with a skin scraping performed by a veterinarian. Mites found solely in the ear can be eliminated with treatments for ear mites (see page 116). Mites in other areas can be controlled with dips effective against *Sarcoptes*.

FLIES

Adult flies are not normally parasitic on dogs. Some biting flies cause irritation and scab formation along the ear edges of dogs that spend a lot of time outdoors. This problem seems to be more common in dogs with erect ears, such as German shepherds. If your dog has this problem, application of commercial antifly ointments designed for horses' ears can reduce the frequency of fly bites.

MYIASIS (FLY MAGGOTS)

Some types of adult flies lay their eggs in raw or infected wounds. When the eggs hatch, the maggots feed on the tissue there, producing a condition called *myiasis*. Maggots are frequently found in infected ears as well as in neglected skin wounds and under matted hair. To treat myiasis, all the maggots must be manually removed, the areas washed with an antibacterial soap (e.g., povidone-iodine [Betadine]), and a topical antibiotic cream or ointment applied to treat any secondary bacterial infection that may be present. It is extremely important to treat the predisposing condition, or myiasis is likely to

119

recur. In regions where fly strike is frequent, thick fur must be kept clean, dry, and unmatted.

Fly maggots are also often found in dog stool that is disposed of frequently. Be careful not to confuse them with internal parasites.

THE VALUE OF PREVENTIVE MEDICINE

Begin to practice preventive medicine as soon as you take a new dog into your home. In a short time the way to take care of a healthy dog and how to keep a dog well will become second nature to you. The effects of poor preventive medicine early in life can sometimes never be completely reversed. On the other hand, a dog that is well fed, groomed regularly, and kept in a clean and parasite-free environment will have a good start on a long and healthy life. Combine these things with proper training and a yearly visit to a veterinarian for booster shots and physical examination, and you should find that living with your dog is a simple, enjoyable, and rewarding experience.

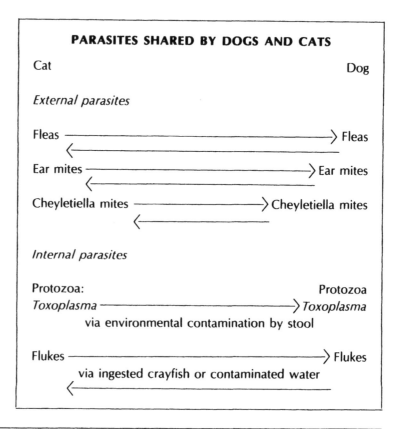

PARASITES SHARED BY DOGS AND CATS

Cat   Dog

External parasites

Fleas ──────────────────────────→ Fleas
      ←──────────────────────────

Ear mites ────────────────────────→ Ear mites
         ←────────────────────────

Cheyletiella mites ──────────────→ Cheyletiella mites
                  ←──────────────

Internal parasites

Protozoa: Protozoa
Toxoplasma ──────────────────────→ *Toxoplasma*
            via environmental contamination by stool

Flukes ──────────────────────────→ Flukes
       via ingested crayfish or contaminated water
      ←──────────────────────────

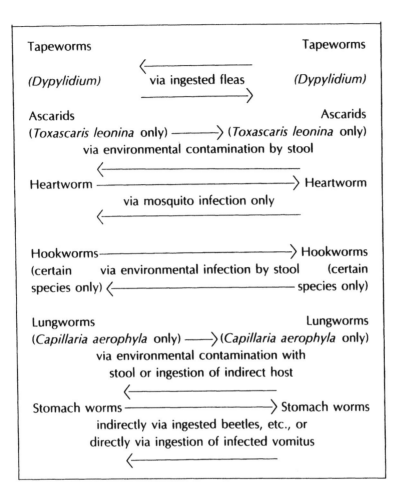

Tapeworms   Tapeworms

              ⟵————————————
(Dypylidium)   via ingested fleas   *(Dypylidium)*
             ————————————⟶

Ascarids   Ascarids
(Toxascaris leonina only) ————⟶ *(Toxascaris leonina* only)
        via environmental contamination by stool
        ⟵————————————————
Heartworm ——————————————————⟶ Heartworm
             via mosquito infection only
        ⟵————————————————

Hookworms———————————————————⟶ Hookworms
(certain   via environmental infection by stool   (certain
species only) ⟵———————————————— species only)

Lungworms   Lungworms
(Capillaria aerophyla only) ————⟶ *(Capillaria aerophyla* only)
        via environmental contamination with
          stool or ingestion of indirect host
        ⟵————————
Stomach worms ——————————————⟶ Stomach worms
        indirectly via ingested beetles, etc., or
        directly via ingestion of infected vomitus
        ⟵————————

3

DIAGNOSTIC MEDICINE:

What to Do When Your Dog Is Sick

**SKIN
(INTEGUMENTARY SYSTEM)**

HEAD

RESPIRATORY SYSTEM

**MUSCLE AND BONE
(MUSCULOSKELETAL SYSTEM)**

**DIGESTIVE SYSTEM
(GASTROINTESTINAL SYSTEM)**

**REPRODUCTIVE AND URINARY ORGANS
(GENITOURINARY SYSTEM)**

EMERGENCY MEDICINE

**GERIATRIC MEDICINE
(CARE AS YOUR DOG AGES)**

TIMES WHEN A VETERINARIAN'S HELP IS NEEDED

Any emergency

Whenever you fail to diagnose the problem

Whenever home treatment fails

For any problem that requires X-ray pictures, ultrasound or other specialized medical equipment, laboratory analysis, or anesthesia

For any problem requiring prescription drugs, including antibiotics

For yearly physical examination and booster vaccination

SIGNS THAT MAY INDICATE PAIN

Decreased appetite

Decreased activity

Shivering, restlessness, sleeplessness, pacing

Vocalization

Dilated pupils

Licking, chewing, or scratching at a specific body site

Rapid breathing

Rapid and/or irregular heartbeat

If you have been giving your dog the kind of good care you have learned about in the first part of this book, but illness occurs, you are not necessarily at fault. Even the best-cared-for dog may become sick or injured. The following pages and the sections on emergency medicine and geriatric medicine are here to help you in such situations. The best way to use these three sections, as with the rest of the book, is to read them through completely and become familiar with the contents. In this way, when a problem occurs you will not have to waste time attempting to digest the new material. You will already know how to deal with the problem, or a quick review will be all that is necessary. Knowing the contents ahead of time will also help you prevent certain problems (see, for example, "Wound Infection and Abscesses," page 133, and "Poisoning," page 190). If your dog is already sick, you can start with the index of signs of illness and the general index for the book.

The Index of Signs is an alphabetical listing of changes that may occur when your dog is sick. *Symptoms* are subjective indicators of disease. Because your dog cannot describe his or her feelings in words, he or she technically has no symptoms, only *signs,* which are any objective evidence of disease or injury you can detect. To use the index, first determine what your dog's signs are, for example: you *see* scratching (not itching, your dog *feels* the itching) and you *see* red bumps on your dog's skin. Then look up these changes in the Index of Signs and turn to the pages listed to find out about the problem and what to do. If you can't find the signs you see or you can't put the signs into words, look in the Index under the part that is involved, for example: "Skin." Use the General Index whenever you want to read about a general subject (e.g., breeding) or a particular disease (e.g., rabies). Some signs are included in the General Index in addition to the Index of Signs. Remember, only *common* problems are discussed here in terms of home treatment. If you cannot find what you are looking for in either index, consult a veterinarian. The problem may or may not be serious but is not one I've considered "run of the mill" for the general dog population.

HOW TO USE THE INDEXES

You should watch carefully for signs of illness. Sometimes a dog is very sick before signs of illness are obvious (even to a practiced eye). Because dogs can't talk, the practice of veterinary medicine is often more difficult than that of human medicine. Since you are closest to your dog, you may be able to notice signs of illness before your veterinarian can find any abnormalities on a simple physical examination. Anything you can tell your veterinarian about signs may be *very* important.

THE VALUE OF SPECIALIZED TESTS A relatively few signs signal the presence of many diseases. Very different diseases cause the same signs and can sometimes be differentiated from one another only by specialized diagnostic aids, such as X-rays, blood tests and urinalysis. Keep this in mind if you think your dog has all the signs of a particular illness but fails to respond to the suggested treatment. Also, keep in mind the value of *intuition* in recognizing that your dog is ill or injured. You are closest to your dog. If "something just doesn't seem right," sit down with your dog, take his or her temperature (see page 221), and perform a physical examination (see page 7). Often you will turn up specific signs that you can read about and deal with at home. If you don't, don't assume that you are wrong and that your dog is okay. Rely on your intuition and get your dog examined by a veterinarian. The doctor may find something wrong on physical examination or can perform specialized tests if necessary.

Three common general signs of illness in dogs are *change in behavior, change in appetite,* and *fever.* Two other general signs you may see are *shivering* and *dehydration.*

CHANGE IN BEHAVIOR Don't take any change in behavior lightly. Although most dogs become less active and more quiet when they are sick or injured (*depression* of activity), any behavioral change can indicate a medical problem. Dogs can have "emotional" problems as well, but they are much less common than illness-associated behavior changes and you will need to consult other books to deal with such problems at home (see page 43).

CHANGE OF APPETITE OR WATER INTAKE Dogs may lose their appetites completely when they are sick *(anorexia).* More often, however, you will notice a *change* in appetite. The sick dog may eat more or less. One day's change, though, is not usually important. Watch your dog's food intake carefully. Once a dog is grown, it should be fairly constant from day to day (see page 76). Changes that persist longer than five days with no other signs of illness should be discussed with your veterinarian. Changes accompanied by other signs should not be allowed to continue longer than twenty-four hours before you or your veterinarian investigates the problem.

The normal resting dog maintains his or her rectal temperature within the range of 101.0–102.5°F (38.3°–39.2°C). (For how to take a dog's temperature, see page 221.) An elevated body temperature *(fever)* usually indicates disease, but keep in mind that factors such as exercise, excitement, and high environmental temperature can elevate a dog's temperature as well. Many kinds of bacteria produce toxins (called *exogenous pyrogens*) that cause the body to release chemical substances called *endogenous pyrogens,* which produce fever. Other agents such as viruses, fungi, antibody-antigen complexes, and tumors produce fever in a similar manner. These exogenous pyrogens induce white blood cells to produce endogenous pyrogens, which pass into the brain and cause the hypothalamus to raise its body temperature set point. **FEVER**

It is important to remember that fever is a *sign* of disease, not a disease in itself. Aspirin may be used to lower an extremely high fever (greater than 106°F [41.1°C]), but the important thing is to find the cause of the fever and treat it. In fact, there are indications that the presence of fever may even be beneficial in some diseases.

Except in puppies less than four weeks of age, lowered body temperature (less than 100°F [37.8°C]), is usually indicative of overwhelming disease and the affected animal needs immediate care.

Shivering may or may not be a sign of illness. Many dogs shiver when frightened, excited, or emotionally upset. This type of shivering is often seen in the smaller breeds of dogs. Dogs also shiver when they are cold. Unless they are accustomed to being outside in cool weather without protection, dogs, like people, get cold and shiver in an attempt to increase body heat. **SHIVERING**

Shivering may also be a sign of pain. It is often seen with the kind of pain that is difficult to localize, such as abdominal or spinal pain. During the early part of a *febrile disease* (illness with fever), shivering sometimes occurs. The heat it produces contributes to the rising body temperature. If your dog is shivering, try to eliminate emotional causes and take his or her temperature before concluding that this sign is due to pain.

All body tissues are bathed in tissue fluids consisting primarily of water, ions, proteins, and some other chemical substances such as nutrients and waste products. Normal tissue fluids are extremely **DEHYDRATION** important in maintaining normal cellular functions. Changes in the body's water composition are always accompanied by changes in other constituents of tissue fluids. Small changes can have important consequences!

The most common tissue fluid alteration seen in sick animals is depletion of body water, or *dehydration*. Dehydration occurs whenever the body's output of water exceeds its intake. One common cause of dehydration during illness is not taking in enough water to meet the body's fixed daily requirements. Water is continually lost in urine, feces, respiratory gases, and evaporation from some body surfaces (minor in dogs). Dehydration also occurs in conditions that cause excessive water and/or *electrolyte* (ion) loss, such as vomiting and diarrhea. Fever also increases the body's water needs.

Although dehydration begins as soon as water output exceeds intake, the signs of dehydration are usually undetectable until a water deficit of about 4% of total body weight has occurred. If your dog has visible signs of dehydration, he or she may have been sick longer than you realize and may need professional veterinary care.

SIGNS OF DEHYDRATION IN ORDER OF INCREASING SEVERITY

1. *Decreased elasticity of the skin.* The tissues beneath the skin contain a large portion of the total body water. Because this water compartment is one of the least important to the body, it is drawn upon first in a situation of dehydration. To test for dehydration, pick up a fold of skin along the middle of the back and let it drop. In a well-hydrated, normally fleshed dog the skin will immediately spring back into place. In a moderately dehydrated dog the skin will move into place slowly. In cases of severe dehydration the skin may form a tent that remains in the skin (fat animals tend to have more elastic skin than thin ones, which can obscure signs of dehydration). The normal dog must be at least 5% dehydrated before any change in skin elasticity is detected.

2. *Dryness of the mucous membranes of the mouth and eyes.* This may be difficult to evaluate until dehydration becomes severe, as panting may also dry the mucous membranes. Normal mucous membranes have a glistening, slightly moist appearance.

3. *Sunken eyes.* This condition can also be due to severe weight loss, but in any case it's serious.

4. *Circulatory collapse (shock).* Capillary refill time (see page 182) is usually two to three seconds with 7% dehydration and more than three seconds at 10% dehydration. Shock occurs with 12%–15% dehydration.

Mild dehydration and its accompanying ion imbalance can be prevented and/or corrected by administering water and nutrients orally. In more severe dehydration, or with diseases that prevent oral intake, fluids must be administered by other routes. In such cases veterinarians administer fluids *subcutaneously* (under the skin) or *intravenously* (directly into the bloodstream), if necessary. Fluids given via these routes are sterile and of varied composition. The fluid your veterinarian chooses will depend on the route of administration and the cause of dehydration. Good fluid therapy is an important part of the care of almost all animals sick enough to require hospitalization.

When you determine the signs your dog has and have read about what they indicate, you will need to begin treatment. (If you do not already know how to proceed with the treatment involved or need more information on the care of a sick dog, see the section "Nursing at Home," page 221.)

SKIN
(INTEGUMENTARY SYSTEM)

In addition to this section, causes of skin disease will be found in the sections on external parasites (see page 104) and nutrition (see page 60).

ALLERGIC DERMATITIS

Some dogs, like some people, are born with a predisposition to develop reactions when exposed to certain substances in their environment. Dogs with allergic dermatitis develop skin disease characterized by signs of itching, such as biting and scratching the skin, when exposed to the material to which they have become allergic. Exposure to the substance may be by inhalation (this route of allergy sensitization is common in a form of allergy called *atopy*), ingestion (e.g., food allergies), inoculation (flea bites, drugs), or direct contact of the skin with the offending substance. You will see reddening of the skin, small bumps, oozing and possibly sticky areas and scabs, and sometimes dandrufflike scales. The reddened skin may feel abnormally warm to the touch. In neglected cases there is hair loss and a thickening of the skin. If these changes go untreated long enough, they can become permanent. Areas where scratching is severe may become infected. Dogs with allergic dermatitis may lick at their feet and legs excessively, which often causes a permanent reddish brown stain on the hair. In addition to these skin signs, dogs with allergic dermatitis may have more general signs of allergy such as a watery nasal discharge and sneezing, and excessive tearing and conjunctivitis. Some may even have vomiting or diarrhea.

ALLERGIC DERMATITIS HAS MANY CAUSES
Fleas are probably the most common cause of allergic dermatitis. If you practice good flea control (see page 104), you may be able to prevent the dermatitis from developing or relieve a case that has already developed. Be careful, however, about putting flea sprays or dips on irritated skin; they sometimes make the irritation worse. If you think you are controlling fleas but your dog continues to scratch, there can be several possibilities, for example:

1. The bite of a single flea (which you may not see) can cause extreme itching in an allergic animal.

2. Dogs can be allergic to many things *other than or in addition to* fleas—among them pollens, house dust, molds, trees, wool, foods, cigarette smoke, and cats!

3. The condition may not be allergic dermatitis (for an example, see page 116).

BATHING IS PART OF THE HOME TREATMENT
Frequent bathing (every one to two weeks) helps control the signs in many dogs and also helps prevent secondary bacterial infection. It removes allergens from the coat and seems to relieve some of the skin inflammation associated with allergic dermatitis. Use a gentle hypoallergenic shampoo (for example, castile shampoo or baby shampoo or a veterinarian-prescribed shampoo, not bar soap or dishwashing detergent) to avoid additional damage to a sensitive skin. If your dog's skin and hair become too dry with bathing, an emollient oil diluted with sufficient water to avoid leaving the fur excessively greasy can be used as a final rinse. Hypoallergenic bath oils for people are satisfactory, or a veterinarian can prescribe a product. If you find that bathing makes your dog's signs worse, don't, of course, continue to use it as a treatment.

Often, once the itching has begun it continues even if you remove the original cause of the irritation. This may be due to scratching, which releases itch-causing substances from the damaged cells. When such a cycle occurs, a veterinarian must administer and/or prescribe drugs such as antihistamines, antiinflammatory fatty acids, or corticosteroids to control the problem. In many allergic dogs drug treatment must be repeated intermittently or administered continuously.

Skin testing, blood testing, and hyposensitization (induction of immune tolerance by the injection of small amounts of allergen) as used in people with certain allergies have been helpful in some dogs with allergic dermatitis induced by environmental allergens such as pollens, molds, and house dust. Special elimination diets, often based on rice or potatoes and lamb or rabbit, are useful to diagnose and treat allergy signs related to food sensitivities. A *minimum* of four weeks' diet restriction is needed to rule out food-induced allergy. Many veterinarians have a special interest in skin disease and can make an effort to find out what allergies affect your dog. Dogs with very difficult allergy problems can be diagnosed and treated by a veterinary dermatologist. For persistent problems, ask your veterinarian for a referral to a specialist.

CONTACT IRRITANT DERMATITIS

Contact irritant dermatitis can occur in *any* dog whose skin comes into contact with an irritating substance such as certain soaps, detergents, plants, paints, insect sprays, or other chemicals. The reaction can look similar to that described for allergic dermatitis, but tends to be limited to the areas that have been in contact with the substance and is more common in sparsely haired skin areas. If left untreated, the affected areas often become moist and sticky.

Contact dermatitis is treated much like allergic dermatitis, but long-term success is more likely since it is usually easier to find the offending substance and remove it permanently. The first thing to do is to remove the cause. If the contact dermatitis is due to a flea collar (see page 109), remove the flea collar. Bathe your dog and rinse the coat thoroughly. If these methods are insufficient to relieve the signs, have a veterinarian examine your dog. Corticosteroids will probably be given and a soothing antibiotic-corticosteroid cream dispensed, if necessary, for home use.

PODODERMATITIS

Pododermatitis is an inflamation of the skin of the foot. It is often a sign of a generalized allergic problem, but is also frequently due to local causes (e.g., a thorn between the toes, excessive running on rocks or pavement, contact with an irritant substance) and may also be due to infection with bacteria, fungi (e.g., ringworm), or parasites (e.g., Demodex). The web of the foot in the affected areas is reddened and usually moist from *exudation* (leakage of fluid from tissue) and licking. It may be swollen. This condition can be painful enough to cause lameness on the affected foot.

Examine the foot carefully in a bright light. Look closely for evidence of foreign bodies. Probe gently for areas of soreness. If you find an invader and can remove it, the pododermatitis may improve quickly. Often the original cause is gone but the problem persists because the dog continues to lick the irritated area. Washing the foot with a gentle antiseptic soap (e.g., chlorhexidine, povidone-iodine) followed by thorough drying and soaking it in warm water for fifteen minutes twice a day is often helpful. Try to prevent your dog from licking the affected area. In addition, the application of a soothing hydrocortisone ointment usually helps clear up the condition rapidly. These products are sold over the counter in drugstores. If the inflammation and/or soreness persists longer than forty-eight hours without signs of improvement, a veterinarian will have to make a diagnosis and administer treatment. Prolonged use of corticosteroid ointments in any but the most simple conditions confounds diagnosis, aggravates certain conditions, and interferes with healing.

RINGWORM (DERMATOPHYTOSIS, DERMATOMYCOSIS)

Ringworm is an infection of the hair, toenails, or skin caused by special types of fungi that may be transmitted to dogs from other animals, people, or the soil. Dogs under one year of age are more often affected than other animals. The "classic" sign of ringworm is a rapidly growing, circular area of hair loss, but it can appear in many other ways—scaly patches, irregular hair loss, crusts, and oozing deformed toenails. A ringworm infection can be present with no evidence of skin disease.

A HUMAN
HEALTH
HAZARD
Certain kinds of ringworm can be transmitted from dogs to humans. Adult humans are relatively resistant to ringworm, however, and are unlikely to become infected if normal hygienic habits are followed. Children should avoid handling animals infected with ringworm because they are more likely to become infected and tend to be less hygiene-conscious.

Veterinarians can diagnose certain cases of ringworm with the use of an ultraviolet light alone (a certain type of ringworm fluoresces green). In other cases microscopic examination of skin scrapings and/or fungal culture may be necessary. An inexperienced person may confuse ringworm with localized demodectic mange (see page 117) or other skin conditions. If you are in doubt, see your veterinarian.

Many uncomplicated cases of ringworm heal spontaneously in

one to three months, so isolated infected areas may be cleared with simple home care. The affected area should be clipped free of hair and washed daily in a miconazole, povidone-iodine (e.g., Betadine) or chlorhexidine shampoo followed by application of an antifungal cream or drops. Products containing 2% miconazole nitrate or 1% clotrimazole, which inhibit the growth of ringworm, can be purchased in a drugstore without prescription. They have been shown to be more effective than over-the-counter products containing tolnaftate. A 0.5% solution of chlorine bleach applied once a day can be effective on localized lesions if more sophisticated products are unavailable. Ringworm cases that do not respond to this simple regime, that have secondary bacterial infections, or that involve the toenails or several body areas need to have more extensive topical treatment as well as treatment with systemic antifungal drugs. Topical treatments include dips of 2.5% lime sulfur, captan (1 oz Orthocide to 1 gallon of water), 0.2% enilconazole, or 0.05% chlorhexidine. *Griseofulvin* is a common systemic drug used for treatment of more serious ringworm cases; it is incorporated into new hair growth to prevent recurrence of the fungus. Other antifungal drugs are also available on prescription by a veterinarian once an appropriate diagnosis is made.

If your dog is diagnosed as having ringworm, clean your house thoroughly and change any air filters in your heating/ventilation system. Wash and disinfect or discard your dog's bedding, collar, leash, sweaters, dog coat, and grooming equipment. Products containing iodophores, chlorhexidine, or 0.5% chlorine bleach (5.25% solution of Clorox, mixed one part to ten parts water) are effective disinfectants that can be mopped or sprayed onto surfaces or used to soak certain washable materials. The ringworm fungus forms spores (something like bread mold does), and thorough cleaning helps remove them and thus prevent reinfection. Untreated ringworm spores may survive in dry environments as long as four years!

WOUND INFECTION AND ABSCESSES

Whether or not your dog needs to see a veterinarian following a wound depends a lot on what kind of wound it is. Short *lacerations* (cuts) or cuts that do not completely penetrate the skin and most *abrasions* (scrapes) usually need only to be washed with mild soap and rinsed with large volumes of warm, clean water. Larger cuts (about a half inch or longer) and punctures, particularly those caused by bites, usually need veterinary attention.

HOW WOUNDS HEAL Wound healing is essentially the same process whether it occurs by *primary* or *secondary* intention. The wound fills with a clot. The wound edges contract, reducing the wound in size. White blood cells called *macrophages* enter the wound and remove dead tissue and foreign material. Blood vessels and connective tissue cells enter the wound, followed by nerve fibers and lymphatic cells. At the same time this is happening, skin cells move in to close the surface defect, and finally the wound is healed. Wounds that are allowed to heal without *apposing* (bringing together) their edges heal by *secondary intention.* Healing by *primary intention* is more rapid. Your veterinarian tries to achieve primary intention healing by suturing wounds closed. Suturing clean wounds closed also helps prevent them from becoming infected while they are healing. A good example of the advantage of suturing a wound is the cut footpad dogs often get. A sutured cut footpad usually heals in about two weeks in spite of the fact that the dog walks on it. Unsutured footpads often take a month or longer to heal, are sore longer, and often bleed. Walking on the unsutured wound causes the edges to pull apart, promotes renewed bleeding, and interferes with healing. Unless the foot is well bandaged, dirt and other foreign material are continually ground into the wound, predisposing it to infection and retarding the healing process.

SIGNS OF WOUND INFECTION Infection interferes with the healing of any wound. Wound infection is usually caused by bacteria. In most clean wounds the body's defenses (white blood cells and lymphatic system) are able to overcome the bacteria present. In some instances the bacteria get the upper hand. They cause *inflammation,* which is characterized by swelling, redness, warmth, and possibly pain, and, if the body is unsuccessful in fighting it, tissue death and pus formation. If resistance is very poor or the bacteria are particularly tough invaders, the infection may reach the bloodstream, causing *septicemia* (bacterial toxins in the blood) or *bacteremia* (actual bacteria in the blood) and sometimes death. All wounds allowed to heal at home should be examined daily for signs of infection. Uninfected wounds may show signs of inflammation, but these signs usually disappear within forty-eight hours. If the swelling, redness, warmth, and pain remain or are getting worse, or if you see unhealthy-looking tissue and/or pus, infection is probably present and you should take your dog to a veterinarian, who can administer appropriate antibiotics (see page 233).

Some wounds are particularly prone to infection. Puncture-type bite wounds are among the worst offenders. It is best to leave most puncture-type bite wounds unsutured to allow a site for drainage if infection occurs. Bite wounds are difficult to wash. Flushing a mild disinfectant into the wound under light pressure (with an eyedropper, turkey baster, or syringe) is one of the best home remedies because this action tends to wash debris out of the wound. Disinfectants that are used in veterinary hospitals and that you can buy there or in drugstores include 0.001%–1% povidone-iodine (the more dilute solutions are actually more potent disinfectants and less damaging to healthy tissue), 0.05% chlorhexidine, and 0.125%–0.5% sodium hypochlorite (one fourth to full strength Dakin's solution), which can be made by diluting household bleach 1:10 to 1:40 with water. Flushing with hydrogen peroxide, once thought to be an effective wound treatment, has fallen into disfavor due to its weak antibacterial properties. Its foaming action is impressive but is best reserved for flushing debris or blood clots from a wound. If used, the concentration of hydrogen peroxide should never be more than 3%. Do not instill oil-based antibiotic wound ointments or those containing the local anesthetic *benzocaine* into the wound cavity. Oily products may interfere with healing. Any benzocaine absorbed through the skin is toxic to red blood cells. If possible, antibiotics should be administered by a veterinarian from the start of treatment (within twenty-four hours of the bite) since bite wounds are so prone to infection. The biting dog (or other animal) should be investigated regarding the status of its rabies immunization.

BITE WOUNDS NEED EXTRA CARE

An *abscess* is a localized collection of pus in a cavity caused by the death and destruction of body tissues. Abscesses are the most common type of infection occurring in improperly treated bite wounds. They usually cause swelling at the wound site. Veterinarians treat abscesses by opening them and removing all visibly dead and infected tissue *(debridement)*. Antibiotics are administered systemically by injection or mouth, and you are usually instructed to clean the wound daily at home. You can often tell when an abscess is formed and ready to be opened by feeling it with your

ABSCESSES

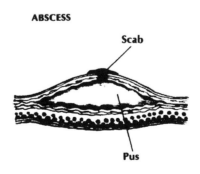

ABSCESS

Scab

Pus

finger. If you can feel a soft spot, it is ready to lance. Sometimes your veterinarian will advise you to put a warm pack on an inflamed, infected area that is not yet abscessed. This tends to transiently increase the blood supply to the area, perhaps helping antibiotics to get into the infection, and, if the wound is likely to abscess in spite of antibiotic treatment, helps to localize the abscess for more effective drainage.

HOME TREATMENT FOR ABSCESSES

If your dog has a well-localized abscess that bursts *and* the animal has *no fever,* you may be able to get the abscess to heal at home. You must determine how extensive the abscess pocket is; any abscess in which you can't reach to clean the full extent of the pocket probably won't heal but will spread or recur and needs a veterinarian's attention. Determine the extent of the pocket by wrapping a finger in a sterile gauze pad and probing the wound *thoroughly.* Be gentle, but be sure to probe to the wound's farthest reaches. A small abscess can be cleaned and probed with a cotton-tipped swab. Clean the abscess thoroughly with a disinfectant once to twice a day (see page 228).

OTHER KINDS OF ABSCESSES

Another common type of abscess in dogs is the *tooth root* abscess caused by an infected tooth, usually found in a neglected mouth. This kind of infection may cause swelling on the face; the swelling may come and go. Treatment usually requires that the infected tooth be removed to prevent recurrent abscessation. So see your veterinarian if you suspect this problem. *Foreign bodies* not removed from a wound can also cause a recurring abscess. *Plant awns* (wild barley "foxtails," on the West Coast) often cause this type of abscess between the toes or in the genital area. These abscesses must be probed by an expert until the foreign object is found and removed. If you are lucky at home, a foreign body abscess will open and, by *expressing* (squeezing out) the contents, you will be able to pop out the foreign body. Infected anal glands frequently abscess (see page 172).

TETANUS

Tetanus is mentioned here with wounds because this disease is usually contracted following a wound that allows entry of the bacteria that cause it. Dogs are much more resistant to infection with *Clostridium tetani,* the bacterium that causes tetanus, than humans are. For this reason veterinarians don't usually vaccinate dogs against tetanus. Vaccination of dogs that live around livestock might be a good idea because the organism is commonly found in manure and manure-contaminated soil. Discuss this question with your veterinarian. Antitoxin and/or penicillin (which kills the tetanus bacteria) can be given by a veterinarian when a dog gets a manure-contaminated wound or acquires a wound in filthy surroundings. Signs of tetanus include progressive stiffness and hyperactivity, difficulty opening the mouth and swallowing, and rigid extension of all limbs. Dogs with tetanus need a veterinarian's care.

BROKEN TOENAILS

Dogs' toenails, particularly those that have been allowed to over-grow, often break. Although this injury is relatively minor, it can produce pain sufficient to cause lameness. Whenever your dog becomes lame, be sure to examine each toenail, including the dew-claw. If you find a broken one, the best course of action is usually to remove it. Calm your dog or have someone else restrain him or her. Grasp the broken nail with your fingertips, a pair of tweezers, or needlenosed pliers and give a quick, hard jerk. The broken part of the nail usually comes off readily, and any pain is of very short duration. Bleeding is usually minimal. If the bleeding seems excessive, apply a pressure bandage to the foot (see pages 183 and 228) and leave it on for twelve to twenty-four hours. If the claw doesn't come off easily, you will have to leave it until it drops off or have your veterinarian remove it. Broken toenails that are very dirty or expose a lot of raw tissue may become infected. These types of nail injuries should be treated with antibiotics if needed, following examination by a veterinarian.

FOOTPAD INJURIES

The three most common injuries to dogs' feet involve the footpads themselves. They are footpad abrasions or blisters, cuts (lacerations), and punctures caused by foreign bodies penetrating the pad.

FOOTPAD ABRASIONS Footpad abrasions and/or blisters occur when dogs are allowed to run vigorously over pavement or rock. Although they are more likely to occur when the hard surface has been warmed by the sun, the heat and friction generated by prolonged running on hard surfaces is itself enough to blister and/or wear away the surface layer of the pad, thus exposing the sensitive tissue below. Dogs with this injury often limp markedly and physical examination reveals raw-looking areas on the pads that may still have a flap of surface tissue attached.

The best treatment for such injuries is get your dog to rest until healing occurs. This may take up to two weeks. However, if there is a loose flap of tissue present, you or your veterinarian should carefully snip it away with scissors close to its attachment to the healthy skin. Done correctly, this procedure is both safe and painless. If your dog must walk a lot, you can bandage his or her feet to protect the raw edges from dirt and further damage and to help relieve pain. Before bandaging, gently rinse away any embedded dirt or gravel with clean water. Areas that are very raw and bleeding should be flushed with a disinfectant solution such as chlorhexidine or povidone-iodine (see page 228). Dry the feet, then apply the bandages (see page 228). No antibiotic treatment is usually necessary, but a topical wound ointment containing neomycin, bacitracin, and polymixin B is safe to apply to raw surfaces should there be any question about infection being introduced. In instances where bandages are unsuitable (e.g., hiking in wet weather), thin, flexible pieces of leather cut to the shape of the raw areas can temporarily be held in place with medical-grade cyanoacrylate glue. Immediate relief from discomfort is usually seen when this procedure is performed correctly.

FOOTPAD CUTS Deep cuts on footpads often cause profuse bleeding, requiring application of a pressure bandage (see page 183) to avoid serious blood loss. Any cut severe enough to require a pressure bandage will probably need stitches to achieve rapid, satisfactory healing and avoid repeated bleeding. Leave a pressure bandage on until a veterinarian's advice can be obtained but no longer than twenty-four hours without reinspection of the wound and rebandaging.

Once bleeding has stopped, minor cuts should be inspected for foreign material, gently washed with disinfectant soap, rinsed, and gently dried. The affected foot should be bandaged to protect the wound from dirt and recurrent bleeding. Change the bandage whenever it becomes wet and at least every third day to allow inspection of the wound for signs of infection and proper healing. Rebandaging can be stopped once the wound is well healed (not just sealed closed). This could be as long as three weeks since weight bearing puts a lot of stress on cut pads, thereby interfering with healing.

FOOTPAD PUNCTURES Thorns and glass shards may cause deep punctures in footpads. Although bleeding is usually minimal, lameness can be severe and persistent and puncture wounds are followed by infection more often than cuts are. Anytime your dog is limping you should perform a thorough inspection of the footpads. Be sure to do this in bright light and use a magnifying glass if necessary. If you see a protruding foreign body, you can carefully try to tease it loose with a sterilized sewing needle. (To sterilize a needle, heat the tip in a flame until it is glowing red, then allow it to cool, or immerse it in rubbing alcohol for ten minutes.) Once the foreign object is loose enough to be firmly grasped with tweezers or needle-nosed pliers, extract it carefully but quickly from the wound. Do not attempt this on an unmuzzled dog (see page 231) unless you are willing to risk being bitten. Success is indicated by immediate improvement of the lameness. If you have any doubt that the object has been fully removed, if the lameness persists after home treatment, or if signs of infection such as swelling around or drainage from the wound occur, consult your veterinarian. Dogs that have received puncture wounds rarely acquire tetanus (see page 136).

CALLUSES

Hairless, thickened, wrinkled areas of skin that often look gray are *calluses*. They are found at pressure points where the skin lies close to the bone—the elbow, outside surface of the hock, bottom (points of the ischia), and occasionally the tail. Calluses occur when a dog lies primarily on hard surfaces. They are usually only cosmetic problems, but they can become infected and then they need treatment. You can prevent calluses or help get rid of those already present by providing your dog with a proper sleeping area. Some good bedding materials include foam padding (1 inch [2.5 cm] or more thick), a thick piece of washable carpet, artificial sheepskin, or a thick washable blanket folded several times.

PUPPY ACNE AND IMPETIGO

Puppy acne and *impetigo* are bacterial infections of the skin in which you see red bumps and bumps filled with pus. Puppy acne occurs on the chin of young dogs (usually under one year), impetigo on the abdomen. Both infections can usually be controlled by washing the affected areas once or twice daily with antibacterial shampoo containing 2.5% benzoyl peroxide soap or by the application of 70% isopropyl alcohol. Be sure to follow soap washing with a thorough rinsing. Although both infections usually clear up as a dog ages, some cases need veterinary attention and antibiotics. If you can't see an improvement within a week of home treatment or if the condition is getting worse in spite of treatment, see your veterinarian.

WARTS (CANINE VIRAL PAPILLOMATOSIS)

Warts on dogs look like warts on people. They are caused by a virus and almost always occur *inside* the mouths of young dogs, although they may occasionally be found on other areas of the skin. They almost always go away without treatment in about two or three months, and should be removed only if they interfere with chewing, swallowing, or breathing. Viral warts are contagious to other dogs, so you should avoid letting unaffected dogs use the food and water bowls of infected dogs.

SEBORRHEA

Seborrhea is a disorder of the formation of the surface layers of the skin and/or the waxy oils *(sebum)* produced by the oil glands of the skin. Dogs affected by seborrhea usually have scaling skin. In one form, *seborrhea sicca,* the white or grayish scales are accompanied by dry skin and a dull, dry coat. In another form, *seborrhea oleosa,* the scales may be more yellow and clumped to the hair and the coat and skin may feel greasy and smell like rancid oil. Many affected dogs have recurrent ear problems, itching skin, and skin infections.

Seborrhea can be a primary skin disorder, especially in certain dog breeds such as cocker and springer spaniels, West Highland white terriers, basset hounds, Chinese shar peis, German shepherds, dachshunds, and Doberman pinschers. More often, however, seborrhea is merely the skin manifestation of some other medical problem such as hypothyroidism or other endocrine disease, dietary deficiency, allergy, internal or external parasites, cancer or other immune disorders, or bacterial or fungal infections.

Primary *(idiopathic)* seborrhea is the dog's equivalent of dandruff and can be controlled (but not cured) by frequent, regular bathing every three to seven days with special medicated shampoos that contain ingredients such as antiseptics, salicylic acid, coal tar, and sulfur. In general, dry scales respond best to a mild, hypoallergenic, emollient shampoo followed by an emollient rinse (e.g., bath oil, one capful to 1–2 quarts of water). Greasy types are best managed with products containing antiseptic degreasers such as benzoyl peroxide and drying agents such as sulfur, salicylic acid, or selenium disulfide. Although some human antidandruff shampoos contain appropriate ingredients for home treatment of dogs, it is safest to obtain an antiseborrheic shampoo designed specifically for dogs from your veterinarian. Some formulations for people can be irritating to some dogs' skin.

If regular bathing and good flea control do not considerably improve or eliminate the skin problem within a month, take your dog to a veterinarian for diagnosis. Extensive testing and analysis are needed to identify any underlying diseases causing the seborrhea, and a precise therapeutic plan must be formulated to ensure successful treatment.

HEMATOMAS

Hematomas are swellings in the skin caused by the accumulation of blood beneath the skin's surface. They occur most commonly on the ears of lop-eared dogs following vigorous head shaking and scratching, which causes a fracture in the ear cartilage. They also occur on other areas of the body, usually following a blow to a skin area that closely overlies bone (e.g., the head or the side of the chest). Dogs with hematomas usually feel and act well (no fever), but you will probably need the aid of a veterinarian for diagnosis and treatment. Hematomas on the head or body are sometimes difficult to distinguish from closed abscesses (see page 135) without removing some of the fluid with a needle. For a good cosmetic result, large hematomas of the earflap may need surgical drainage and suturing. Small ear hematomas not associated with an underlying ear infection can be allowed to heal slowly on their own without veterinary intervention.

MASTITIS

Mastitis is an inflammation of one or more of the *mammary glands* (breasts). While it may be due to abnormal drainage of milk from the gland or to trauma, it is usually caused by bacterial infection. Affected glands look enlarged, may be discolored red, purplish, or blue, and often feel hard and warm. They are often painful, making the female a little reluctant to let her puppies nurse. If you express some milk from the infected gland, it may be blood-streaked, pink, gray, or brown. Often, however, the milk does not look unusual to the unaided eye. If left untreated, the gland may abscess or the female may develop more generalized signs of illness.

In order to prevent sick puppies, do not allow them to nurse from infected glands. Placing a piece of adhesive tape over the nipple of the gland will usually effectively prevent nursing. Infected glands should be milked out three to four times a day. Ask your veterinarian to show you how to do this properly. Warm packs applied to the gland seem to relieve discomfort and speed the localization of infection. Infected glands must be treated promptly with an antibiotic to avoid systemic illness. Your veterinarian will prescribe the appropriate one.

INFANTILE PUSTULAR DERMATITIS

This skin condition, which usually affects young puppies, is discussed on page 268.

UMBILICAL HERNIA

An *umbilical hernia* is a defect involving the body wall that is usually first noticed in young dogs as a lump in the skin over the abdomen. Its diagnosis and treatment are covered on page 267.

TUMORS (CANCER)

Tumors are often noticed as growths on a dog's skin. (For more information, see page 213.)

HEAD

EYES

The eyes are very important and delicate organs. Mild and unobtrusive conditions can rapidly become severe, and many untreated conditions can cause irreversible damage. *Don't ignore even minor evidence of irritation.* Any minor eye problem that doesn't clear up rapidly (within twenty-four hours), as well as any obvious change you see in an eye, should be brought to the attention of an expert. *Do not* use anything in the eye not specifically labeled for *ophthalmic* use, and do not use a preparation in the eye just because you had it left over from an eye problem you or your dog had in the past. Ophthalmic drugs have very specific uses, and the use of a drug for a condition for which it was not specifically intended can cause serious injury or complication.

EPIPHORA (TEARING)

Epiphora is the abnormal overflow of tears from the eye. It has *many* causes because tearing is the eye's response to irritation. Among the causes are allergy, infections, *conjunctivitis,* corneal injuries, misplaced eyelashes, and plugged tear ducts. In poodles, in particular, and some other miniature or toy breeds, epiphora may be mainly a cosmetic problem with no serious underlying physical cause. If you can eliminate other causes of epiphora, staining can be controlled by frequent washing of the affected area and by clipping away stained hair and any facial hairs that may protrude into the eye. Animals that have congenital membranes across the openings of their tear ducts, abnormally formed eyelids, or abnormally placed eyelashes can be helped with surgery. Dogs with very prominent eyes sometimes form inadequate tear pools that cause the tears to be squeezed onto the face instead of draining down the *nasolacrimal* (tear) canal. These dogs may sometimes be helped by reconstructive surgery of the eyelid. In the past, surgical removal of all or a portion of the tear gland located on the back surface of the third eyelid was used to stop or improve the tearing condition. This procedure is no longer recommended as it may reduce tear production below normal and therefore be detrimental to eye health.

CONJUNCTIVITIS

Conjunctivitis is an inflammation, sometimes accompanied by infection, of the membrane *(conjunctiva)* that lines the lids and covers part of the eye. It is probably the most common eye problem of dogs because the conjunctiva is exposed to so many irritants. The first obvious sign is often an excessive amount of sticky, yellowish discharge that accumulates at the *medial* corners (see illustration, page 19) of the eyes. There are many degrees of inflammation. Very mild cases, with just a slight reddening of the conjunctiva and small amounts of discharge, may clear up without drug treatment. Other cases that are persistent and cause inflammation of the lids and/or extreme discomfort must be treated by a veterinarian to avoid permanent damage to the eye.

In mild cases the first step in home treatment is to examine the eyes thoroughly to look for the cause and remove it. Dogs who ride with their heads out of the car window or who spend a lot of time outside in wind, dust, or pollen frequently suffer from eye irritation followed by conjunctivitis. Dogs can also have an allergic irritation of the eyes, just as people do. Diagnosing the primary cause of irritation and avoiding it will prevent recurrent problems and is much better than symptomatic treatment with over-the-counter remedies or repeated treatment with antibiotics for secondary infection. Dogs with anatomical abnormalities such as lower eyelids that roll out excessively *(ectropion)* also need diagnosis and are best treated by surgical correction of the predisposing condition.

Two common causes of recurrent conjunctivitis in dogs are "dry eye," or inadequate tear production *(keratoconjunctivitis sicca, KCS)* and chronic infection of the nasolacrimal tear drainage system *(dacryocystitis)*. A veterinary consultation is needed for proper diagnosis and treatment of these conditions.

"DRY EYE" MAY PREDISPOSE TO CONJUNCTIVITIS

143

For KCS, a simple test of tear production can be performed in the veterinarian's office (Shirmer tear test) and treatment with immunosuppressive (cyclosporine) eye drops often successfully restores tears to normal levels. In nasolacrimal infections, flushing of the tear duct system is often necessary to remove infectious debris or foreign material that has lodged in the tear canal. After this procedure, your veterinarian may prescribe both systemic and topical antibiotics to clear up the problem permanently.

Conditions as diverse as glaucoma, tooth root abscesses, and systemic disease can cause signs of eye irritation that may be confused with simple conjunctivitis. Be sure to consult your veterinarian when redness of the conjunctiva is persistent, recurrent, or accompanied by signs of pain such as squinting, tearing, and/or eye rubbing. Difficult problems will need help from a veterinary opthalmalogist.

FOREIGN OBJECT IN THE EYE

Epiphora and conjunctivitis may be signs of a foreign body in the eye. So it's a good idea to examine your dog's eye for foreign objects whenever there are such signs. If epiphora and/or conjunctivitis is *unilateral* (on one side) only and accompanied by squinting, pawing at the eye, or other signs of pain, a thorough examination for a foreign body *must* be made.

The first thing to do when looking for a foreign body in your dog's eye is to get under a good light. In dim light slight but extremely important changes in the eye are easily overlooked. Place the thumb of one hand just below the edge of the lower lid of the affected eye and the thumb of the opposite hand just above the edge of the upper lid. Then gently pull the lower lid downward and the upper lid upward. This rolls the lids away from the eyeball, allowing examination of the conjunctiva and most of the cornea. The surface of the cornea should look smooth and completely transparent. If necessary, compare it to the opposite (probably uninjured) eye to be sure the corneal surface is normal. Be sure to look along the edge of the third eyelid to see if there is anything protruding from behind it. It is a good idea to look under the third eyelid, but most dogs with a painful eye will not allow

EXAMINING THE EYE
FOR FOREIGN OBJECT

you to lift it without administration of some form of anesthesia. You can, however, moisten a cotton-tipped swab and move it *very gently* along the inner surface of the lids and under the third eyelid. Occasionally a foreign body will cling to the swab and be removed, or the swab will sometimes bring a hidden foreign body into view. This must be done with *extreme* care to avoid injury to the cornea. If you see a large object (e.g., a foxtail), you can grasp it with your fingertips or a pair of tweezers and remove it. Small foreign bodies are most easily removed with a moistened cotton swab or a piece of tissue. Any foreign object not easily removed should be entrusted to a veterinarian, and *any* sign of irritation following removal of a foreign body that persists more than a few hours is reason to have the eye examined by an expert.

The majority of foreign bodies are most safely removed by a veterinarian. Since a dog can't tell you when there is eye irritation, it is often easy to overlook small but significant eye damage. Veterinarians use special eye stains to color the surface of the cornea. These stains show corneal damage not evident to the unassisted eye. Veterinarians can also give local or general anesthetics to relieve pain during examination, thus allowing a more thorough search.

EARS

EXTERNAL EAR INFLAMMATION (OTITIS EXTERNA)

Otitis externa is a medical term used to describe an inflammation of the external ear (outside the eardrum). It has many causes, but the signs are usually the same. Head shaking and scratching at the ears are probably the most common signs. In mild cases your dog may like to have his or her ears rubbed more than usual; in other cases touching the ear causes signs of pain. The inside of the pinna is usually abnormally red and there may be swelling. Large amounts of waxy discharge are often present; in severe cases there may be actual pus. (See page 20 if you are not familiar with a normal dog ear.) The normal smell of a healthy dog ear becomes fetid as the inflammation gets worse.

All ear inflammation should be treated promptly and vigorously with the aid of a veterinarian if possible. If left neglected, changes occur in the ear, making conditions that could have been easily cured at first difficult or impossible to treat successfully, and the infection can progress to include the middle and inner ear. If you are unable to obtain the services of a veterinarian or choose first to attempt treatment at home and don't think a foreign object is in the ear (see page 147), try using 70% isopropyl alcohol, 10% povidone-iodine solution, or 0.5% chlorhexidine solution. First, clean out the affected ear thoroughly (see page 227). Then, twice a day, after a more minor cleaning, instill several drops of the disinfectant into the ear canal and massage the base of the ear to spread the medication all the way down the canal (see page 227). If you see improvement within three or four days, continue the treatment for two weeks. If there is no improvement or if the treatment seems too irritating to your dog's ear, be sure to seek professional help.

YEAST INFECTIONS ARE COMMON AMONG DOGS A very common type of recurrent otitis externa in dogs is associated with a yeast, *Malassezia pachydermatis*. Signs of discomfort that may range from mild to severe are often associated with a brown, waxy discharge when excessive numbers of these organisms are present. This form of otitis externa often crops up during humid weather or after a dog has been swimming, as this yeast thrives in a warm, moist environment. A microscopic examination of debris associated with this type of ear inflammation is needed to be sure the yeast is present and significant. Ears that are kept clean, dry, and slightly acid in pH are less likely to develop excessive numbers of yeast, so predisposed dogs often need a routine of home ear care to prevent repetitive problems. Commercial products containing alcohol and boric acid instilled into the ears once or twice a week, especially after bathing, can prevent yeast-associated otitis externa. Home remedies for prevention are white vinegar (5% acetic acid) diluted 1 to 1 with water or 70% isopropyl alcohol instilled once or twice a week and after swimming or bathing.

MANY OTHER MEDICAL CONDITIONS CAUSE EAR INFLAMMATION Certain breeds are noted for their predisposition to otitis externa, among them poodles, German shepherds, and spaniels. Dogs with seborrhea (see page 140) often have an accompanying ear condition that can be controlled, but not always cured. Keeping such dogs' ears clean on a routine basis is very important. A veterinarian can prescribe various antifungal, antibiotic, and steroidal medications for use in these dogs as well as for the treatment of acute bacterial or fungal problems. Bacterial or fungal cultures of the ear may be necessary, particularly in recurrent inflammations accompanied by infection. Often a general medical evaluation is needed to rule out underlying predisposing conditions such as hypothyroidism or allergy, which may be responsible for recurrent ear problems. Otitis not controlled by other methods must be treated surgically. *Lateral ear resection* (surgery that changes the external

146

ear structure) often cures or improves a condition that hasn't responded to any other treatment. However, it should be employed only as a last resort since surgery will not work well if other predisposing factors are not controlled.

Foreign bodies in the ear usually cause a sudden onset of signs of otitis externa. The dog will often tilt his or her head with the affected ear toward the ground as well as scratch or paw at the ear. In many geographic areas, foxtails (plant awns) in the ear are a problem, particularly among long-haired dogs. If you can see the object at the opening of the ear canal, you can sometimes grasp it with your fingers or tweezers and remove it. When the object has traveled all the way down the ear canal, it should be removed by a veterinarian, who can use an otoscope to examine the entire canal and eardrum. If you think your dog has a foreign object in his or her ear but can't get to a veterinarian right away, a few drops of mineral or baby oil placed in the ear and massaged around will often soften the object sufficiently to relieve the signs until it can be removed. Prevent foreign bodies in the ear by checking the hair around the ears each time your dog goes outside and frequently during hiking. Cotton wads placed firmly in the ears will often help prevent access of foreign bodies to the ear canal if used during hikes in brushy country. **FOREIGN BODIES IN THE EAR**

Parasites in the ear can also cause inflammation. Ear ticks *(Otobius megnini)* can cause a sudden onset of signs similar to that of other foreign bodies. Like many foreign objects, they must usually be removed by a veterinarian. Ear mites and trombiculid mites are usually more insidious (see pages 116 and 119).

NOSE

Major conditions involving the outside of dogs' noses are uncommon. Minor skin irritations with signs of raw skin, discharge, or scabs are often caused when a dog uses his or her nose as a tool to dig with or to poke through a fence. You should be able to correct such irritations by observing and modifying your dog's behavior (or the fence). Thickening of the nose skin commonly occurs as dogs age. You cannot prevent this but can help keep the surface soft by applying petroleum jelly or emollient creams made for humans. Any condition of the nose skin (unaccompanied by other signs) that doesn't disappear or improve within two weeks with such simple treatment should be examined by a veterinarian.

Conditions involving the inside of the nose cannot be treated at home. (For more information see "Sneezing," page 151, "Canine Distemper," page 86, "Normal Appearance of Nasal Discharge," page 32, and "Dry Nose," page 15.)

MOUTH

FOREIGN OBJECT IN THE MOUTH

Dogs who have gotten foreign objects stuck in their mouths usually paw at their mouths and make unusual movements with their lips and tongues. They may sometimes, but not always, make gagging motions and drool. Try not to get excited if you think your dog has gotten something stuck in his or her mouth. Try to reassure and calm your dog, then perform a thorough mouth examination in good light (see page 25). Be sure to examine the areas of the mouth around the molars thoroughly; look under the tongue, at the soft and hard palates, and far into the back of the mouth (pharynx). If you see the foreign body, grasp it with your fingertips or tweezers and remove it quickly and cautiously to avoid injury to yourself. If your dog is uncooperative or if you can't find anything but the signs persist, you will have to have your dog examined by a veterinarian. (If your dog is choking and you can't remove the foreign object, see page 209).

TOOTH ROOT ABSCESS

A tooth root abscess often causes swelling on the face. (For more information, see page 136 and below.)

BROKEN TOOTH

A broken tooth can become the cause of serious medical problems in a dog if it is neglected. When the inside chamber of the tooth (pulp cavity chamber), which contains the blood supply and nerve, is exposed by breakage, the tooth dies and may develop an abscess (localized infection) around its root. Such localized infections may be associated with facial swelling, pain, and reluctance to eat or chew on hard objects. However, many dogs show no specific signs of discomfort and the broken tooth is found only incidentally on physical examination. Some dogs develop serious systemic bacterial infections from infected broken teeth, so it is important always to examine the mouth for evidence of infected teeth whenever the presence of any kind of bacterial infection is diagnosed.

Some tooth fractures are very minor and do not expose the pulp chamber or kill the tooth. They require no special veterinary care unless there are sharp edges on the break that need to be smoothed. The more usual type of break is severe enough to expose the pulp cavity. If this type of break has been present for some time, a dark gray-black spot is seen in the area normally occupied by the pulp. The surrounding part of the tooth may be the normal creamy white color, or it may also be discolored pinkish brown or grey. Should you notice a broken tooth at this stage, a veterinarian's examination is indicated but not urgent. A freshly broken tooth with pulp exposure has a bright, reddish-pink pulp area that may bleed if touched. This type of tooth injury calls for a veterinarian's examination within a few hours if an attempt to preserve its vitality is desired. Veterinarians with special training in dentistry will take steps to seal the freshly exposed pulp chamber in the hope that the broken tooth will survive without abscessation.

Since it is relatively rare for a dog owner to discover a freshly broken tooth, the more usual treatments administered are extraction or root canal therapy. Dogs tolerate tooth extraction well since, unlike in humans, their teeth have little tendency to migrate out of their normal position when an opposing tooth is removed. Root canal therapy is performed when tooth preservation is important for cosmetic or functional reasons. Ask your veterinarian for more information if you think your dog may require treatment for a broken tooth.

DENTAL TARTAR

Dental tartar is hard white, yellow, or brown material on your dog's teeth. (For more information, see pages 24 and 58.)

GINGIVITIS/PERIODONTAL DISEASE

Red or bleeding gums, which may be accompanied by unpleasant mouth odors, may be signs of *gingivitis* or periodontal disease. (See pages 23 and 59 for more information.)

RESPIRATORY SYSTEM

KENNEL COUGH (INFECTIOUS TRACHEOBRONCHITIS, CANINE RESPIRATORY DISEASE COMPLEX)

Kennel (canine) cough is the common name given to a group of respiratory diseases of dogs caused by a variety of different viruses and bacteria that infect the cells lining the windpipe *(trachea)* and airways *(bronchi);* hence the designation *infectious tracheobronchitis.* Its common name stems from the fact that dogs often develop signs of respiratory infection when boarded at a kennel, where they are under stress and exposed to other dogs carrying disease or to contaminated premises.

Canine parainfluenza virus, canine adenovirus type 2, and *Bordetella bronchiseptica* bacteria are infectious agents often associated with kennel cough. Bacterialike organisms called *mycoplasmas* and *canine adenovirus type 1, reovirus,* and *herpesvirus* have also been found in dogs with signs of infectious tracheobronchitis. In most cases, infection with any single agent results in only mild to moderate illness. However, severe symptoms may occur with simultaneous infection by both a virus and a bacterium.

SIGNS OF KENNEL COUGH

Dogs with kennel cough are usually bright and alert and eat well. They have a dry, hacking cough or bouts of deep, harsh coughing, often followed by gagging motions. The gagging sometimes produces a foamy mucus. When external pressure is applied to the trachea or larynx, coughing is usually easily produced. Exercise or excitement will also readily trigger the cough. Most dogs with uncomplicated kennel cough do not have a fever.

KENNEL COUGH TREATMENT

The mildest cases of kennel cough heal without treatment in about two weeks. Many cases benefit by the administration of appropriate antibiotics, which your veterinarian will prescribe if indicated. Use your judgment on whether or when to go to the veterinarian. Be sure, however, to take your dog's temperature daily if you decide to rely on home treatment. Cough suppressants (children's over-the-counter or prescription preparations containing dextromethorphan hydrobromide, 1 mg/lb body weight [2.2 mg/kg] every six hours) may be administered if the cough is overly frequent and tires your dog. Remember, however, that a cough is a protective reflex designed to clear secretions from the larynx and airways and therefore should not be unduly suppressed. Cough suppressants mask signs but do not treat any disease.

To help prevent the development of pneumonia and to lessen coughing bouts, dogs with kennel cough should be rested and kept in a relatively warm environment. They should be quarantined from other dogs to prevent exposing uninfected dogs to this very contagious disease. Don't assume that just any cough is kennel cough. Use home treatment only if your dog's signs are exactly those described and there is no fever. If there is fever, your dog is less active than normal, has a decreased appetite, has discharge from the eyes and/

or nose, or has difficulty breathing (possible signs of pneumonia), or if your dog is younger than five months or older than three years, a physical examination by a veterinarian is indicated to be sure a more serious problem is not present.

Modern-day vaccination procedures can prevent many cases of infectious tracheobronchitis in dogs. Parainfluenza virus vaccine is usually administered during a dog's initial vaccination series starting at six to eight weeks of age with booster doses given every three to four weeks until the pup reaches fourteen to sixteen weeks of age. Annual revaccination then follows.

VACCINES CAN PREVENT KENNEL COUGH

Canine adenoviruses types 1 and 2 cross-protect, so vaccines effective against infectious canine hepatitis (see page 88) will prevent infection with the respiratory form of adenovirus. *Bordetella bronchiseptica* vaccines are also available for dogs expected to have significant exposure to infection at kennels, grooming parlors, or dog shows. A unique form of this *bacterin* (antibacterial inoculation) is given by instillation of nose drops, which induces local immunity in the upper respiratory tract, the normal path of entry for infection. Such vaccines can be given to dogs as young as six weeks of age, and annual revaccination is recommended.

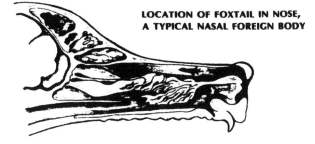

LOCATION OF FOXTAIL IN NOSE, A TYPICAL NASAL FOREIGN BODY

SNEEZING

Sneezing is a *sign* rather than any particular disease in itself. Its presence usually indicates a problem in the nasal passages or sinuses. One of the most common causes of sneezing is the presence of a foreign body in the nose. In these cases sneezing is often violent and *paroxysmal* (recurring in intense bouts). There is often a blood-flecked and/or pure blood discharge from the nostril containing the foreign body. A foreign body in the nose must almost always be removed by a veterinarian with the dog under general anesthesia or physically restrained and the nasal passages locally anesthetized.

(The procedure is not painful, but the "sneeze reflex" usually prevents a good look up an awake dog's nose.) If you can see the object protruding from the nostril, gently try to pull it out. If it resists you, get a veterinarian's help.

Sneezing accompanied by watery, clear nasal discharge from both nostrils in a seemingly healthy dog may be allergic in origin or may even be due to infection with nasal mites *(Pneumonyssoides caninum)* or nasal worms (*Linguatula serrata* or, rarely, *Capillaria*). If sneezing is persistent (lasts longer than three days), the discharge is milky, bloody, or sticky, and/or your dog is acting ill, be sure to have an examination performed by a veterinarian.

REVERSE SNEEZING

For lack of a better term, this phrase is applied to the paroxysmal occurrence of forced efforts to inhale that produce a loud snorting type of noise. It is usually pretty frightening the first time you hear it, but most attacks last only a few seconds to a minute and cause no permanent damage. The attacks are usually brought on by water drinking, excitement, or collar pressure. It is thought that they occur in dogs sensitive to pharyngeal irritation due to incomplete opening of the epiglottis after swallowing. No treatment is necessary. If the attacks are very frequent and severe, consider discussing the problem with a veterinarian to be sure you have made the correct diagnosis. In some cases surgical removal of the free border of the epiglottis has provided some relief.

MUSCLE AND BONE (MUSCULOSKELETAL SYSTEM)

Many musculoskeletal diseases can be difficult to diagnose, even by an experienced veterinarian. Proper diagnosis often requires the use of X-rays as well as a thorough physical examination. It may be impossible to distinguish among fractures, dislocations, and sprains without the aid of X-rays. In general, however, it should not be too difficult to distinguish the presence of a fracture or dislocation from the presence of a mild sprain, strain, or bruise. Keep in mind that although musculoskeletal injuries often cause marked signs, they themselves are usually not emergencies (see page 180). Review the musculoskeletal section beginning on page 8; read this section thoroughly, and become familiar with your dog's normal stance and gait in order to prepare yourself in case there is an injury to your dog's muscles and/or bones.

When the actual injury occurs, keep calm and proceed with an examination in a thorough, deliberate manner. First try to localize the site of injury. To accomplish this, stand back and look at your dog as a whole. Try to determine the area (or areas) causing the change in posture or gait. If the legs are involved, which ones? Which hurt, are distorted, or are being protected by the dog? Swelling is often fairly well confined to the injured area, but is sometimes extensive. The posture of the affected leg *may* be fairly normal above, but not below, the affected area. Once you have a general idea of the location of the problem, examine each part of the limb, including each joint, gently and carefully. All legs should be examined thoroughly, but you will probably want to go over the most obviously damaged one first. Review how to perform a leg examination in the anatomy section if you feel unsure, and remember that comparing an injured leg to its (probably) uninjured mate can be very helpful.

SPRAINS, STRAINS, AND BRUISES

Sprains, strains, and bruises (contusions) consist of damage to the soft tissues surrounding and supporting the bones, usually without loss of weight-bearing ability. In these injuries swelling and signs of pain are often quite diffuse, so you may not be able to determine the exact size of injury, only the general area involved.

A *contusion* occurs when a blow causes the capillaries (small blood vessels) in the affected soft tissues to bleed. You may see skin discoloration, abrasion, or other skin injury at the site of a bruise. However, dogs' fur often obscures the outer signs of injury. Expect a contusion to be free of significant pain in seven to ten days following injury.

Strains result from unaccustomed or excessive activity that overstresses the involved muscle, tendon, and/or site of the attachment of the tendon to the bone. Signs of a strain are often most obvious two or three days after the actual injury occurs. Strains often take one to three weeks of enforced rest to heal.

Sprains are ligament injuries that occur when these soft tissues, which directly surround and stabilize the joints, are stretched (mild or first-degree sprain), partially torn (moderate or second-degree sprain), or completely torn apart (severe or third-degree sprain). *All sprains heal slowly* even if the signs of pain disappear quickly. Radiographs (X-ray pictures) are often necessary to the diagnosis of sprain as the more severe forms can easily cause signs of pain, swelling, deformity, and inability to bear weight that are indistinguishable from signs of a bone fracture. Splinting, casting, or surgery is sometimes needed to return the affected joint to normal stability.

If your dog has a mild to moderate lameness due to soft tissue injury, enforced rest is the best treatment, and it should result in rapid improvement in two to seven days. Ice packs and aspirin can be used to relieve inflammation and discomfort. Consult your veterinarian in more severe cases.

FRACTURES

Complete fracture (break) of any of the major limb bones usually results in an *inability to bear weight* on the affected limb, as well as some visible *deformity* of the limb. The deformity may consist simply of swelling or include *angulation* (formation of an abnormal angle), usually at the fracture site, rotation or shortening of the affected limb, or other deviations from the normal position. The sound or feel of bone grating against bone *(crepitus)*, if present, is almost always indicative of a fracture. Unless sensory nerves have been damaged or the dog is in deep shock (see page 182), evidence of *pain* can be elicited by manipulating the fracture. Signs of pain, however, are unreliable because they are also present in other conditions, because many sensitive dogs overreact to relatively mild pain, and because "stoic" dogs may be less likely to react strongly to painful stimuli.

**COMPOUND
FRACTURES
ARE
EMERGENCIES**
A fracture is classified as *simple* if there is no communicating wound between the outside of the skin and the broken bone. A *compound* fracture communicates to the outside. If your dog has a compound fracture with bone protruding from a wound, you should have no difficulty diagnosing the condition. Compound fractures become infected easily and should be given immediate attention by a veterinarian, if at all possible.

If your dog is in fairly normal general condition, a simple fracture is not necessarily a veterinary emergency. The best thing to do is to localize the fracture site, then call your veterinarian for further advice. Fractures of the foot bones are rarely emergencies and can usually be left unsplinted until X-ray pictures can be taken. Whether or not you splint other limb fractures depends on the site of the fracture and the mobility of the bone ends. In many cases, splinting causes more trouble for you and pain for the dog than it's worth. In obviously mobile fractures, where you see the leg below the break dangling freely and twisting, heavy cardboard cut to the appropriate shape, roll cotton, and elastic bandage can be used to prevent bone movement, interruption of blood supply, and nerve damage. Wrap the padding (even a diaper can be used) gently and *thickly* around the injured part. Then apply the splint and top it with the bandage. Compound fractures should have a clean bandage applied over the exposed bone ends if splinting is unnecessary or not possible.

A special case of fracture (or dislocation) is fracture of the spine. This requires professional veterinary care *at the earliest possible time* as well as careful first aid. Spinal fractures usually result in partial or complete paralysis of the rear legs and sometimes the front legs as well, often with remarkably little evidence of pain. If your dog shows such signs following trauma, *immediate* and *absolute* (if possible) restriction of movement is necessary. If you can get the dog to lie quietly, transport on a stretcher or board is best. Do not, however, attempt to tie a frightened and struggling dog to a board—you may make the damage worse. Small dogs, in particular, can be lifted in your arms if you are careful to prevent back movement. Small and medium-sized dogs can be placed in a box for transportation to a veterinarian. A less satisfactory carrier is a sheet or blanket used as a sling.

SPINAL FRACTURES ARE EMERGENCIES

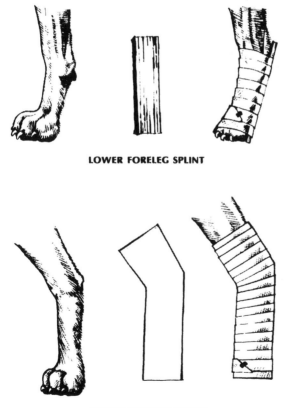

LOWER FORELEG SPLINT

LOWER HINDLEG SPLINT

The method a veterinarian chooses to repair a fractured bone depends on the type of fracture present, the fracture site, and the age and size of your dog. External devices, such as casts and splints, can in some cases be used alone. In many others surgery to place a metal pin, plate, or other internal fixation device into the fractured bone is necessary. A good veterinarian will radiograph the fracture, evaluate all the possibilities for repair, and tell you what he or she thinks is necessary to achieve the best healing. If you feel you cannot afford the best repair, a veterinarian should offer alternative methods that may not be as ideal for healing but more within your means. (Keep in mind that the alternatives may be slower healing or complete failure to heal.)

DISLOCATIONS

**DISLOCATED
ELBOW JOINT**

Dislocations *(luxations)* are seen much less frequently than fractures in most veterinary practices. They occur whenever a bone is displaced from its normal position in relation to another bone at a joint. *The signs of dislocation are similar to those of fractures, but usually milder.* Dislocations are not usually emergencies in the sense that they endanger a dog's life or limb. However, they should be examined by a veterinarian within twenty-four hours of occurrence because they are most easily corrected without surgery during this period. All suspected dislocations should be radiographed to determine the true extent of body damage. General anesthesia is given to relax the muscles and provide relief from pain while the bones are manipulated back into their proper positions. Some dislocations require surgery for permanent correction as the supporting and surrounding soft tissues may be completely disrupted.

KNEECAP DISLOCATION (PATELLAR LUXATION)

Recurrent dislocation of the kneecap is most commonly a problem in small breeds of dogs such as poodles, Pomeranians, Yorkshire terriers, and Chihuahuas; however, many larger breeds are also affected. It results from malformation of the bones forming the knee joint, which causes the kneecap to move intermittently or permanently out of its normal position in the joint. Very mild cases cause no apparent lameness or only mild, intermittent lameness and do not need treatment. Dogs with a mild condition are often described as "skipping" in the rear legs. More severe cases can cause serious lameness and must be treated surgically. To avoid this problem, have puppies of breeds predisposed to patellar dislocation thoroughly examined by a veterinarian before the final purchase agreement is made. Should a marked tendency to patellar luxation be discovered in a growing dog, early intervention is required to prevent extreme leg deformity. Correct surgical procedures can prevent lifelong problems. Ask your veterinarian for further information should you suspect patellar dislocation in your dog.

HIP DYSPLASIA

Hip dysplasia is a deformity of the hip joint in which the joint socket is abnormally shallow and the head of the femur is malformed. Although in affected dogs both hips are usually malformed, it is not unusual for only one hip to be abnormal (18% of affected dogs in one study). Hip dysplasia is a complex, genetically influenced disease, and some breeds (e.g., Saint Bernards, Newfoundlands, bull mastiffs, German shepherds) have a notably higher incidence of hip dysplasia than others (Chihuahuas, greyhounds). It has been shown that the bony changes of this condition follow developmental changes that produce a looseness in the hip joint. Studies indicate that exercise, vaccines, and diet do not change the course of the disease once present. However, dogs who are overfed and overweight during their growth period may be more likely to develop dysplastic hip changes if the genetic propensity preexists. Also, dogs who are genetically predisposed to hip dysplasia may be less likely to develop its bony abnormalities if during their growth they are strictly confined to pens that enforce long periods of sitting. (However, this is *not* recommended for healthy psychological development!)

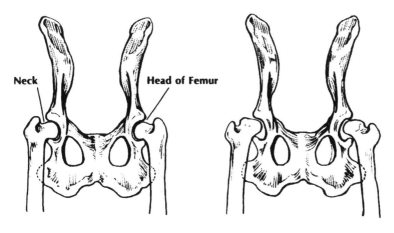

Neck   Head of Femur

NORMAL HIPS   **HIP DYSPLASIA**

Dogs with hip dysplasia may or may not show outward signs of disease. Some dogs with hip dysplasia show signs of pain in the hip joint when handled or exercised. Some have an abnormal swaying gait or a restricted range of motion when running. Others have difficulty rising. But the presence or absence of any or all of these signs or other lameness is not alone sufficient to diagnose the condition. Other diseases, especially those involving the lumbosacral spine, may cause symptoms that can easily be confused with those of hip dysplasia. The only way to properly diagnose the presence or absence of hip dysplasia is to take X-ray pictures of the dog's hips.

The average pet with a normal gait doesn't need to be examined for hip dysplasia. However, if your dog is to be used for breeding, an X-ray examination should be performed and the status of the hips determined before any breeding is allowed. *Only* dogs with normal hips should be used for breeding. The Orthopedic Foundation for Animals (OFA) and the Institute for Genetic Disease Control in Animals (GDC) maintain a staff of veterinary radiologists who evaluate X-ray films of dogs' hips for dysplasia and a registry of purebred dogs certified free of hip dysplasia. Registration with a foundation improves the value of a breeding animal. OFA radiologists will evaluate films of dogs one year of age or older, but films taken for OFA certification must be taken after twenty-four months of age because the changes characteristic of hip dysplasia may not be present in younger dogs. If your dog's hips are examined at less than one year of age and the signs of hip dysplasia are present, there is no need for X-rays later—once present, hip dysplasia does not go away.

Young dogs with hip dysplasia may experience a period of rear-limb lameness as they are growing, then be just fine. Other dogs seem to experience discomfort only after strenuous exercise. Most dogs with hip dysplasia develop degenerative joint disease (arthritic changes) of the hip joint as they age (as do some dogs with normal-looking hips); these changes may or may not cause signs of discomfort and lameness.

Don't believe anyone who says your dog must be "put out of its misery" because of hip dysplasia. There is no correlation between the degree of primary hip dysplasia and secondary arthritis and the amount or persistence of discomfort or disability an affected dog exhibits. Euthanasia should be used only in cases of disability and extreme discomfort that have not responded to other care. If you have a dysplastic dog who shows persistent signs of discomfort, there are several things that may provide relief:

1. Provide warm, dry quarters (minimizes the effects of osteoarthritis).

2. Do not allow the dog to become overweight (extra weight is an extra stress on the hips).

3. Allow the dog to control his or her exercise (don't encourage excessive jumping or forced exercise).

4. Aspirin can relieve some pain associated with hip dysplasia.

5. Prescription drugs can be used to provide intermittent relief when aspirin is insufficient.

6. Acupuncture may provide pain relief during the growth phase or later when osteoarthritis has occurred if other traditional forms of pain relief fail. For a list of certified veterinary acupuncturists, contact the International Veterinary Acupuncture Society.

7. Surgery:

Corrective *osteotomy* (bone cutting) is the only procedure that may create a more normal, stable hip in an animal developing hip dysplasia. This major surgical procedure involves cutting and repositioning the bones of the leg, hip, or pelvis and it must be performed on an immature dog before bony abnormalities are very significant (usually between six and ten months of age). Therefore, it is of value only when the diagnosis is made very early, the owner is willing to go to considerable surgical expense, and a veterinary orthopedic surgeon is available to perform the procedure. Consider an early hip screening radiograph for pups of predisposed breeds if you would like to take advantage of this treatment option. All other surgical procedures are useful only for relief of pain that does not respond to conservative medical management.

Total hip replacement can provide pain relief and improved mobility for both primary hip dysplasia and the secondary arthritic changes it may have caused. In this operation, the head and neck of the femur and the pelvic hip joint are removed and replaced with an artificial joint. Again, considerable surgical expense and the availability of an experienced veterinary orthopedic surgeon limit its usefulness. However, most veterinary teaching hospitals and some sophisticated private practices can offer this procedure to owners who are willing to give their dogs this opportunity to regain normal function.

A less sophisticated and less expensive procedure, *excisional arthroplasty* or *femoral head and neck resection* (removal) is an excellent method of pain relief when discomfort is a major problem for the dog and total hip replacement is not possible. It works best on dogs under 40 pounds of body weight and should be used when other medical treatment is ineffective.

Pectineous myectomy (myotomy) has been most effective in providing temporary relief from pain not responsive to aspirin or other drugs or other medical approaches. In this operation a portion or all of the small pectineous muscle, which is located on the upper inside surface of the rear leg, is removed. Although it can provide dramatic pain relief, it does not alter the course of the disease over the long run, and similar results can usually be achieved with medical treatment and the passage of time, especially in young dogs whose pain in any case often passes with growth.

OSTEOCHONDRITIS DESSICANS (OCD, OSTEOCHONDROSIS)

Osteochondritis dessicans (osteochondrosis) is a developmental abnormality of bone formation that occurs in rapidly growing cartilage and results in abnormally thickened joint cartilage that is subject to trauma from shear forces that are normally transmitted harmlessly across the joints. The defect in cartilage maturation (osteochondrosis) usually occurs in medium- and large-sized breeds of dogs (e.g., Swiss or Bernese mountain dogs, Kuvaz, Newfoundlands, Great Pyrenees, golden retrievers, Labrador retrievers, Rottweilers) and most often affects the shoulder joint. It may also affect the hip joint, knee, tarsal joint, elbow, distal radius, and neck vertebrae.

Early in the course of the disease, cracks develop in the joint cartilage, releasing breakdown products into the joint that irritate it (the actual osteochondritis) and cause pain, usually indicated by lameness. Later, a flap of cartilage may be formed, followed by degenerative changes in the joint leading to arthritis (secondary degenerative joint disease).

Affected dogs often become lame between four and nine months of age, but early signs are easy to overlook or to attribute to other causes as the lameness associated with OCD often improves with rest. Therefore, it is not unusual to diagnose OCD in dogs older than one year.

Although the shoulder form of osteochondritis dessicans often presents itself as a one-sided foreleg lameness, up to 50% of dogs are affected on both sides. Males (generally the larger and heavier sex) are at least two to three times more likely to be affected with OCD than females, and the heavier, faster-growing dogs of a litter also seem to be affected more frequently. Because of these facts and the fact that the actual cartilage defect of OCD occurs in weight-bearing joints, it is recommended that particular attention be paid to keeping a puppy (especially of a large breed) from becoming overweight or overexercising during its rapid growth phase (from two to six months of age) in the hope of preventing clinical OCD.

Radiographs of the suspect joint will be needed to confirm the diagnosis of OCD. The corresponding opposite joint should also be X-rayed for comparison. In difficult cases, special contrast X-ray joint studies may be necessary.

Treatment of osteochondritis dessicans includes rest, pain relievers (e.g., aspirin), and surgery to remove any loose or free-floating pieces of cartilage in the joint. Although some dogs' lameness resolves with conservative treatment, excellent results are obtained with surgical intervention and it is recommended for large lesions, free fragments within the shoulder joint, older patients, and dogs of any age who do not remain pain-free after a period of enforced rest.

ELBOW DYSPLASIA

Elbow dysplasia is a developmental disease that is generally the result of one or more defects in the growth of the elbow bones that cause instability of the joint, abnormal joint contact and weight distribution, and subsequent degenerative joint disease. Common defects associated with elbow dysplasia are *osteochondrosis,* an *ununited anconeal process,* and a *fragmented coronoid process.* Like other developmental bone problems, elbow dysplasia occurs most often in large dog breeds such as the Rottweiler, German shepherd, Labrador retriever, Bernese mountain dog, Saint Bernard, and Newfoundland and is generally accepted to be an inherited disease affected by a number of genes *(polygenetic).*

Most dogs with elbow dysplasia will develop lameness before six or seven months of age. Signs of pain may vary from a mild gait change, where the elbow is held out away from the body during a stride, to severe restriction of motion, enlargement of the joint, and reluctance to bear weight on the painful leg. Exercise usually aggravates the symptoms, while rest and pain relievers help lessen them.

Diagnosis of elbow dysplasia relies on evaluation of multiple, well-positioned radiographs, so any dog with a recurrent or persistent foreleg lameness suspected of elbow disease should be examined by a veterinarian. The Orthopedic Foundation for Animals (OFA) and the Institute for Genetic Disease Control in Animals (GDC) maintain elbow registries to provide standardized evaluation of elbow joints and a means of identifying dogs that should not be allowed to reproduce. Preliminary examinations may be evaluated when the dog is six months of age, but dogs will be certified free of elbow dysplasia only on the basis of X-ray films taken at twelve (GDC) to twenty-four (OFA) months of age or older.

Treatment for elbow dysplasia is similar to that for hip dysplasia (see page 158) except that the value of surgery for pain relief and to prevent progression of the degenerative joint disease is controversial. The best results are obtained when mildly affected dogs respond quickly to strictly enforced rest (dogs who do not respond quickly to enforced rest usually do not respond well to any treatment).

PANOSTEITIS

Another disease of large dog breeds, notably young German shepherds, is *canine panosteitis.* Although this disease is self-limiting, and resolves spontaneously with the passage of time, it can be responsible for persistent and/or recurrent lameness that may begin as young as two months of age or as late as five years. Characteristically, an affected dog suddenly becomes lame on one leg (usually in the front) and may also be lethargic and reluctant to eat. Finger pressure over the affected bone will elicit signs of discomfort such as pulling away or biting at the area. After a few days of improvement, the lameness often shifts to another limb and then another every two to three weeks for as long as nine months. All these symptoms are caused by a cyclic degeneration of the bone marrow *adipocytes* (fat cells) and internal bone remodeling, which is later followed by regrowth of the marrow cells.

Since it is easy to confuse other, more serious causes of lameness with panosteitis, all dogs suspected of it need a veterinarian's examination and X-ray pictures to confirm or refute the diagnosis. Pain relievers such as aspirin may be needed only if the signs of discomfort become severe.

INTERVERTEBRAL DISC DISEASE

The *intervertebral discs* are anatomic structures that normally function to absorb shock and distribute pressure along the spinal column. The intervertebral discs undergo degenerative changes in all dogs as they age and in certain breeds (dachshunds, Pekingese, beagles, Welsh corgis, Lhasa apsos, Shih Tzus, cocker spaniels, French bulldogs) at a relatively early age. The degenerative changes result in a fibrous disc that has lost its elasticity and often becomes calcified. The outer covering of the disc *(annulus fibrosis)* also undergoes degenerative changes that make it less efficient at keeping the disc material in its normal position. Signs of disease result when the degenerating disc begins to protrude from its intervertebral space, causing pressure on the spinal cord or on the roots of the spinal nerves. What signs appear depend on the area in which the protrusion occurs and the type of protrusion. If you are the owner of a breed predisposed to this problem or if you own an older dog, you should be alert to the possible signs.

I.V. DISC DISEASE

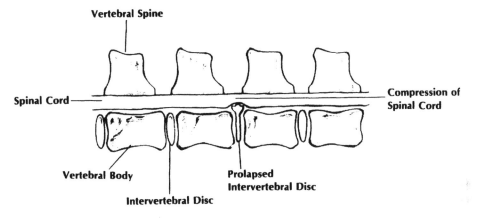

Vertebral Spine

Spinal Cord

Compression of Spinal Cord

Vertebral Body

Prolapsed Intervertebral Disc

Intervertebral Disc

CERVICAL DISC PROTRUSION (NECK REGION)

Protrusion of a disc in the neck region often causes extreme pain. Your dog may hold his or her neck rigid with the head in a lower-than-normal position. Signs of front-leg lameness may be present (due to effects on front-leg nerves that originate in the cervical region of the spinal cord) or may accompany neck signs. This type of disc protrusion is common in beagles. Similar signs accompanied by dysfunction in the rear legs are also seen in larger breeds such as Doberman pinschers and Great Danes when malformation of the neck vertebrae *(cervical spondylopathy)* causes compression of the spinal cord.

THORACO-LUMBAR PROTRUSIONS (REAR LEGS)

Disc protrusion in the thoracic or lower back regions often causes symptoms in the hindlegs. If the onset is slow, you may see only a reluctance to move (e.g., to go up- and downstairs or jump) or a mild hindleg "lameness." In severe or progressive protrusions, complete rear-leg paralysis and loss of bladder and anal control may be seen.

If your dog shows signs of disc protrusion, immediate enforced restriction of exercise is necessary. This will help prevent complete disc protrusion and possible paralysis as a sequel. If the protrusion is minimal and strict inactivity is enforced for several weeks, recovery from a mild episode may occur even without a veterinarian's care. Do not be overly concerned with the administration of drugs to relieve pain. Pain relievers often make a dog feel sufficiently comfortable to exercise, causing undue stress on a *herniating* (protruding) disc.

If the signs progress, persist, or recur, or the herniation of the disc is sudden and severe, causing signs of leg weakness or paralysis, the help of a veterinarian is important. Cases with rapid progression of signs or paralysis are emergencies. Veterinarians will often confine your dog in the hospital and administer antiinflammatory and/or pain reliever medications. Medication also may be given to relieve the swelling of the spinal cord that follows its compression. X-rays will be used to determine the site and extent of the problem. Acupuncture is used occasionally for pain relief when more traditional medicines are contraindicated or ineffective.

Surgical operations are available for disc protrusions so severe that medical treatment alone is insufficient. Surgical procedures are also available to help prevent additional protrusions in dogs that have had disc trouble in the past. This type of surgery is called an *intervertebral disc fenestration* and involves removal of the contents of the degenerated discs to prevent their future protrusion.

Physiotherapy is important in the recovery of many dogs with disc disease. Whirlpool baths, swimming, and passive muscle and joint exercise may be given at the veterinary hospital, or you may be requested to employ these measures at home. *Paraplegic* (paralyzed in the rear legs) dogs can be provided with a cart that supports their rear legs.

DIGESTIVE SYSTEM (GASTROINTESTINAL SYSTEM)

VOMITING

Vomiting is the forcible expulsion of stomach and/or intestinal contents through the mouth. It is important to try to distinguish between true vomiting and *regurgitation,* which is the passive act of return of the contents of the esophagus or pharynx through the mouth. This distinction will help your veterinarian make a diagnosis if home treatment is unsuccessful. Vomiting is a *sign* of various illnesses, not a disease in itself.

Vomiting occurs commonly in dogs. It seems to be caused most often by irritation of the stomach, which veterinarians call *acute* or *simple gastritis.* Gastritis is usually caused by the ingestion of an irritant substance—for example, decomposed food, grass, aluminum foil, paper, or bones. The dog often first vomits food or another irritant material and later vomits clear or yellow fluid. Dogs with gastric irritation may seek grass to eat, but grass eating is often an "enjoyable pastime" for dogs and not a sign of illness. They may or may not be interested in their normal food. If your dog vomits once or twice, has no fever or obvious abdominal pain, and is no more than slightly depressed (inactive), you can probably treat the vomiting at home.

Do not feed your dog for twelve to twenty-four hours following vomiting. At the end of twelve hours (if you can't stand to wait longer), you can offer a very small amount of soft, bland food such as cooked rice, pasta, or potatoes mixed with low-fat cottage cheese (9-to-1 ratio). If your dog keeps this small meal down for about four hours, another small meal can be offered, then another about four hours later. If no further vomiting occurs, the next day's meals can be normal-sized portions of bland food and the following day you can return your dog to a regular diet. Water should be offered only in small amounts but frequently in order to combat the tendency to dehydration that accompanies vomiting. Large amounts of food or water distend the already irritated stomach and usually cause vomiting to recur. An easy way to have water available in small portions is to place ice cubes in the water bowl and allow the dog to drink the liquid that accumulates as the cubes melt. **HOME TREATMENT FOR VOMITING**

Antacid liquids for humans containing aluminum and/or magnesium hydroxide may help soothe the irritated stomach lining; however, the most important part of treatment is fasting! (Dose aluminum hydroxide antacids to provide 10 mg per pound [22 mg/kg] of body weight every six hours.) If vomiting is present with diarrhea *(gastroenteritis),* drugs containing bismuth subsalicylate are best (see page 167). Do not give any preparations containing aspirin.

If your dog vomits more than a few times, if the vomitus is ejected extremely forcefully (*projectile* vomiting), if there is blood in the vomitus or obvious abdominal pain, or if your dog seems particularly depressed or weak, has a fever, or retches unproductively, *do not* attempt to treat the condition at home. **TIMES TO SEEK VETERINARY HELP FOR VOMITING**

Even simple gastritis cannot always be treated successfully without the help of a veterinarian, and there are many other serious causes of vomiting, among them intestinal foreign bodies, bowel or stomach torsion (twisting), inflammation of the pancreas, kidney failure, and even certain forms of idiopathic seizure disorders (epilepsy).

Some dogs, particularly young dogs used to eating several times a day, vomit during the hours preceding their regular meal. The vomitus usually looks like a frothy white or yellow fluid and is usually present in small amounts. This type of vomiting may be due to excess gastric acidity and can be controlled in several ways:

1. Feed two meals a day (morning and evening).
2. Allow free-choice feeding.
3. Administer an antacid before the time when vomiting usually occurs. This last method is the least desirable since prolonged use may stimulate even greater secretion of gastric secretions.

Another not-very-serious type of vomiting experienced frequently by young dogs occurs following meals, usually those who gobble their food, overeat, and/or exercise excessively immediately following eating. If your dog is an after-meal vomiter, you can try the following:

1. If your dog normally eats with other animals, feed the one who vomits by him- or herself. Competition encourages food gulping.
2. Feed smaller meals more frequently.
3. Enforce rest after meals.
4. Try a food that has to be chewed before swallowing (e.g., large-size kibbles).

MOTION SICKNESS Some dogs become nauseated and vomit when they ride in cars. The first sign of nausea is usually excessive *salivation* (drooling). If the car is stopped and the dog is exercised at this point, the signs often subside and the trip can be resumed for at least a short time. Most young dogs with this problem seem to outgrow it, particularly if they are taken for short but frequent automobile rides. If your dog is prone to motion sickness, avoid feeding for eight hours before traveling, stop for frequent exercise, and be sure there is adequate ventilation in the vehicle. If these measures aren't sufficient to prevent vomiting, motion sickness pills for people containing *dimenhydrinate* (1 milligram per pound [2.2 mg/kg] of body weight), given about thirty minutes before car rides, will help some dogs. In other cases prescription drugs (certain tranquilizers) that act on the "nausea centers" in the brain must be used to control the problem. Ask your veterinarian about these drugs.

DIARRHEA

Diarrhea is the passage of abnormally soft and/or frequent stools. This sign is often associated with vomiting, but may be present alone. It has *many* causes; the most common are dietary. All-meat diets or diets containing milk (see page 64) often cause diarrhea. High-fat or spicy table scraps and decomposed food are other common offenders. Intestinal parasites (e.g., worms) may cause diarrhea (see page 92), but this is much less common in adults than in puppies. Diarrhea may be caused by psychological stress such as a trip to the veterinarian's office or new animals in the house, but this type usually subsides quickly and needs no treatment.

Home treatment for diarrhea consists of withholding food for twelve to twenty-four hours (don't be too worried if your dog is not hungry at first), then offering a bland, easily digestible diet for three to five days. Use nine parts cooked white rice, pasta, or potatoes mixed with one part low-fat cottage cheese or cooked, skinned chicken and feed only small meals three or four times a day. Although in the past intestinal protectants and absorbents such as Kaopectate (2 teaspoonsful per 10 pounds [2 ml/kg] of body weight every six hours) were thought to be important to the treatment of diarrhea, most cases resolve as quickly with fasting alone followed by a restricted diet. It is especially important to be careful to make the return to a normal diet gradually over about a week's time by mixing in small quantities of the normal food with the bland diet before returning to full feeding of the usual diet. A change back to a normal diet before healing of the bowel is complete will result in a relapse.

HOME TREATMENT FOR DIARRHEA

Bismuth subsalicylate (Pepto-Bismol, ¼ teaspoonful per ten pounds [≈¼ ml/kg] of body weight every six to eight hours) is a useful nonprescription medication for mild diarrhea of unknown cause, as is loperamide hydrochloride (Immodium, 0.5 milligrams per 10 pounds [≈0.1 mg/kg] of body weight every six to eight hours). Both can be administered together, if necessary, for symptomatic relief of nonspecific diarrhea. However, neither should be administered at home for longer than forty-eight hours without the advice of a veterinarian.

Diarrhea that persists longer than twenty-four to thirty-six hours without improvement, bloody diarrhea, diarrhea accompanied by persistent vomiting, fever, listlessness, lack of appetite, or diarrhea that seems to clear up and then returns should not be allowed to continue without seeking help from a veterinarian. In severe forms of hemorrhagic (bloody) diarrhea, death may occur within eight to sixteen hours following onset. A typical case of a dog who had been allowed to vomit and have diarrhea for two weeks resulted in an intestinal puncture by a bone and the dog's death from *peritonitis* (inflammation of the membrane lining the abdomen).

TIMES TO SEE A VETERINARIAN FOR DIARRHEA

If you decide to take your dog to a veterinarian for treatment of diarrhea, try to bring along a stool sample when you go. This can be very helpful in diagnosis and treatment of the problem. The color, composition, and consistency of the stool are important, and an examination for parasites may have to be performed.

CONSTIPATION

Constipation is the difficult or infrequent passage of feces. This sign occurs infrequently in healthy dogs and, like diarrhea, is most commonly caused by diet. Dogs who do not ingest sufficient bulk or who eat indigestible foreign material such as bones often become constipated. Most normal adult dogs have one or two bowel movements a day, but since each dog is an individual and diet has a great influence, a routine must be established for each dog. One day without a bowel movement is not a crisis. However, forty-eight hours without a stool passage may be reason for concern, especially if there are other signs such as lack of appetite, vomiting, dehydration, a hunched-up abdominal appearance, or repeated and/or unsuccessful attempts to defecate.

HOME TREATMENT MAY HELP MILD CONSTIPATION   If constipation is mild, a change in diet may relieve the problem. Dogs should be given only bones that can be chewed on, not eaten. Constipation due to bone ingestion is often associated with crumbly, hard white, or light-colored stools. Feeding dry dog food will help some dogs who have trouble with mild constipation since most dry foods have more bulk than canned diets do. Water and bran (up to 5 tablespoonsful [30 g] daily) added to the food may help. You can try commercial preparations containing psyllium (e.g., Mucilose and Hydrolose); they are designed for humans and are sold in drugstores to add bulk to one's diet. If you find that you must add such preparations to your dog's diet frequently, discuss the problem with a veterinarian as there is likely to be an underlying physical problem.

Mineral oil (1 teaspoonful per 10 pounds [1 ml/kg] of body weight) will sometimes relieve more severe constipation. It works by softening and lubricating the stool. Like all laxatives, it should not be used on a continuous or frequently repeated basis. Mineral oil interferes with the absorption of oil-soluble vitamins, and prolonged use can cause vitamin deficiency as well as treatment-induced abnormal bowel function. Mineral oil should be administered in food. *Do not* attempt to force it orally; if inhaled, it can cause severe pneumonia.

An enema may be necessary to relieve *impaction* of the colon (hardened stool lodged in the colon). This is best performed by a veterinarian, who should give your dog a thorough physical examination before treatment. Docusate sodium (DSS) enemas, which come in adult and pediatric sizes, can be purchased in drugstores if the services of a veterinarian are unavailable. To administer an enema, insert the lubricated nozzle of the enema into the rectum and administer the liquid at a rate not to exceed 10 ml (2 tsp) in small dogs, 20 ml (4 tsp) in medium-sized dogs, or 30 ml (6 tsp) in large dogs. Other kinds of enemas are too dangerous for home use.

ENEMAS ARE BEST GIVEN BY VETERINARIANS

In long-haired dogs straining is frequently associated with hair matted over the anus, not constipation. The dog sometimes cries continuously or when making attempts to defecate. If you have a long-haired dog who strains at defecation, be sure to examine his or her anus before concluding that the problem is internal constipation. Clip away any matted hair with scissors or clippers and wash the anus gently with an antiseptic shampoo. If the anus is very inflamed, a soothing antibiotic-steroid ointment may help relieve discomfort. Prevent recurrent problems by keeping the hair around the anus clipped short.

ANAL HAIR MATS

Straining associated with bladder infection (see page 176), and with severe diarrhea and intestinal inflammation, are also commonly confused with constipation. Be sure you know what the problem is before attempting to treat it. (If necessary, insert a gloved and lubricated finger into the rectum to feel the stool.) Constipation may become so severe that the stool cannot be passed at all *(obstipation)* without physical manipulation of it under general anesthesia.

FLATULENCE (INTESTINAL GAS)

Having a flatulent dog around is more of an inconvenience than a real medical problem. Excessive gas formation can usually be controlled by changing the diet. Some dogs gulp air with their meals that is later passed as intestinal gas, so changing the physical form of the food can help these cases. Although some veterinarians blame excessive carbohydrate intake, many flatulent dogs are fed high-protein or high-fat diets (e.g., large quantities of canned meat). You may find that feeding certain types of table scraps causes the problem. Most dogs who eat dry food are not excessively gassy unless the dog cannot digest oligosaccharides such as raffinose or stachyose, two carbohydrates contained in soybeans, which are a common ingredient in dry foods. (Dry cat food when fed to dogs may cause a problem because of its high protein and soy content.) Oligosaccharide intolerance is similar to lactose intolerance, which occurs when a dog is unable to digest milk sugar (lactose) and bacteria in the gut ferment the excess carbohydrates, causing excessive gas production and sometimes diarrhea. The best antiflatulence diet needs to be chewed (e.g., dry food), is easily digestible, and is low in fiber with moderate protein and fat levels. Try a rice, corn, and/or wheat-based diet if you suspect your dog is having trouble digesting soy-based dog foods and avoid giving milk to flatulent dogs.

Increased exercise, activated charcoal administered orally, or other human antiflatulence products containing *simethicone* (20–40 mg every eight hours) may help minimize any discomfort associated with flatulence in dogs in which diet changes have not helped. Discuss their use with your veterinarian as persistent flatulence may occasionally be associated with more serious medical problems.

STOOL EATING (COPROPHAGY)

Coprophagy is the act of eating stool, either your dog's own or another animal's. It is a common problem, particularly among young dogs. Some veterinarians believe that coprophagy of a dog's own stool is due to a lack of certain digestive enzymes and is a method the dog uses to conserve the enzymes that are in short supply. Thiamine (vitamin B_1) deficiency can cause coprophagy under experimental conditions. On occasion stool eating occurs in dogs who have abnormally increased appetites due to disease, such as diabetes mellitus, hyperthyroidism, or hyperadrenocorticism. Many healthy, well-nourished dogs eat other animals' stool because they seem to like the taste. Many dogs will also eat horse manure and cat feces. The ingestion of cat or dog stool should be prevented not only for aesthetic reasons, but because it can be a source of infection from intestinal parasites.

If you let a young dog know that coprophagy is not acceptable by voicing "no" in a firm and disgusted tone of voice when you catch the dog eating stool, this punishment plus the maturing process is often enough to stop the habit. While working to change the behavior, it is critical that the dog not have the opportunity to eat stool when unsupervised, so he or she cannot be left alone for long periods of time or allowed to run off the leash. Dietary changes may also help prevent dogs from eating their own stool. Self-feeding, allowing free access to food, instead of scheduled meals helps some dogs. In dogs fed a high-carbohydrate diet, try adding good-quality protein—eggs, cottage cheese, skeletal muscle meat. Diets consisting mainly of canned meat–type foods should be changed to include more car-bohydrates—the addition of dry kibble is the easiest, most balanced method. Adding the enzyme *papain* to the food will also sometimes prevent coprophagy. This can be done at home by sprinkling meat tenderizer containing papain on food. Veterinarians often supply drugs that when added to the diet make the stool unpleasantly bitter. Ask your veterinarian for one if other methods fail to stop coprophagy.

ANAL SACCULITIS

Impaction of the anal sacs, often accompanied by infection, is a frequent problem in dogs. It can occur in any dog but seems to be most common in smaller breeds, such as the toy and miniature poodles, Chihuahuas, and cocker spaniels. (The function of the anal sacs is explained on page 15.)

The most common signs of anal sac impaction are scooting along the ground on the anal area and licking excessively at the anus. Occasionally affected dogs will chew at their tail bases or lower backs or develop more generalized skin problems. Scooting is only rarely a sign of "worms." At an early stage expressing the contents of the sacs will usually relieve the problem. You can do this yourself. Use one hand to hold up the dog's tail and pull it gently toward the head. (This makes the sacs easier to feel.) Hold a disposable cloth or tissue in the other hand. Place your thumb externally over one anal gland and your fingers over the other. Press in and apply firm pressure as you pull your fingers posteriorly over the glands. This causes the contents to be expressed out through the anus into the tissue so they can be discarded. If you cannot empty the sacs this way, empty each sac separately. Place your thumb externally over the sac and your gloved index finger over the same gland 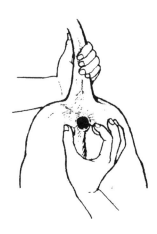 inside the rectum, then compress the sac between your thumb and finger. Normal anal sac fluid should come out slightly yellow or brown in color, perhaps with a few brownish flecks in it. Impacted sacs will be very difficult to express and the material may be pasty in texture and colored gray or black.

ANAL SAC ABSCESSES If impacted anal sacs are not emptied, one or both may become infected. Infected sacs are usually painful, and you may be able to express blood-tinged material or greenish yellow pus from the sac. The odor of infection often attracts the affected dog's or other dogs' attention to the area. If you don't notice the infection at this stage, you may later see an abscess or swelling externally at one side of the anus or the other. The abscess may open and drain to the outside. Infected anal sacs are best treated by a veterinarian. If they have not yet abscessed, it may be possible to treat them with antibiotics alone. If they are abscessed, surgical drainage is often necessary. Chronically inflamed and/or infected anal sacs may have to be removed.

HICCUPS

Hiccups that occur in dogs are the same as those people get. They are caused by a sporadic contraction of the diaphragm. They are seen most often in puppies and usually stop spontaneously without treatment. A dog with continuous hiccups that don't stop spontaneously within twenty-four hours needs to be examined by a veterinarian.

OBESITY

Obesity (fatness) in dogs is almost always an owner-induced disease caused by overfeeding and inadequate exercise. Excessive fat puts excessive stresses on your dog's joints, heart, and lungs and often results in an inactive dog who is a poor companion. An obese dog, as you may have discovered, is more difficult to examine thoroughly than a normally fleshed one, since excess fat interferes with listening to or feeling the heartbeat and feeling the pulse and abdominal organs. An obese dog is a poorer surgical risk and is more likely to develop cancer, skin disease, diabetes mellitus, heat stress, liver malfunction, and decreased resistance to infectious diseases. If your dog is overweight, have a veterinary examination if you want to be sure that his or her general health is good and that the obese condition is not caused by a hormonal imbalance such as hypothyroidism (this requires blood tests); then start a diet. This important single step can prolong your dog's life, as calorie restriction (providing the diet itself is nutritionally adequate) is the *only* dietary manipulation scientifically shown to improve longevity.

An obese dog is 15% or more above optimum body weight. Since dogs vary so much in size, shape, and weight, obesity is best judged by feeling over the ribs for the fat layer. Normal dogs have only a thin layer of fat between the skin and muscles covering the ribs, and each rib can be easily felt but not seen. They also have a clearly defined abdomen, which is normally tucked up higher than the bottom of the rib cage.

Choose the weight to which you want your dog to reduce. Then feed 60%–70% of the daily caloric requirement to maintain that weight until the desired weight is reached. This could take several months. Small breeds need about 40 calories per pound ($\approx$18 calories/kg) per day, medium-sized breeds need about 30 calories per pound ($\approx$13.7 calories/kg) per day, and large breeds need about 20 calories per pound ($\approx$10 calories/kg) per day. You can use the following as a rough guide to how much commercial food will provide the proper amount of calories, but remember, an individual dog's calorie requirements may vary up to 20% more or less than the average.

TYPE OF FOOD	CALORIES PER POUND OF FOOD	CALORIES PER KILOGRAM OF FOOD
Dry (maintenance type)	1,700 (about 350/ 8 oz measuring cup)	3740 (about 350/240 ml measuring cup)
Semimoist	1,300 (about 250/ 8 oz measuring cup)	3960 (about 250/240 ml measuring cup)
Canned mixed diet	550	1210
Canned meat	600	1320

If you make your dog's food yourself, you will have to determine its calorie content. You can feed the calculated amount of food in as many meals as you desire each day and experimental studies indicate that several small meals may result in greater weight loss than one or two large ones, but remember *more total food is not allowed.* If your dog is accustomed to begging and you can't resist, offer small pieces of raw vegetable such as carrots or iceberg lettuce or a rawhide bone for chewing. At the same time, gradually increasing periods of exercise help tone the muscles and are a better alternative to food when begging occurs.

Special low-fat, relatively high-fiber, complete and balanced diets are now commercially available for dogs. Such products are reduced in calories compared to maintenance foods while still providing the proper ratio of protein to fat and all the other nutrients a dog needs. These products allow an obese dog to consume a relatively large volume of food, thereby providing a greater degree of satiety than that provided by portions of a usual maintenance diet. Although most dogs can easily maintain a normal body weight when given appropriate quantities of regular commercial diets without snacks or table scraps, weight control products are useful to dog owners who have difficulty resisting their pet's demands for food. Also, dogs who are not exercised regularly will maintain their weight much more easily when fed diets lower in fat (therefore lower in calories) than the usual maintenance diets, which are designed for normally active dogs.

Weigh your dog weekly. Small dogs (less than 20 pounds [9 kg] body weight) should lose up to ½ pound (227 g) per week. Medium dogs (between 20 and 40 pounds [9–18 kg] body weight) should lose up to 1 pound (454 g) per week. Dogs heavier than 40 pounds (18 kg) should lose no more than 3 pounds (1.4 kg) per week. If you are following the rules set out above and your dog is not losing weight, consult your veterinarian for further help. Once your dog has reached the desired weight, you can relax the rules a little. Weigh your dog once a month thereafter and make small adjustments in the diet whenever your dog starts to gain weight.

DESIRED WEIGHT	DAILY MAINTENANCE CALORIE REQUIREMENT
5 lb (2.3 kg)	250
10 lb (4.5 kg)	420
15 lb (6.8 kg)	560
20 lb (9.1 kg)	700
30 lb (13.6 kg)	900
40 lb (18.2 kg)	1,200
50 lb (22.7 kg)	1,350
60 lb (27.3 kg)	1,500
70 lb (31.5 kg)	1,750
80 lb (36 kg)	1,960
90 lb (40.5 kg)	2,160
100 lb (45 kg)	2,300

An example: Your dog weighs 30 pounds (13.6 kg), but should weigh 20. The daily maintenance calorie requirement for a 20-pound (9 kg) dog is about 700 calories × 60% = 420 calories to be fed while reducing. This is about 12 ounces (350 g) of canned complete diet, 4 ounces (112 g) of dry food (about 1¼ cups [280 ml]), or 5 ounces (106 g) of semimoist food (about 1⅔ [404 ml] cups). When the desired weight of 20 pounds is reached, the food intake could be raised to about 20 ounces (578 g) of canned complete diet, 6.5 ounces (187 g) of dry food, or 8.6 (177 g) ounces of semimoist food. Keep in mind that all calculations are approximate as individual differences in metabolism affect the actual maintenance requirements significantly.

GENITOURINARY SYSTEM (REPRODUCTIVE AND URINARY ORGANS)

If your dog has any of the following signs, *genitourinary* (reproductive or urinary) system disease may be present and immediate, thorough examination by a veterinarian is indicated:

Drinking increased amounts of water
Urinating very frequently
Urinating abnormally large or small amounts
Difficulty or inability to urinate
Bloody urine
Inability to hold his or her urine (urinary incontinence)
Blood and/or puslike material dripping in quantity from the penis or vulva
Abdominal pain or walking with an arched back

BALANOPOSTHITIS (INFLAMMATION OF PENIS AND PREPUCE)

A small amount of opaque white or yellowish discharge from the *prepuce* (skin covering the penis, sheath) is present in almost all mature male dogs, and is generally considered normal. When this discharge is excessive, perhaps greenish or odorous, and the dog licks at his prepuce excessively, these are signs of inflammation of the lining of the prepuce and of the surface of the penis that veterinarians call *balanoposthitis.* If you protrude the penis (see page 29) and examine its surface and the lining of the sheath, you may see small, smooth lumps, which are enlarged *lymphoid follicles,* and the surface of the penis may look abnormally red. If the puslike discharge is dripping directly from the penis opening, the condition is probably more serious than a simple preputial infection (see "Prostatitis," page 178). You should look for foreign material, such as foxtails, inside the prepuce of affected dogs. If you see one and remove it, your dog's problem may be solved without the aid of a veterinarian. If you cannot find an obvious cause and get rid of it, simple balanoposthitis without the presence of a foreign body is treated by flushing the prepuce with an antibiotic solution or instilling antibiotic ointment that your veterinarian can prescribe.

VAGINITIS

Vaginitis is an inflammation, often with accompanying infection, of the vagina similar to the vaginal inflammations common in humans. Females with vaginitis have a sticky .yellowish, greenish, or gray discharge often seen on the hairs at the vulva. They may lick excessively at their vulvas and may be unusually sexually attractive to male dogs. If you examine the mucous membrane (skin) inside the lips of the vulva, you may find it abnormally red or bumpy.

Vaginitis in females who have not reached puberty may be characterized by a small amount of discharge only, and often does not need treatment. It usually disappears at the time of first heat. If your young female has only mild signs at the vulva, no accompanying urinary signs, and seems generally healthy, you may choose to wait for treatment.

Vaginitis in older females should always be examined by a veterinarian because more serious diseases, such as *pyometra* (see page 179), can be confused with it, and it may be associated with abnormalities of the genitalia and of the urinary tract. It is treated with systemic antibiotics, douching, antibiotic suppositories, and estrogen hormones. Vaginitis in both puppies and adult females may be accompanied by a bladder infection *(cystitis).*

CYSTITIS (BLADDER INFECTION)

Cystitis is an inflammation of the bladder most often caused by bacterial infection. It can occur in both male and female dogs, but is more common in females. Dogs with cystitis often urinate frequently or strain to urinate frequently without passing much urine. (This sometimes causes cystitis to be confused with constipation.) The urine may look normal to you, or it can appear cloudy or bloody. Females with cystitis may lick at their vulvas excessively and may have a vaginal discharge. Cystitis may also be due to causes other than bacterial infection, such as bladder tumors or stones.

If you think your dog may have cystitis, immediate examination by a veterinarian is indicated. Urinalysis will be necessary, so you can help by bringing a clean, recently caught urine sample with you. To obtain a clean urine sample, begin with a clean, dry jar, pan, or pie tin. Wash your dog's genital area with mild soap and rinse with lots of clear water, then dry. Take your dog outdoors on a leash, and when the dog squats or lifts a leg to urinate, quickly slip the pan into the stream to catch the urine. You only need to catch about one-fourth cup of urine for a complete urinalysis. Transfer the urine to a clean container and take it in for analysis within the hour. If you have to wait longer than an hour, refrigerate the urine. If you can plan ahead, ask your veterinarian to provide you with a urine container and preservative if necessary. Try not to contaminate the urine with hair, dirt, grass, or other foreign materials. Many veterinarian prefer to obtain the screening urinalysis sample in the office by a safe, relatively painless and quick procedure called *cystocentesis.* A fine needle attached to a syringe is passed through the abdominal wall and into the bladder, where a small sample of urine is withdrawn. This procedure avoids inconvenience for you as well as contamination of the urine sample, which can confuse the interpretation of lab results.

HOW TO OBTAIN A URINE SAMPLE

If your veterinarian finds evidence of bladder infection, he or she will probably want to take a sterile sample for bacterial culture. This helps determine the preferred drugs for treatment. After your dog is treated, you will want your veterinarian to examine another urine sample since sometimes signs of cystitis disappear after treatment even though the infection is still present. Abdominal X-rays may be necessary to rule out other diseases that may mimic a simple bladder infection, such as bladder stones, bladder tumors or enlargement, tumors, or infection of the prostate gland. It is extremely important that cystitis be treated promptly and properly to prevent retrograde infection of the kidneys and other possible permanent damage to the urinary system. (For more information on urinary tract disease, see page 216).

PROSTATITIS

Signs very similar to cystitis may often be seen when a male dog is affected by *prostatitis,* an inflammation of the prostate gland with or without concurrent bacterial infection. Also, prostatic disease must be ruled out whenever a male dog is diagnosed with urinary tract infection. Dogs with prostatitis often pass blood-tinged urine. Sometimes the blood is observed only at the end of urination, when the last urine is being squeezed from the bladder, or only at the opening of the prepuce or penis. Other times there is no visible blood in the urine but the dog has difficulty with urination itself or defecation. In more severe cases, the dog may exhibit a painful abdomen, difficulty walking, fever, vomiting, lethargy, and loss of appetite. Some dogs with prostatitis even develop painful, swollen testicles.

If you suspect that your dog may have prostatitis, take him in for a veterinarian's examination. Urinalysis, culture of the urine and/or prostatic fluid, X-ray examination, and other more sophisticated diagnostic procedures such as ultrasound examination and prostatic biopsy may be necessary to rule out prostate diseases such as cancer, cysts, or age-associated enlargement *(benign hyperplasia),* which can accompany or mimic simple infection. Antibiotics are the mainstay of treatment for prostate gland infection, but surgery on the gland itself is sometimes needed. Castration is often necessary in the treatment of long-term or recurrent prostatitis and in the treatment of other prostate diseases.

SWELLING OF THE VULVA

Swelling of the vulva normally precedes the onset of heat, often by as much as a month and occasionally more. This change in the vulva can be recognized only if you become familiar with the appearance of your dog's vulva while she is in the *anestrous* state (see page 241). Other swelling in the genital area is uncommon. However, foreign body abscesses sometimes occur in this region (see page 136). If you cannot find an obvious cause of swelling and don't think the time of your female's heat is near, be sure to have her examined by a veterinarian.

BLEEDING AT THE VULVA (PROESTRUS)

Proestrus is the time during which a bloody discharge first appears at the vulva of the sexually mature female. (For more information, see page 241.) If your female dog is not "in heat," any bloody vulvar discharge should be cause for examination by a veterinarian.

ESTRUS (MATING READINESS)

For signs of mating readiness, see page 241.

FALSE PREGNANCY

For signs of false pregnancy, see page 253.

UTERINE INFECTION

PYOMETRA

Pyometra is a type of uterine infection that most commonly occurs in older unspayed (or partially spayed, see page 246) females. It usually occurs following estrus and is probably due to a hormonal imbalance. In cases of pyometra where the cervix is open, there is usually a sticky reddish to yellow, abnormal-smelling discharge from the vulva. *Other cases have no discharge.* A female with pyometra is often listless, lacks appetite, and shows increased water intake and increased urination. She may vomit and *sometimes* has fever. If not treated, this condition can cause death. Ovariohysterectomy (see page 244) is the treatment of choice for pyometra. In rare instances of pyometra in valuable breeding animals, methods other than spaying have been used. Females with pyometra are poor surgical risks, so consider having an ovariohysterectomy performed when your dog is young to avoid pyometra later, and rush your dog to a veterinarian if you think pyometra may be present.

ENDOMETRITIS

A retained placenta or fetus, or a lack of cleanliness during delivery, can result in a later infection of the uterus, *acute metritis (endometritis)*. A female with acute metritis is usually depressed and febrile, lacks appetite, and may seem uninterested in her puppies. She may seem excessively thirsty, vomit, and/or have diarrhea. The discharge from the vulva is often odorous, reddish, and watery, later dark brown and puslike. This condition calls for immediate treatment by a veterinarian. Puppies may have to be raised by hand (see page 261) since females with acute metritis often do not have enough milk, or the milk produced may be toxic.

179

EMERGENCY MEDICINE

An *emergency* is any situation that requires immediate action in order to prevent irreversible damage to or death of your dog. Each of the following signs indicates an emergency situation:

Uncontrollable bleeding
Extreme difficulty breathing (including choking)
Continuous or recurrent convulsions
Inability to urinate
Unconsciousness
Shock
Sudden paralysis
Repeated or continuous attempts to vomit, repeated unproductive vomiting, and/or diarrhea

Conditions such as injury to the eyeball or snakebite are usually emergencies; others, such as certain leg injuries, are not so clear-cut. Therefore, in many cases you will have to use your intuition to make a good judgment about the best action to take.

It is to both you and your veterinarian's benefit that you be able to recognize a genuine emergency. No veterinarian I know enjoys being taken away from dinner, pulled from the bathtub, or awakened in the middle of the night by a hysterical pet owner who obviously does not have an emergency. Most veterinarians value their leisure time more than any emergency fee they may collect. Rational pet owners are often unhappy to find out, upon reaching the veterinary hospital, that the "emergency" could safely have waited until morning and the emergency fee saved. Usually, getting emotionally upset leads to restricted judgment. Try to remain calm and use this section as a reference.

THE BEST EMERGENCY TREATMENT IS PREVENTION Most emergencies are the result of trauma (hit by a car, dogfights) or poisoning. Most could have easily been prevented if the owners had confined their dogs to a yard or run when unable to provide supervision. Medical emergencies due to failure of a vital organ could often have been prevented by consulting a veterinarian soon after the earlier signs appeared. Look ahead. If a weekend or holiday is coming up, it may be a good idea to take your dog in for an examination even if the signs seem minor. An emergency could follow directly.

It is also a good idea to make up a first-aid kit to have on hand and to take with you on trips during which your pet will be far from veterinary care. It should include the following:

A SIMPLE FIRST-AID KIT FOR PETS

Instruments:

   Rectal thermometer
   Penlight flashlight
   Scissors
   Fine-toothed tweezers
   Nontoothed tweezers
   Magnifying glass
   Needlenose pliers
   Small wire snips
   Sewing needle

Antiinfectives:

   Povidone-iodine solution and scrub (shampoo) and/or
   Chlorhexidine solution and scrub
   Neomycin/polymixin B/bacitracin topical cream (or ointment)
   Rubbing alcohol (70% ethyl or isopropyl alcohol)
   3% hydrogen peroxide (poor disinfectant but good for removal of blood)

Poisoning antidotes:

   Syrup of ipecac
   Activated charcoal liquid

Bandaging materials:

   Nonstick wound pads (2" × 2", 3" × 3", 4" × 4")
   Gauze squares (2" × 2", 3" × 3", 4" × 4")
   Roller gauze (1", 2" wide)
   Roll cotton (disposable diaper or sanitary pad pieces can often be substituted in an emergency)
   Adhesive tape (½", 1", 2" wide)
   Elastic bandage (2", 3" wide)

Miscellaneous:

   Cotton-tipped swabs
   Styptic powder (or pencil)
   Toenail trimmer
   Medical-grade cyanoacrylate glue (rarely needed)

All of these materials should be easy to obtain in any well-stocked drugstore, except for the needlenose pliers, metal snips, and medical glue. Commercial first-aid kits intended for people can easily be expanded to make them appropriate for use with pets. Ask your veterinarian for instructions for the use and purchase of medical glue.

SHOCK

The term *shock* is one that is frequently misused. It is extremely important to know whether or not shock is truly present, because its presence or absence often determines whether or not a condition is an emergency. Shock can be simply defined as *the failure of the cardiovascular system to provide the body tissue with oxygen.* There are several causes of shock, among them severe infection and severe allergic reaction; the most common cause in veterinary medicine is blood loss. The following are signs that may indicate the presence of shock:

SIGNS OF SHOCK IN ORDER OF INCREASING SEVERITY

1. Depression (quietness and inactivity) and lack of normal response to external environmental stimuli. This may progress to unconsciousness.

2. Rapid heart and respiratory rate.

3. Rapid pulse that becomes weak and may become absent as shock progresses.

4. Poor capillary refilling time. To test for capillary refilling time, press firmly against the gums, causing them to blanch (whiten) beneath your finger. Lift your finger away and see how long it takes for the color to return to the blanched area. The normal refilling time is no more than one or two seconds. Poor capillary filling is an early and constant sign in shock. It precedes the pale, cool mucous membranes present in advanced shock.

5. Lowered body temperature. The extremities (legs and paws) and skin become cool to the touch, and the rectal temperature often drops below 100°F (37.8°C).

If your dog shows signs of shock following injury or prolonged illness, contact a veterinarian immediately. But first wrap your dog in a towel or blanket (if available) to preserve body heat.

EXTERNAL BLEEDING AND HOW TO STOP IT
(HEMOSTASIS)

Most cuts through the skin will stop bleeding within five or six minutes of occurrence. Those that do not or that are bleeding profusely
need some kind of immediate care, especially if it's going to be a
while before you can enlist professional veterinary aid.

A *pressure bandage* is the best way to stop bleeding. If a gauze pad **PRESSURE**
is available, place this directly over the wound; then apply the ban- **BANDAGE**
dage over it. Any clean strip of material can be used for a bandage.
Gauze roller bandage, a strip of sheet, or an elastic bandage are best
since persistent bleeding causes seepage that you can see through
such bandages. If the wound is on the trunk or you plan to bandage
a limb only temporarily, apply several wraps of bandage firmly but
not tightly directly over the wound. If the bandage is to be left on
a limb for several hours or more, it should be applied over the wound
and down the leg to cover the foot as well. This will prevent swelling
and *ischemia* (loss of blood flow) of the part of the limb below the
bandage. This rule applies to bandaging the tail as well. If you cannot
apply a pressure bandage, firm, *direct* pressure (with your bare hand,
if necessary) over the wound for several minutes will often stop
bleeding.

If a pressure bandage successfully stops the bleeding and no other
problems are apparent, you can usually wait several hours or overnight, if necessary, to have the wound examined and treated by a
veterinarian. An exception is a chest wound in which there are air
bubbles in the blood or that is accompanied by the sound of air
moving in and out of it. Wounds like this may be associated with
air leakage into the chest cavity from outside, which can cause
difficult breathing and fatal lung compression. Once covered, such

APPLYING A PRESSURE BANDAGE TO THE TAIL

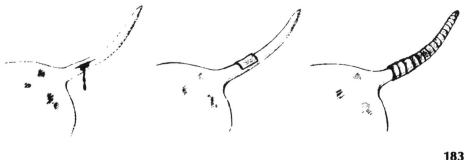

183

wounds should remain so and immediate veterinary aid sought. Do *not* disturb any foreign body protruding from such a wound before seeking a veterinarian's advice. Most wounds severe enough to require a pressure bandage will need *suturing* (sewing closed) for proper and most rapid healing. (Any wound that gapes open is likely to benefit from suturing.)

TOURNIQUET

A *tourniquet* is a second and *much less desirable* method of hemostasis. Tourniquets are useful only for bleeding involving a limb or the tail, and they should be loosened *at least* every fifteen minutes to allow reoxygenation of the tissues. Use any strong cord, rope, bandage strip, or even a piece of panty hose to form a tourniquet. Form a loop and apply it to the extremity between the body and the wound. (It is easiest to apply it at a joint to prevent slippage.) Watch the change in blood flow to determine how tightly to tie the tourniquet. Proper application will usually cause an immediate and definite slowing of blood seepage. When you achieve sufficient slowing, stop tightening the tourniquet. Then consider replacing the tourniquet with a pressure bandage if at all possible.

HIT BY A CAR

REMAIN CALM The first thing to do if you find your dog hit by a car is to try to remain calm. This isn't easy, since your animal is so important to you, but hysterics will not help you or your dog. Try to assess the damage that has been done. You must gather information to help your veterinarian decide on the seriousness of the injuries before you get to the hospital. So concentrate your attention on this plan of action while administering first aid.

Many seriously injured animals try to run from the scene of the accident in fright, thereby increasing their injuries or becoming lost and unavailable for veterinary care. *Do not* leave your dog unattended for one second. If necessary, ask a bystander to telephone your veterinarian, or carry your animal with you to the telephone. (Before moving your animal, check for possible fractures or spinal cord damage; pages 154–155.)

First, evaluate your dog's vital signs. Look for signs of shock, con- **EVALUATE VITAL SIGNS** sciousness, airway obstruction, breathing, and heartbeat. If the airway is obstructed, the dog is not breathing or seems unconscious, and you cannot detect a heartbeat, cardiopulmonary resuscitation (CPR) may be needed (see page 187). A fracture or large cut can be spectacular and frightening, but this matter takes secondary consideration. If signs of shock are present, be sure your dog gets professional veterinary care *at once*. If this is not possible and shock is present, indicating the possibility of internal bleeding, an elastic bandage wrapped firmly around the abdomen can be effective in raising the blood pressure and limiting blood loss until veterinary aid can be obtained. Be sure any wrap you apply is firm but does not further compromise the breathing.

Even a small amount of blood can make a wound appear to be more **EXTERNAL AND INTERNAL BLEEDING** serious than it is. Try to determine the source of the blood loss. When you find the site, you will often find that the bleeding has stopped.

If there is a great deal of bleeding from the wound, apply a makeshift pressure bandage or direct pressure to it (see page 183). Persistent bleeding from the nose and/or mouth requires immediate veterinary care, as does blood in the urine or signs that indicate internal bleeding and/or injury (shock, abdominal pain, difficulty breathing).

A veterinarian should be consulted if you think your dog has a **FRACTURES** fractured limb, but the fracture itself may not be an emergency if the dog is otherwise doing well (see page 154). *Paralysis or partial paralysis may indicate spinal cord damage* and requires that you keep the vertebral column as immobile as possible from the time of the accident until you arrive at the veterinary hospital (see page 155). A nose muzzle (see page 231) is important to protect yourself if the animal is frightened and uncooperative. A stretcher or board is the best means of carrying a severely injured dog. If you can't determine the extent of injury and do not have a makeshift stretcher available, carry the dog as illustrated, being careful not to bend the dog's back in any direction.

If you find that your dog seems essentially normal following the **INTERNAL INJURIES** accident, you may not need to see a veterinarian. You should be aware, however, that certain major internal injuries may not be apparent for several hours (sometimes days) following such trauma, for example, diaphragmatic hernia.

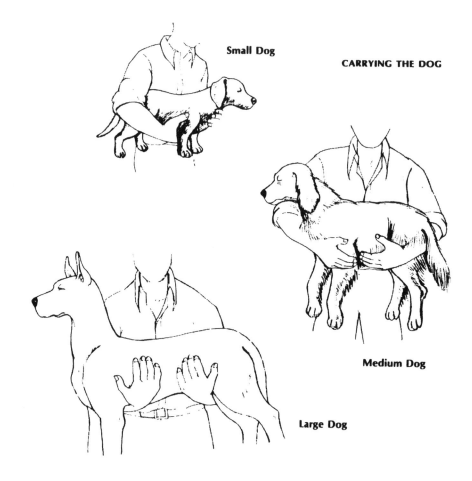

Small Dog

CARRYING THE DOG

Medium Dog

Large Dog

DIAPHRAGMA-TIC HERNIA

A *diaphragmatic hernia* results when a tear in the diaphragm allows the abdominal organs to move through it into the chest. If the tear occurs at the time of an accident but the actual hernia does not (or is mild), you may not see any signs. When the abdominal organs herniate (or a small hernia gets worse), strained respiration ensues. Lack of appetite, vomiting, or difficulty in swallowing may be seen. If you try to hear the heart sounds, they may be absent or muffled. If a large portion of the abdominal organs has moved into the chest, you may notice a "tucked-up," relatively empty-looking abdomen. Watch for signs indicating a possible diaphragmatic hernia for several weeks following any severe accident.

URINARY INJURIES

Be sure to watch for signs of normal urination following incidents involving abdominal trauma, such as that suffered when a dog is hit by a car. Dogs with ruptured bladders or other injuries to the kidneys and/or ureters may act normally at first, then later develop abdominal pain. Their abdomens may be very tender when examined. If urination is completely absent or blood-stained, or if normal-looking urine is passed with some difficulty, suspect a ruptured bladder or other urinary tract injury. Any such injury is likely to be a surgical emergency.

If your dog is not examined by a veterinarian following an accident, be sure to perform a thorough physical examination yourself, and watch closely for signs of shock for twenty-four hours. Don't forget to examine the abdomen thoroughly by palpation. If your dog shows signs of pain such as *tensing* (contracting) the abdominal muscles more than usual or crying out, or if the abdomen feels unusual to you (too few, too many, or unusually shaped masses present), be sure to arrange for an examination by a veterinarian.

CARDIOPULMONARY RESUSCITATION (CPR)

Cardiopulmonary resuscitation (CPR) is an important emergency life-saving technique to know, although it is rarely needed by pet owners. CPR is used whenever there is an event or illness that causes the breathing or heartbeat to stop, such as drowning, electrical shock, or choking. It can also be used to assist severely impaired breathing or heart function. Signs that indicate the need to employ CPR include unconsciousness accompanied by absence of a heartbeat, absence of a pulse, mucous membranes that are gray, blue, or white (a pale pink or normal pink color may be present if aid is administered immediately), dilated pupils, and failure to breathe. CPR must be administered within three to five minutes of respiratory and/or cardiac arrest to be effective. Its two components, artificial respiration and external heart massage, are described below.

ARTIFICIAL RESPIRATION

Any occasion on which you have to resort to artificial respiration is an emergency (except perhaps in a newborn puppy that is slow to start breathing). Don't spend all your time trying to revive the dog on the spot. As soon as your veterinarian is contacted, head for the clinic while continuing attempts at resuscitation.

Artificial respiration serves no purpose in an already dead animal. **SIGNS OF** Place your ear on the unconscious dog's chest and listen for a heart- **DEATH** beat; feel for a pulse (see page 33). If no pulse or heartbeat is detectable and the pupils are dilated and nonresponsive to light, it is probable that death has already occurred and that your first aid will be useless. However, you can try external heart massage (see below).

To administer artificial respiration, open the mouth, pull out the tongue, and look as far back into the pharynx as possible to see if there are any obstructions. If you can't see anything, it is a good idea to feel for obstructions with your fingers and remove any you find. However, you must take extraordinary care when doing this, as a bite from a semiconscious animal can be severe. Wipe away excessive mucus or blood in the pharynx that might interfere with the flow of air. Extend the dog's head and neck. Then close the dog's mouth. Inhale. Holding the dog's mouth closed, place your mouth over his or her nose (cover it completely) and exhale, forcing the exhaled air through the dog's nose into the chest. In small dogs your mouth may cover the whole *anterior* (front) part of the muzzle. Then watch for the chest to expand as you blow. After inflating the lungs in this manner, remove your mouth to allow the chest to return to its original (deflated) position. Repeat the inflation-deflation cycle twelve to twenty-four times per minute as long as necessary. If the heart is beating and you have been quick to relieve an airway obstruction, respiration may resume within a few minutes. These procedures put the resuscitator at significant risk of accidental injury and should be undertaken only by those willing to assume such risk.

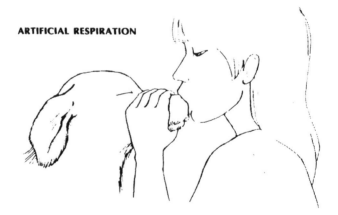

ARTIFICIAL RESPIRATION

EXTERNAL HEART MASSAGE
(EXTERNAL CARDIAC COMPRESSION)

External heart massage is used in an attempt to maintain circulation when cardiac arrest has occurred. If you cannot feel a pulse or heartbeat in an unconscious and nonbreathing dog, you may try external cardiac compression. Heart arrest automatically follows re-

EXTERNAL CHEST (HEART) COMPRESSION

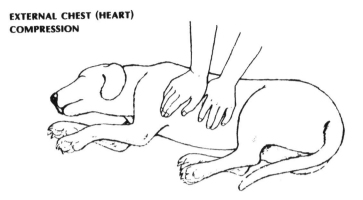

spiratory arrest; when heart arrest occurs first, breathing soon stops. Therefore, *cardiac massage must be combined with artificial respiration if any benefit is to be gained.* Irreversible damage to the brain is said to occur after three minutes without oxygen. This implies that heart compression must be started within three to five minutes following cardiac arrest to be of benefit.

Place the dog on his or her side on a firm surface. For small- and medium-size dogs, place your hands on the side of the chest over the heart and compress the chest firmly. Then completely release the pressure. For larger dogs, compression works best when it is applied on the side of the chest at the point where the diameter of the chest is greatest. The very largest dogs are compressed most effectively when placed on their backs with pressure applied over the distal one-third of the sternum (see page 9). Don't worry too much about damage to the chest: getting effective circulation going is more important, and it has been shown that chest compression, not actual heart compression, is probably most important in maintaining blood circulation. The compression/release cycle should be repeated 60 to 120 times per minute. In puppies or very small dogs, you can achieve effective cardiac massage by applying pressure on the heart area with one hand on each side of the chest wall or with the fingers of a single hand wrapped around the chest. If your actions are effective, you should be able to feel a pulse (see page 33) with each massage. If you are unassisted, try to intersperse an artificial respiration for every ten cardiac compressions. Otherwise have your assistant give a respiration at the same time as every other heart compression, since simultaneous chest compression and lung inflation have been shown to provide the best circulatory results.

While attempts to restart the heart are being made, try to get the animal to a veterinarian. Don't expect the animal to revive during your attempts at resuscitation before obtaining veterinary services. If consciousness resumes, however, keep the dog warm and quiet and proceed to a veterinary hospital where observation can continue.

CONVULSIONS

Convulsions (seizures) include a wide variety of signs consisting primarily of abnormal behavior and/or abnormal body movements. The most easily recognized signs are *loss* (or disturbance) *of consciousness, loss of motor control,* and *involuntary urination* and/or *defecation*. Convulsions fall into two main categories, in terms of whether or not they are emergencies:

1. The single convulsion, which lasts for a minute or two and does not recur for at least twenty-four hours
2. Repeated or continuous convulsions

Convulsions in the second category require immediate veterinary attention. Dogs with convulsions in the first category should be examined by a veterinarian, but may not require emergency care.

RESTRAIN A DOG HAVING A CONVULSION The most important thing for you to do if your dog is having a convulsion is to provide gentle restraint so he or she will not become injured. One of the best ways is to place a light blanket or towel over the dog. It's not a good idea to place your hand in or near the dog's mouth unless you are willing to risk a serious bite. Airway blockage by the tongue rarely occurs. While one person restrains the dog, another can try to reach a veterinarian. Seizures in the first category are often past by the time you get in touch with a veterinarian.

POISONING

Emergency situations involving convulsions commonly occur following poisoning. Snail bait *(metaldehyde, metaldehyde-arsenic,* or *metaldehyde carbamate)* and *strychinine* are the two poisons that most frequently cause convulsions.

SNAIL BAIT POISONING *Never* put snail bait anywhere where there is the slightest possibility that your dog may come in contact with it. There are snail bait holders designed to keep bait away from pets. And if necessary, you can resort to "old-fashioned," environmentally sound methods of snail and slug control such as hand picking, the use of beer in a shallow container as bait, or a pet duck. Some snail baits contain only metaldehyde (also found in compressed tablets for small heaters); others contain arsenic or carbamates as well as metaldehyde. Some brands claim to be nontoxic to dogs, but don't assume this about any garden pesticide product. In cases of poisoning, even with the combination products, metaldehyde seems to be the toxic agent that causes the immediate signs. The first signs of toxicity are uneasiness and muscle tremors, which worsen until apparent convulsions occur. Vomiting may also be seen.

INDUCED VOMITING

If you see your dog eat snail bait, immediate induction of vomiting can prevent poisoning. The most reliable way to cause vomiting is to administer *syrup of ipecac, USP* (2% alcohol, 7% ipecac in glycerine, sold over the counter in drugstores), about 1 teaspoonful per 5 pounds (2 ml/kg) of body weight. Vomiting should occur in ten to thirty minutes. Another home remedy for induction of vomiting is *3% hydrogen peroxide* by mouth; give about 1 teaspoonful per 5 pounds (2 ml/kg) of body weight. If vomiting does not occur within five to ten minutes, you can repeat the dose up to two more times. A much less effective way to cause vomiting is to place a teaspoonful of salt on the back of the dog's tongue. As this method itself is potentially toxic, avoid it unless induction of vomiting is critical and there is no other product available. If signs of poisoning are already apparent when you first see the animal, *do not* try to induce vomiting, but rush your dog to a veterinarian. General anesthesia must usually be used for treatment of severe signs of snail bait poisoning.

STRYCHNINE POISONING

Strychnine is a potent poison often used in mole, gopher, and wild animal baits, and for malicious poisonings of other animals. The best way to protect your dog from strychnine poisoning is not to allow unsupervised roaming. Unsupervised dogs are more likely to come into contact with attractive baits set out for pests or to become pests themselves, thus encouraging malicious poisoning.

How quickly signs of poisoning follow the ingestion of strychnine varies depending on the fullness of the stomach and the form of the poison. Initially there may be restlessness and incoordination, progressing to convulsions in which the legs are extended and the body is rigid. A sudden stimulus such as a touch or noise will often initiate convulsions. At the onset of *any* signs indicative of poisoning, contact your veterinarian. Intensive care including general anesthesia is usually necessary.

You can prevent poisoning by common household products by reading their labels carefully and using them appropriately. Any product labeled hazardous for humans should be assumed to be toxic for your dog as well. As with small children, keep human medications and household products of all kinds out of dogs' reach, as these categories of chemicals are often involved in dog poisoning. Dogs should also be trained never to put anything into their mouths that is not their toy, their own food, or an item provided directly by their owners.

GENERAL TREATMENT OF POISONING

1. If you see your dog ingest a toxic substance, read the label to see if specific instructions for treatment are given. If not, induce vomiting unless the material is corrosive (a strong acid or alkali or a petroleum distillate, e.g., kerosene). Then give milk mixed with a raw egg at ¼ cup per 10 pounds (13 ml/kg) of body weight. If milk is not available, plain water can be used (see the poisons chart for treatments and times to use activated charcoal as the universal antidote). *Do not induce vomiting if your dog is already losing consciousness or is beginning to convulse.* If veterinary care is immediately available, *do not waste time on home treatment.*

2. If your dog gets a toxic substance on his or her skin or in the eye, flush with large volumes of water while (or before) someone calls a veterinarian. Be sure to protect yourself from toxic exposure when rinsing or washing toxins from the fur.

3. If convulsions occur, try to restrain the dog.

4. Try to bring a sample of the suspected poison *in its original container* to the hospital. If this is not possible, bring a sample of any vomitus you find.

LEARN TO USE POISON CONTROL CENTERS FOR HELP

There are thousands of potentially toxic substances in the environment and new toxins are developed every day, making it impossible for any single textbook to provide current information on every toxic substance. The National Animal Poison Control Center was formed to provide specific animal-oriented poisoning information. This pioneer animal poison control center provides a 900 number and a 24-hour toll-free number—(800) 548-2423—to assist with poisoning problems in animals. Information is available to both pet owners and veterinarians for a fee that must be paid at the time the call is made (credit cards are accepted). Local human poison control centers can also provide information on toxic ingredients in pesticides, insecticides, medicines, and numerous other commercial products.

COMMON HOUSEHOLD POISONS AND THEIR IMMEDIATE TREATMENT

POISON	TYPICAL PRODUCTS CONTAINING IT	SIGNS THAT MAY OCCUR AFTER EXPOSURE	IMMEDIATE TREATMENT
Acids	Car batteries, some metal cleaners, antirust agents, swimming pool cleaners	Local white, gray, or black burns; pain, shock, vomiting, respiratory distress, other	*Externally*: Flush copiously with water. *Internally*: Do not induce vomiting, give milk or water to dilute.
Alkali	Cleaning products, lye, drain openers	Local white, gray, or black burns; pain, shock, vomiting, respiratory distress, other	*Externally:* Flush copiously with water. *Internally:* Do not induce vomiting; give milk or water to dilute.
Amphetamines, caffeine	Diet and stimulant pills	Dilated pupils, restlessness, rapid heartbeat, muscle tremors, vomiting, seizures, coma	Induce vomiting; follow with activated charcoal.*
Arsenic	Ant poisons, herbicides, insecticides	Vomiting, restlessness, abdominal pain, diarrhea (may be bloody)	Induce vomiting; follow with milk or tea.

POISON	TYPICAL PRODUCTS CONTAINING IT	SIGNS THAT MAY OCCUR AFTER EXPOSURE	IMMEDIATE TREATMENT
Brodifacoum, bromadiolone, diphacinone, fumarin, pindone, valone, warfarin, chloro-phacinone	Rodent poisons	Hemorrhage, mainly internal; pale mucous membranes, weakness, vomiting or diarrhea (may be bloody), pain, difficulty breathing	Induce vomiting; consult veterinarian immediately. No effective home remedy. Signs may not appear for hours or days.
Bromethelin	Rodent poisons	Weakness, paralysis, tremors, seizures	Induce vomiting; consult veterinarian immediately. No effective home remedy. Signs may not appear for hours or days; repeated doses of activated charcoal* necessary.

POISON	TYPICAL PRODUCTS CONTAINING IT	SIGNS THAT MAY OCCUR AFTER EXPOSURE	IMMEDIATE TREATMENT
Carbamates	Antiflea sprays, powders, foggers; slug and snail bait; ant, roach, and water bug baits	Drooling, small pupils, abdominal pain, vomiting, diarrhea, difficulty breathing, muscle tremors, weakness, paralysis, restlessness, seizures, coma	*Externally:* Flush copiously with water followed by mild detergent baths. *Internally:* No good home remedy; rush to veterinarian. If veterinary care not available, induce vomiting before convulsion stage. Follow with activated charcoal.*
Cholecalciferol	Rodent poisons	Vomiting, depression, not eating, excessive thirst and urination, kidney pain	Induce vomiting; consult veterinarian immediately. No effective home remedy. Signs may not appear for hours or days.
Ethylene glycol	Antifreeze (2 tsp. will kill a 5-lb. animal)	Immediate treatment necessary to prevent death; *do not* wait for signs to appear	Induce vomiting and rush to veterinarian.

POISON	TYPICAL PRODUCTS CONTAINING IT	SIGNS THAT MAY OCCUR AFTER EXPOSURE	IMMEDIATE TREATMENT
Fertilizer (NPK)	Houseplant and garden plant food	Vomiting, diarrhea, dehydration	Give water or milk to dilute. Take to veterinarian if signs develop.
Lead	Paints, solder, fishing weights, used motor oil, food or water fed from improperly glazed pottery	Lack of appetite, vomiting, diarrhea, constipation, abdominal pain, behavioral changes from subtle to seizures and blindness	*Externally:* Bathe thoroughly using nonalcohol-based detergent. *Internally:* Induce vomiting followed by Epsom salts (250–500 mg/kg diluted in 5–10 volumes water). All exposure suspects need a veterinarian's evaluation as signs may not develop until long after exposure.
Metaldehyde	Snail bait	Restlessness, incoordination, muscle tremors, vomiting, convulsions	Induce vomiting if signs not yet present.

POISON	TYPICAL PRODUCTS CONTAINING IT	SIGNS THAT MAY OCCUR AFTER EXPOSURE	IMMEDIATE TREATMENT
Methanol, other alcohols	Windshield washer fluid; automotive, medicinal, and cleaning products; fuels, wood finishes	Excitability, incoordination, depression, coma, respiratory and cardiac arrest	*Externally:* Flush copiously with water followed by soap baths. *Internally:* Activated charcoal.* Rush to veterinarian.
Nonsteroidal anti-inflammatory drugs (NSAIDs)	Pain, cold, cough, or allergy remedies containing, e.g., acetaminophen, aspirin, ibuprofen	Vomiting, diarrhea, gastrointestinal bleeding, lack of appetite, abdominal pain, death	Induce vomiting followed by activated charcoal.* Consult veterinarian.
Organochlorines	Antiflea dips, insecticidal shampoos, ant and roach baits, garden insecticides	Drooling, small pupils, abdominal pain, vomiting, diarrhea, difficulty breathing, muscle tremors, weakness, paralysis, restlessness, seizures, coma	*Externally:* Flush copiously with water followed by mild detergent baths. *Internally:* No good home remedy; rush to veterinarian. If veterinary care not available, induce vomiting before convulsion stage. Follow with activated charcoal.*

POISON	TYPICAL PRODUCTS CONTAINING IT	SIGNS THAT MAY OCCUR AFTER EXPOSURE	IMMEDIATE TREATMENT
Organophosphates	Antiflea sprays, powders, foggers, dips, collars; ant and roach killers; dewormers, pest strips	Drooling, small pupils, abdominal pain, vomiting, diarrhea, difficulty breathing, muscle tremors, weakness, paralysis, restlessness, seizures, coma	*Externally:* Flush copiously with water followed by mild detergent baths. *Internally:* No good home remedy; rush to veterinarian. If veterinary care not available, induce vomiting before convulsion stage. Follow with activated charcoal.*
Petroleum distillates, turpentine	Kerosene, gasoline, solvent carriers for pesticides, wood finishes, furniture polishes, lighter fluids, lamp oils	Difficulty breathing, vomiting, diarrhea, skin irritation	*Externally:* Bathe thoroughly with nonalcohol-based detergent. *Internally:* Do not induce vomiting. Consult vet. Minimal exposure may not be serious.

POISON	TYPICAL PRODUCTS CONTAINING IT	SIGNS THAT MAY OCCUR AFTER EXPOSURE	IMMEDIATE TREATMENT
Phenol (carbolic acid)	Household disinfectants and antiseptics, wood preservatives, fungicides, herbicides, photographic developer	Incoordination, muscle tremors, depression, unconsciousness	Wash with soap and water. Induce vomiting.
Phosphorous	Strike-anywhere matches (safety matches are nontoxic), rat poison, fireworks	Vomiting, diarrhea, abdominal pain; apparent recovery may be followed by relapse and death	Induce vomiting followed by activated charcoal.* Consult veterinarian.
Salicylate (aspirin)	Aspirin	Weakness, lack of appetite, vomiting, fever, incoordination, convulsions	Avoid use; spontaneous consumption unlikely
Strychnine	Rodent poisons, malicious poisonings	Restlessness, incoordination, muscle tremors, convulsions	Induce vomiting if signs not yet present.

POISON	TYPICAL PRODUCTS CONTAINING IT	SIGNS THAT MAY OCCUR AFTER EXPOSURE	IMMEDIATE TREATMENT
Theobromine	Chocolate (3 oz. baking or 1.5 lb. milk chocolate can kill a 20-lb dog) Cacao bean mulch	Dilated pupils, restlessness, rapid heartbeat, muscle tremors, vomiting, seizures, coma	Induce vomiting; follow with activated charcoal.*

*Do not waste time trying to administer activated charcoal if veterinary aid is nearby. It can be both difficult and messy to administer. Activated charcoal is available over the counter in drugstores in tablet or liquid form. The recommended initial dose is 1 to 4 grams per pound of body weight (2 to 8 gm/kg body weight). Multiple capsules are needed even for small pets. The liquid form is more effective. Familiarize yourself with the appropriate dose for your pet.

See page 111 for chemical names of typical insecticidal poisons.

The list of potentially dangerous garden and houseplants is extremely long. The best rule to follow to avoid problems is to teach dogs to chew only on their own toys. If you supervise your dog whenever he or she is in an area where there are plants (especially during the puppy teething stage), the dog can usually learn quite readily to regard plants as only a part of the landscape.

Although some plants have only certain poisonous parts, consider all parts, *including the roots, tubers, and bulbs,* dangerous until proven otherwise. Many plants considered poisonous have only local irritant properties, so a reasonable strategy to follow if there is no veterinary care available when a pet is found chewing on a plant is to rinse the mouth carefully with a stream of water. If there is evidence that some of the plant has actually been consumed, induce vomiting and follow with activated charcoal. When local veterinary care is unavailable, a call to the regional or veterinary poison control center may also yield advice.

Poinsettia *(Euphorbia pulcherrima), Philodendron* species, dumbcane (*Diffenbachia* species), members of the *Rhododendron* family including azaleas, and mushrooms are the potentially poisonous plants pets consume most often. Although once thought to be highly toxic, poinsettias are now regarded as plants that are mainly gastrointestinal irritants. Most pets who chew on poinsettias develop no signs. A few begin to drool or vomit and have diarrhea. Similarly, a minimal exposure to philodendron or dumbcane may cause local irritation followed by drooling or vomiting. However, moderate exposure can result in swelling of the lips, tongue, and throat, which may produce laryngitis, tongue paralysis (rarely), and difficulty breathing (rarely). In rare cases, ingestion of philodendron or diffenbachia has resulted in later death from kidney failure.

Members of the *Rhododendron* family and wild-growing outdoor mushrooms have great potential to cause death in any pet who eats them. As there are no specific antidotes for the toxins they can contain, a veterinarian's emergency aid is needed for animals poisoned by these plants.

TYPICAL POISONOUS PLANTS

Araceae family—dumbcane (*Diffenbachia* spp.), *Philoden-dron* spp., ceriman (*Monstera* spp.), elephant's ear (*Alocasia antiquorum*), calla lily, caladium, skunk cabbage, wild calla or water arum, malanga (*Xanthosoma* spp.)

Algae—blue-green algae bloom contaminates pond water in hot weather (*Microcystic aeruqinosa, Anabaena flos-aquae, Aphanizomenon flos-aquae*)

*Azalea (*Rhododendron* spp.)

Black locust (*Robinia* spp.)

Bleeding Heart (*Dicentra* spp.)

Bulbs—narcissus, daffodil, jonquil (*Narcissus* spp.); *Amaryllis* spp., naked lady amaryllis (*Brunvigia, Iris* spp.); Easter lily (*Lilium longiflorum*); glory lily (*Gloriosa* spp.); autumn crocus (*Colchicum* spp.)

Buckeye (*Aesculys* spp.)

Buttercups (*Ranunculus* spp.)

*Castor beans—castor oil plant, palma christi (*Ricinus communis*)

Chinaberry (*Melia azedarach*)

*Chokecherry (*Prunus virginiana*)

Daphne (*Daphne* spp.)

English ivy (*Hedera helix,* fruits especially)

*Foxglove (*Digitalis* spp.)

Golden chain (*Laburnum*)

Helleborus

Hydrangea

Larkspur (*Delphinium* spp.)

Lily of the valley (*Convallaria* spp.)

Marijuana (*Cannabis* spp.)

Mistletoe (*Phoradendron flavescens*)

*Monkshood (*Aconitum* spp.)

*Mushrooms—*Amanita, Gyromitra, Coprinus, Inocybe* spp., *Clitocybe* spp.

Nettles—*Urtica* spp., *Laportea* spp., *Cnidoscolus* spp.

Nightshade family—*Solanaceae* spp. all contain toxic agents at some growth stage or in some plant part: *Datura stramonium* (thornapple, jimsonweed); *Datura inoxia* (tolguacha, trumpet vine, angel's-trumpet); *Datura arborea*; *Nicandra physalodes* (apple-of-Peru); *Solanum nigrum* (black nightshade, common

nightshade); *Solanum dulcamara, Atropa belladonna, Pseudo capsicum* (deadly nightshade, Jerusalem cherry, European bittersweet, climbing nightshade); tobacco, potato; and tomato leaves and stems
*Oleander—*Nerium oleander;* yellow oleander, yellow bestill tree (*Thevitia peruviana*)
Poison hemlock (*Conium maculatum*)
Pokeweed (*Phytolacca*)
*Precatory beans (*Arbus precatorius*)
Spurges—snow-on-the-mountain, crown of thorns, candelabra cactus, tinsel tree, poinsettia (*Euphorbia* spp.)
Walnut hulls (*Juglans regia, Juglans nigra*)
Water hemlock (*Cictua maculata*)
*Yew (*Taxus* spp.)

*Extremely toxic; ingestion of *very* small amounts often results in death.

SNAKEBITE

If your dog is bitten by a poisonous snake, prompt action by you and your veterinarian is necessary. Bleeding puncture wounds or small tooth marks are common signs of envenomation. Bites of poisonous snakes may also cause severe pain if venom has been injected, so a bitten dog will often become excited and run. You should attempt to prevent this response, since exercise helps spread the venom. Immobilize the dog as soon as possible.

If the bite is on an extremity, apply a flat tourniquet between the body and the wound (nearest the wound). The tourniquet should be applied firmly but not tightly, loose enough barely to slip one finger under, and it *should not* be fully loosened until the bite is treated by a veterinarian or until two hours have passed. (This type of application allows some oxygen to reach the tissues beyond the tourniquet while inhibiting flow of the venom in the lymph and venous blood.) If possible, keep a bitten limb on a level horizontal with the heart. Then make a linear incision (not *X*-shaped) over the fang wounds and apply suction for at least thirty minutes, preferably not by mouth but with a suction cup. The value of suction in limiting the spread of venom is controversial. For coral snake bites, in particular, copious flushing of the wound with water and germicidal soap is recommended. Another excellent alternative is to apply a tight compression bandage that includes both the bite wound and a wide area on both sides of it. Elastic bandage material or strips of panty hose are good for this purpose. Do not remove the bandage before getting veterinary aid within twenty-four hours. If veterinary care is nearby, don't waste time with prolonged attempts at first aid. The successful treatment of serious snakebite requires a prompt antivenin injection and prolonged intensive supportive care in a veterinary hospital.

Get your dog to a veterinarian as soon as possible. The veterinarian will administer antivenin, antibiotics, and pain relievers and can administer other medical treatment as called for. It may be necessary to remove a large portion of the wound surgically. Even if this is not done, snakebites often cause large portions of skin to die and slough off, leaving a large wound that must be treated. Plan on your dog being hospitalized for a minimum of twenty-four to forty-eight hours. If you are traveling to a snake-infested area, discuss with your veterinarian the possibility of your carrying a supply of antivenin, and of course get a good snakebite kit.

TOAD POISONING

Toads have glands in their skin that secrete substances that are bad-tasting to dogs and that can cause local irritation and drooling. At least two toad species, the Colorado River toad *(Bufo alvarius)* and the marine toad *(Bufo marinus)* are very toxic. Should you observe your dog mouthing or playing with a toad, flush his or her mouth thoroughly with water (a carefully directed stream from a garden hose can be effective). Contact with poisonous toads requires *immediate* veterinary care as well since heart irregularities often develop that can result in death less than thirty minutes after contact.

FISHHOOK IN THE SKIN

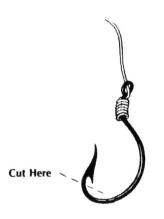

FISH HOOK

Cut Here

Fishhooks are foreign bodies that become embedded in dogs' skin relatively frequently. Once the barb has passed under the skin, a hook will not fall out on its own. The only way to remove it is to push the barb through the skin. Once it is through, cut the curved part of the hook just below the barb and pull the rest of the hook back out through the original hole. Often this procedure is too painful to be done without anesthesia, so don't be surprised if you need the help of a veterinarian. Veterinary services are needed to administer antibiotics as well; unless the hook was *extremely* clean, this type of wound is likely to become infected.

PORCUPINE QUILL IN THE SKIN

The important thing to remember about a porcupine quill in the skin is to remove the *whole* thing. Grasp the quill with a pair of pliers near the point where it disappears into the skin; then, with a quick tug, pull it out. If the quill breaks off as you try to remove it or if some of the quills break off before you have a chance to try to remove them, you may need a veterinarian's help. *Do not* ignore pieces of quill you cannot pull from the skin. They can migrate long distances (sometimes into bone or internal organs), carrying infection with them. And remember to check for quills inside the mouth as well as on the body surface.

INSECT BITE OR STING

Owners usually become aware of insect bites or stings long after they have happened. Usually a large swelling of the muzzle is noticed with no particular evidence of pain. Other times hives *(wheals)* appear. These are allergic reactions to the bite or sting. If there is no fever and the dog acts normally (even though abnormal in appearance), no treatment is usually necessary, but pull out the stinger if you see it. The swelling caused by a sting should go away in about forty-eight hours. With spider bites, the swelling may last for days or weeks and may sometimes be accompanied by death and sloughing off of tissue at the site of the bite. If you catch the bite early, if your dog receives multiple stings from bees, wasps, or hornets, or if the signs are progressing to severe allergic reaction, *anaphylaxis* (e.g., difficulty breathing, vomiting, diarrhea, urination followed by shock and collapse), consult a veterinarian. Emergency supportive care may be needed, and corticosteroids may be administered to prevent signs or further progression of signs that are already apparent.

BURNS

Burns may be thermal, chemical, or electrical (electric shock). The severity of *thermal* (heat) burns in dogs may be underestimated because their appearance differs considerably from those in humans. The type of blister characteristic of superficial burns in humans may not form in the burned skin of a dog. In a superficial burn, the hair remains firmly attached. If you pull on the hair in the area of a burn and it comes out easily, the burn is deeper and more serious.

THERMAL BURNS

Immediate treatment of thermal burns consists of applying cold water or ice compresses for twenty minutes. The affected area should then be washed with povidone-iodine or chlorhexidine disinfectant. Neomycin–polymixin B–bacitracin cream can then be applied topically if the burn is minor. Deep burns or burns covering large areas need emergency veterinary care. Because of the difficulty in evaluating the severity of burns in dog skin immediately after their occurrence, it is a good idea to have all burns examined by a veterinarian within twenty-four hours.

ELECTRICAL BURNS (ELECTRIC SHOCK) Electrical burns occur often in puppies who chew on electric cords. They can cause severe damage to the skin of the mouth and may result in *pulmonary edema* (fluid in the lungs). Dogs sustaining such burns should be thoroughly examined by a veterinarian as soon as you become aware of the injury. If difficulty breathing or cough occurs, pulmonary edema may be present. In severe cases the tongue and gums may look bluish. If you find your dog unconscious and not breathing after electric shock, administer artificial respiration (see page 187) once you have carefully and safely removed the dog from the electrical source. Even if general signs do not develop after electric shock, mouth tissue damaged by the burn often dies and sloughs off several days later and needs veterinary attention. Electrical burns are characteristically cold, bloodless, pale yellow, and painless.

CHEMICAL BURNS

For information on chemical burns, see "Acids and Alkali" in the chart of common household poisons, page 193.

HEAT STRESS (HEATSTROKE)

Heat stress occurs most often in dogs that have been confined to a car (or other enclosure) with inadequate ventilation on a warm day. Temperatures inside a parked, poorly ventilated car can rapidly reach over 100°F (37.8°C) on a relatively mild 75–80°F (23.9–26.7°C) day even in the shade. Heat stress can also occur in dogs suddenly transported to a hot climate to which they have not previously been acclimatized. It may even occur in dogs well adjusted to hot climates if they are overexercised during humid, hot weather. Puppies, *brachycephalic* (short-nosed) dogs, fat dogs, and older dogs are more subject to heat stress than others are.

Signs of heatstroke are panting, increased pulse rate, congested mucous membranes (reddened gums), and *an anxious or staring expression.* Vomiting is common. Stupor and coma may occur if the stress is allowed to continue long enough. Rectal temperatures are elevated (106–109°F [41.1–42.8°C]). Immediate treatment by immersion in cold water is necessary. If you cannot immerse the dog, soak the fur and skin with cold water. Massage the skin and flex and extend the legs to return blood from the peripheral circulation. Then get your dog to a veterinary hospital where treatment can be continued. Dogs whose body temperatures reach 110°F (43.3°C) usually die.

USE COLD WATER TO TREAT HEAT STRESS

Dogs sustaining heat stress should always be examined by a veterinarian, but if this is impossible, the temperature should be taken frequently over a twenty-four-hour period because elevation of the rectal temperature often recurs after the initial drop and first signs of improvement. It has been suggested that if the rectal temperature has not reached 103°F (39.4°C) in ten to fifteen minutes after starting treatment, a cold-water enema should be given. Following this treatment, however, the rectal temperature is no longer accurate.

Prevent heatstroke by carrying water with you on hot days and by giving your dog small amounts frequently. Wet towels placed over your dog or wetting the dog's fur itself will provide cooling by evaporation. Open car windows when a dog is left inside, or better yet, don't leave the dog in the car. And contrary to some opinions, clipping a long-haired dog is *not* an effective way to prevent heat stress.

YOU CAN PREVENT HEAT STRESS

FROSTBITE AND/OR HYPOTHERMIA

Dogs who experience frostbite (cold injury caused by freezing of tissue) and hypothermia (lowered body temperature) have usually been left outdoors for several hours in freezing weather. Short periods of cold exposure such as that needed for elimination are usually harmless if the dog has been acclimatized gradually. However, even short periods can be dangerous for animals who have recently moved from a warm climate to a cold one, for very young, very small, short-haired, sick, and/or old dogs, and for any animals whose fur is wet in cool and/or windy weather. Puppies under four weeks of age may become hypothermic at room temperatures between 65°F and 85°F (18.3°C and 29.4°C) if they are separated from their mother or littermates (see page 262). Although frostbite and hypothermia often occur together, a severely frostbitten pet may not become hypothermic and vice versa. Prevent frostbite and hypothermia by never leaving your pet outdoors in cold weather that you would consider unsafe for a child unless your dog has free access to warm, dry, draft-free shelter.

SIGNS OF
FROSTBITE Frostbite usually affects the tips of the ears and tail, the footpads, and, in male dogs, the scrotum. When first frostbitten, the skin looks pale and feels cool to the touch, and it is insensitive to painful stimuli. Later the skin may die and fall off (slough). In less serious cases of frostbite, the skin may never slough, but hair may fall out and grow back white although it was previously dark colored.

SIGNS OF
HYPOTHERMIA Signs indicating hypothermia may not be accompanied by frostbite. They include decreased mental alertness, shivering, weak or absent pulses, slowed heart rate, and slowed, shallow respiration. Shivering stops when the body temperature drops below 90°F (32.2°C). Animals whose temperatures drop to 75°F (23.8°C) usually die.

HOME
TREATMENT
FOR COLD
INJURY Rewarming is treatment for both frostbite and hypothermia. If veterinary care is immediately available, do not attempt home treatment. Wrap your pet (and a hot-water bottle, if available) in a blanket, warm jacket, or other insulator to retain any remaining body warmth, and rush to the veterinary clinic for treatment. Should veterinary care be unavailable, home care will be necessary.

If frostbite is unaccompanied by signs of hypothermia, treatment is directed only at the injured areas. Do not rub the areas but apply moist heat by immersing the part in warm water (102–104°F [38.9–40°C]) or by applying warm, moist towels. Rapid return of sensation, pink color, and warmth to the skin indicate successful treatment.

If the dog's temperature is above 86°F (30°C), simple home treatment for hypothermia is often successful. Bring the pet into a warm room and cover him or her. Warm water bottles (102–104°F [38.9–40°C]) placed inside a blanket wrapped around the dog help speed rewarming. Be sure to rewarm the fluids as soon as their temperature drops below 100°F (37.8°C). This can be done in a microwave oven to avoid repeated refilling of bottles. Electric heating pads may also be used if they are well insulated with toweling, set on low, and the animal is turned frequently to prevent burns. Water-circulating heating pads or chemical gel warming bags are safe and ideal for providing heat. Immersion of the body in warm water (102–104°F [38.9–40°C]) can also be done if a hair drier or heater is available to prevent re-chilling on removal of the pet from the water. The body temperature should be maintained just above 100°F (37.8°C) until thermoregulation resumes and the animal's temperature returns to normal.

CHOKING

Most dogs have a highly developed gag reflex that prevents choking. Occasionally dogs that gobble their food (especially if they have short faces like pugs, Pekingese, or boxers) choke and may suffocate if the airway remains obstructed. Should the dog be unconscious, follow the procedure for artificial respiration (see page 187). If you can't reach the obstruction and the dog is small enough, grasp the dog by the abdomen, turn him or her upside down so the nose is facing the ground, and give a quick squeeze to the abdomen to cause a forced exhalation, which may dislodge the object. (This is a Heimlich maneuver for dogs.) Avoid swinging a dog by his or her hindlegs to lower the head as you may dislocate the hips.

Dogs too big to be turned nose down should be laid with chest and abdomen to the ground. Stand over the dog and wrap your arms around the abdomen near the chest, elevate the hindquarters, and give a quick squeeze accompanied by an upward thrust of your clenched fists to achieve the forced exhalation needed to dislodge the foreign material. Then proceed with cardiopulmonary resuscitation as needed.

ECLAMPSIA (PUERPERAL TETANY, MILK FEVER)

Eclampsia *(puerperal tetany)* usually occurs within two or three weeks after delivery, although it can occur before delivery and even after four weeks postpartum. Although the exact cause is unknown, it is due to a defect in calcium metabolism that results in an abnormally low blood calcium level. Heavily lactating females with large litters seem predisposed to the disease, perhaps due to excessive calcium loss through the milk.

The first signs are often restlessness, whining, and rapid breathing. The bitch may be irritable and appear to lose her motherly instincts. Spontaneous recovery may result, or the signs may progress to stiffness, recumbency, convulsions, and fever. *Progressive tetany is an emergency* that must be treated by a veterinarian. Calcium preparations are given by injection. Puppies are removed from nursing for at least twenty-four hours. They may be returned to restricted nursing later, but this must be supplemented by hand feeding. Puppies old enough to eat solid food are weaned. Calcium–phosphorus–vitamin D supplements are often prescribed for mothers who must continue restricted nursing.

Certain females seem predisposed to milk fever, and it may be advisable not to rebreed these females. A ration adequate in calcium, phosphorus, and vitamin D should be fed throughout pregnancy. Some veterinarians, however, feel that oversupplementation may help to induce milk fever. Therefore, any supplementation during pregnancy should be done only with balanced vitamin-mineral preparations used cautiously. Discuss this in detail with your veterinarian if your female is to be bred.

GERIATRIC MEDICINE
(CARE AS YOUR DOG AGES)

The life expectancy of dogs varies considerably among breeds and with the kind of health care received throughout their lives. In general, large dogs age faster than small dogs. Giant breeds, such as Great Danes or Saint Bernards, are considered "old" at eight or nine years. Small breeds, such as the Chihuahua or miniature poodle, often live until fifteen or sixteen.

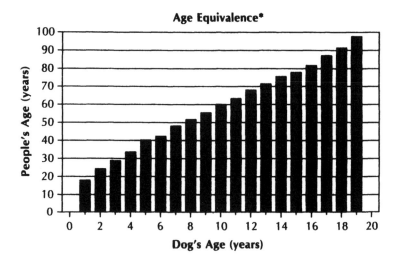

*Reprinted by permission from *California Veterinarian*, Reichenbach, Tom, "Aging In Canine Pets", July/August 1989.

The record for dog longevity has been reported to be twenty-nine years, five months! Although an age equivalence factor of seven human years for each year of a dog's life is often used, a dog ages from birth to puberty in his or her first year of life. Other aging changes are also disproportionate, so comparison with a population-based aging chart (see opposite) is a somewhat more accurate method of comparing a dog's age to a human's. No matter how old your dog is in "human years," though, the most important thing to his or her quality of life is general good health.

In general, an old dog is less adaptable to stress. Sudden changes in diet, routine, or environment are probably best avoided if they have not been part of the dog's routine in the past. Many old dogs do not adapt well to hospitalization and therefore need special care when ill. Good veterinarians are aware of this and provide special attention or make special arrangements for the care of such older animals. **OLD DOGS MAY NOT ADJUST WELL TO CHANGES**

Special diets need to be provided for old dogs with degenerative changes of the kidney and heart or other major organs. In many other cases the addition of a balanced vitamin-mineral supplement to the normal diet is sufficient to meet any special needs caused by the aging process. Since each dog is an individual, the need for a special diet should be discussed with a veterinarian familiar with your aging dog. **GERIATRIC DIET**

Exercise should be continued as your dog ages to the degree the dog desires, unless a specific condition (e.g., heart disease) exists that requires that exercise be restricted. Again, a veterinarian familiar with your dog can advise you best. **GERIATRIC EXERCISE**

Some conditions that are likely to develop in dogs with age are covered in this section. Not all are disabling or progressive, and most, if recognized early, can be treated at least palliatively. To use this section for diagnosing signs, refer to the Index of Signs, as well as to the General Index.

LENS SCLEROSIS

The formation of new fibers in the lens of the dog's eye continues throughout life. As new fibers are formed, the older ones are compressed and pushed toward the center of the lens. This results in a continually increasing density of the lens. The lens also loses water as it ages, another factor contributing to increased density. This process is called *nuclear sclerosis* and should be recognized as a normal part of the aging of the dog's eye. It results in a bluish or grayish-white haze in the part of the lens that can be seen through the pupil. It *does not* normally interfere with vision and does not need treatment. This condition is often erroneously referred to as a *cataract* (a lens opacity that interferes with transmission of light to the retina).

CATARACTS In truth, senile cataracts, which can cause loss of vision, occur much less commonly. If your dog does develop cataracts as an aged (or sometimes young) dog and loss of vision begins, there are surgical procedures that can be used to remove the opacity and restore vision. Surgery is best performed by a specialist because cataracts are relatively uncommon and the best results are obtained only by those individuals who perform the operations most frequently. Most dogs adjust completely to gradual loss of vision should surgery be unavailable or contraindicated.

DEAFNESS

Gradual loss of hearing commonly occurs as dogs age. The anatomical changes responsible for this loss are not well defined. However, a significant number of old dogs appear to be affected by loss of the peripheral nerve fibers associated with hearing. Treatment is not often possible. Inattentiveness or slowed response to commands is often one of the first signs of hearing loss. Unfortunately, these signs are often mistakenly attributed to stubbornness and the dog is punished instead of accommodation being made for the hearing loss. A crude test of hearing ability is to stand behind the dog and make a sudden sound such as a whistle, handclap, or sharp call. Most dogs will cock their ears toward the sound or turn around. Hands clapped near the ears (but not near or in front of the eyes) may cause both eyes to blink in response to the sound.

A sound-amplifying hearing aid has been developed that can effectively improve the hearing providing there is not absolute deafness. The device is placed in the ear or attached to the dog's collar with sound-transmitting tubes leading to the ear. In order to use the hearing aid successfully, the dog must be trained to leave the device in place. Ask your veterinarian for more information if you think a hearing aid could help your dog.

OSTEOARTHRITIS (ARTHRITIS)

Osteoarthritis is a joint disease in which the *cartilages* (fibrous caps) covering the articular surfaces of the bones degenerate and bony proliferation (excess bone growth) occurs. This condition usually results in pain and lameness of the joints involved. It may occur in single joints of young dogs with congenital joint defects (e.g., *hip dysplasia*) or following any kind of joint trauma. When it occurs as an aging change, it usually affects several joints, although lameness may not be apparent in all those affected. The lameness present with arthritis is often most severe on arising and improves with mild exercise. If you gently move the affected joints, you may hear or feel *crepitus* (cartilage or bone grating against cartilage and/or bone). X-ray pictures can be taken to show the affected joints and the severity of bone changes. Although you may not become aware of the disease until signs occur, the changes characteristic of arthritis have usually been developing over a long period.

There is no effective means of arresting the progression of simple osteoarthritis in older dogs, so treatment is usually symptomatic and directed at relieving any significant pain. Mild intermittent lameness or lameness that is present only on arising usually needs no treatment. Aspirin is the preferred pain reliever for more severe pain because of its low cost and lack of major side effects in most dogs. Your veterinarian may prescribe other antiinflammatory medications if aspirin is inappropriate. Weight reduction often significantly improves lameness in obese dogs with osteoarthritis. Soft bedding, warm, dry quarters, and regular but nonstrenuous exercise are also helpful. Acupuncture may help some dogs who don't respond to more conventional treatment, as do some nutritional supplements with antiinflammatory effects. Ask your veterinarian what is appropriate for your dog.

TUMORS (NEOPLASMS, CANCER)

A *tumor* is an abnormal growth of tissue (*neoplasm* means "new growth"). *Benign tumors* are those that are likely to remain at the site of their original growth. *Malignant tumors* (cancer) are neoplastic growths that invade the surrounding tissue and travel via blood vessels or lymph channels to other body sites, where they start to grow anew. As dogs age, the likelihood of a tumor occurring increases.

Many tumors occur internally, where you would not be likely to be aware of them until they have grown quite large. You should, however, watch carefully for growths in the mouth and on the outside of your dog's body. On females it is wise to check each mammary gland periodically (e.g., once a month) for new growths as the dog has the highest incidence of breast cancer among domestic animals and humans. In male dogs, especially those over six years of age, it is important to palpate the testicles for changes in size that may indicate tumor formation. (Tumors may be present in the testicle, however, without external change in size. If they secrete hormones, an older male dog may develop tumor-associated hair loss, changes in skin pigmentation, prostate enlargement, and enlarged nipples and may become sexually attractive to other male dogs.) If you find a tumor in either a young or an old dog, it is always best to discuss its removal with a veterinarian. If you don't feel that you can see a veterinarian, watch the tumor carefully for growth. If you notice growth, be sure to investigate the possibilities for removal. Some malignant tumors *metastasize* (spread) while the original tumor is still very small, and for some tumors, such as melanomas, microscopic examination by a pathologist is the only reliable way to differentiate benign from malignant growths.

SEBACEOUS ADENOMAS Old dogs are subject to the growth of tumors of the oil-producing skin glands *(sebaceous adenomas)* in particular. These are usually small, light-colored, hairless growths that look as if they are stuck onto the skin. They are often described as wartlike or cauliflowerlike. They are benign and do not usually need to be removed except for cosmetic reasons. Adenomalike masses that bleed or become irritated should be inspected by a veterinarian to rule out malignancy.

COMMON SIGNS OF CANCER IN ANIMALS

1. Abnormal swellings that persist or continue to grow
2. Sores that do not heal
3. Unexplained weight loss
4. Loss of appetite
5. Bleeding or discharge from any body opening
6. Offensive odor
7. Difficulty eating or swallowing
8. Hesitation to exercise or loss of stamina
9. Persistent lameness or stiffness
10. Difficulty breathing, urinating, or defecating

Source: The Veterinary Cancer Society

HEART DISEASE

There are several forms of heart disease in the older dog that are similar to those in people. The most common type is *endocardiosis,* in which the valves that separate each ventricle from its atrium (see page 32) become thickened and contracted so that they no longer form an adequate seal against the backflow of blood. It is often accompanied by myocardial fibrosis, in which the heart muscle itself becomes riddled with microscopic scars. Together these changes cause the heart to become progressively more inefficient as a blood pump until it is no longer able to supply the needs of the body tissue *(heart failure).* It is important to understand that heart disease (of many types) can be present long before actual failure occurs. Heart disease generally progresses through several stages where it can be treated and the signs ameliorated before heart failure, requiring emergency treatment or resulting in death, occurs.

A *murmur,* which is a sound caused by abnormal turbulence of blood in a heart with "leaky valves," may be the first sign of heart disease in an older dog. Your veterinarian may mention the presence of a murmur at the time of your dog's yearly physical exam and shots. Or you may hear a murmur as a "shh" interposed between the normal *lub-dup* of the heartbeat when you are examining your dog. If the murmur is intense enough, you may even be able to feel it through the chest wall as the heart beats. The presence of a murmur in a dog of any age is not necessarily something to be alarmed about, but it is something that requires examination by a veterinarian. Your veterinarian may suggest chest X-rays, an electrocardiogram, an echocardiogram (ultrasound examination of the heart), blood pressure measurement, or other tests. **HEART MURMURS**

In cases where you are unaware of a murmur or a murmur is not present, you may first notice easy tiring with exercise or a low-pitched, deep cough. You may notice the cough more frequently in the morning or at night. Sometimes it will occur when the dog is excited and pulls on the leash, exercises, or drinks water. Mucus may be gagged up. Some dogs suffer short periods of weakness or fainting. If your older dog has any such signs, consult your veterinarian. If left untreated, heart disease progresses over a variable period of time to complete heart failure with severe difficulty in breathing, coughing even while at rest, bluish-colored tongue and gums, rapid heart rate, and inability to exercise. **SIGNS OF HEART FAILURE**

Treatment of canine heart disease in the older dog is generally directed at improving circulatory function, since the aging process
cannot be arrested. In the earliest stages no treatment is necessary.
As your veterinarian follows the progression of the disease, you will
probably be asked to feed your dog a low-sodium diet (to help
prevent fluid retention), which can either be purchased already prepared or made up at home. Medical treatment includes drugs that
dilate the airways, *digitalis*-like drugs to increase the strength of heart
contractions, drugs that alter blood pressure, and *diuretics* to help
control the sodium and water retention that accompanies heart failure. With the help of a good veterinarian, treatment of heart disease
in the older dog can be relatively easy. The benefits of keeping a
close watch on an older dog's heart function can be substantial—
including a longer, more comfortable, and more active life.

KIDNEY DISEASE

Many older dogs have decreased kidney function due to aging
changes and/or urinary tract disease processes that have gone un-
detected earlier in life. Because the kidneys have a large amount of
tissue reserve, signs attributable to progressive kidney disease are
often not apparent without laboratory tests until damage is severe
and often irreversible. Special testing is also necessary to detect high
blood pressure, which may cause or result from kidney disease.

Increased water drinking accompanied by increased volume of urination are often the only external signs of kidney disease. As the
kidneys degenerate, less functioning tissue is available to excrete the
same amount of wastes produced by the body as when the kidneys
were healthy. In an effort to maintain a normal physiological state,
a larger volume of urine in which the wastes are less concentrated
must be excreted and the dog must drink more water. The need to
excrete large volumes of urine will sometimes cause an old (or
young) dog without free access to the outside to urinate in the house.
This dog has not "forgotten his or her housetraining" or "grown
senile"; the volume of urine is just too great to be held for several
hours. The only way to remedy this situation is to take the dog for
walks more frequently or to provide free access to the yard. Restricting water will not help but can actually make the dog sick since it
interferes with waste excretion. When the dog can no longer compensate for failing kidneys, vomiting, lack of appetite, and weight loss
are other signs that may develop.

If your dog has any signs of failing kidneys, consult your veterinarian immediately. Other diseases (e.g., *diabetes mellitus*) may have similar signs and diagnosis requires laboratory tests including urinalysis and blood tests. Your veterinarian will try to find out if the disease process can be arrested and advise you on care that can prolong your dog's comfortable life in spite of diseased kidneys. The cornerstone of treatment for chronic kidney disease is a diet that provides only restricted quantities of high-quality protein, phosphorus, and sodium. Drugs that adjust blood pressure may be used when kidney disease is associated with high blood pressure.

EUTHANASIA

It would be nice if all old pets who died did so peacefully in their sleep with no previous signs of illness. This doesn't always happen, though, and sometimes you must decide whether to end your dog's life or allow a progressive disease to continue. This is never an easy decision. A mutually close and trusting relationship with a veterinarian established when your dog is still young may help if you ever have to face this problem. A veterinarian familiar with your dog's medical history can tell you when a condition is irreversible and progressive and give you an opinion as to when that condition is truly a burden for your dog.

It is unfair to you, your dog, and the veterinarian to take an animal to a new veterinarian and request euthanasia. A veterinarian who does not know your dog may perform euthanasia because you requested it when the condition was actually treatable. A veterinarian unfamiliar with you may refuse to carry out this heartrending act because your dog seems healthy, not knowing that continuing to live with the dog is an extreme burden on you. Most veterinarians enter the profession to make animals well, not kill them. Many people react emotionally without knowing the facts and insist that their pet be "put to sleep" for a condition that can be treated and with which their dog can live happily. In other cases euthanasia is requested because buying a new pet is less expensive than treatment. For most people the joy of life outweighs minor discomforts, and this is probably true for most pets. The monetary value of a pet's life, of course, depends on each individual's point of view. If you decide you just don't want a healthy animal anymore, give the dog to a friend who does want it or take the dog to a shelter or pound where humane euthanasia is performed only after all other avenues for adoption are explored.

When you and your veterinarian are in agreement about ending the life of a pet, you need not worry about discomfort. Euthanasia in veterinary hospitals is performed by the intravenous injection of an overdose of an anesthetic drug. Death is both rapid and painless.

It's a good idea to approach the subject of euthanasia with your veterinarian soon after the possible need for it enters your mind. Your veterinarian should be willing to discuss the procedures used and to explain all the options available for disposal of the remains. Local laws prescribe whether dead pets may be buried. Veterinary hospitals and humane organizations often offer cremation services with or without return of the dog's ashes.

Many veterinarians allow an owner to remain with the pet at the time of euthanasia. A request for this service should not be considered unusual at any small animal hospital. Again, a discussion regarding its pros and cons is important to your and your dog's well-being at such an emotional time.

A useful book that explores the subject of euthanasia and grief more extensively is *When Your Pet Dies: How to Cope with Your Feelings,* by Jamie Quackenbush and Denise Gravine, Pocket Books, New York, 1985. Also, many veterinary associations and veterinary schools sponsor pet loss support groups for grieving owners. Feel free to ask your veterinarian for a referral to an appropriate group.

4

HOME MEDICAL CARE

NURSING AT HOME

DRUG INFORMATION

NURSING AT HOME

O ver the course of a lifetime, the average dog has few illnesses for which hospitalization is necessary. Most veterinarians are anxious to have your dog recuperate at home if you can provide adequate nursing. In some cases there are no alternatives to hospitalization, but when there are, when the sick animal can convalesce at home, there are several procedures with which you should be familiar.

RECORD KEEPING

If your dog has a serious illness, regular and accurate record keeping is invaluable in helping your veterinarian help you treat your dog at home. Take your dog's temperature at least once a day (preferably at the same time) and record it. Record how much your dog eats and drinks, the frequency of urination, and the types of bowel movements passed. An indication of the times and amounts of medication given is also helpful, as is as a record of any unusual signs (e.g., vomiting) or any other change in condition.

TEMPERATURE

THERMOMETER

Use a rectal thermometer to take your dog's temperature. An oral thermometer can be used in a pinch, but the bulb is more likely to break off. Before inserting the thermometer into the rectum, shake the mercury column down below 99°F (37.2°C) and lubricate the tip of it with any nontoxic greasy substance (petroleum jelly, lubricant jelly, vegetable oil). Hold your dog's tail up with one hand and insert the thermometer into the rectum with a firm, gentle push. This is most easily done with the dog standing, but can be done while he or she sits or lies down.

How far you need to insert the thermometer to get an accurate rectal temperature depends on the

YOUR DOG'S MEDICAL RECORD

Date	Temp-era-ture	Appetite/ Water Intake	Stool	Urine	Miscellaneous—include here medication, times given, times wounds cleaned, unusual signs, changes, etc.

Photocopy this page to use for record keeping while nursing your pet at home.

size of the dog—in small dogs an inch may be adequate, for large dogs it takes half the length of the thermometer or more. If you feel the thermometer go into a fecal mass when you insert it, try again. The thermometer should be left in two or three minutes, although many thermometers will register an accurate temperature in about a minute. (Helpful information if you have a squirmy dog!)

To read the thermometer, roll it back and forth between your fingers until you can see the thin mercury column inside. The point where the column stops is the temperature. Each large mark indicates one degree, each small mark two tenths of a degree. Normal is usually 101.0°–102.5°F (38.3–39.2°C).

PULSE, HEART RATE

For how to take your dog's pulse and measure the heart rate, see page 33.

HOW TO GIVE YOUR DOG PILLS

The only way to be sure your dog has really swallowed medication in pill, capsule, or tablet form is to administer it in the following way:

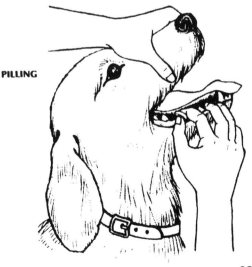

PILLING

Grasp your dog's muzzle with one hand and tilt the nose upward at about a 45° angle. Gently press inward on the upper lips; this usually causes the mouth to open at least slightly. Keep the upper lips rolled inward between the dog's teeth and your fingers; this keeps most friendly dogs from clamping their mouths completely closed on your fingers. If you have a large dog, insert your opposite, pill-containing fingers into his or her open mouth and place the pills as far back over the base of the tongue as possible. Quickly remove your

223

hand, letting the dog close his or her mouth. Try to keep your dog's nose pointed upward during the whole procedure; it seems to encourage swallowing. If your dog licks his or her nose, you can be fairly certain the medication has been swallowed.

If your dog is one of the smaller breeds, you will have to modify the procedure a little. Grasp the pill between your thumb and forefinger and, as you use your third finger to hold the lower jaw open, place the pill over the base of the tongue. If your dog is extremely tiny or your fingers large, you will have to take aim and drop the pills over the back of the tongue instead of placing them there.

PILLING

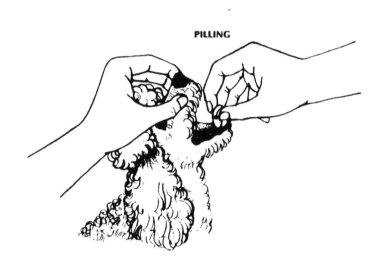

Most dogs are extremely easy to give pills to, particularly if you have been handling and examining them from a young age. If you do not get the pills in the center of the tongue or far enough back, your dog will spit them out and you'll have to start again. If the pills are not slippery enough or seem relatively large, buttering them may help you administer them. If you absolutely cannot get the pills down in the way described, you can resort to wrapping them in a piece of cheese or meat. If your dog gulps food, he or she will gulp the pill down easily. You can try crushing a tablet (pill cutters and crushers are available at drugstores) or emptying the contents of a capsule, then mixing the drug thoroughly with a small portion of meat or some other favorite food. Most medications taste so bad that a sick dog will not take them this way. *If it can be avoided, do not use these methods of administration.* You can never be sure that your dog has taken all the medication when it is administered in food, and some drugs are inactivated in the presence of food. If you grind an *enteric-coated* (coated to be absorbed by the intestine) tablet or empty the contents of a capsule into food, you may be preventing normal absorption from the gut. Coverings are often designed to remain intact until the drug reaches the part of the gut where it is best and most safely absorbed.

LIQUID MEDICATION (FORCE-FEEDING)

The simplest way to give your dog liquid medication is by placing it in the space between the outside surfaces of the molar teeth and the inside surface of the cheek. If you place your finger into this area and pull the cheek slightly outward, you can pour liquids directly into it from a bottle or spoon. This works best if the dog's muzzle is tipped slightly upward and held in this position until your finger is removed and a swallow occurs. A syringe, eyedropper, or turkey baster can also be used to give liquid medication. Fill it and place it directly into the cheek space. Slowly administer the liquid as you hold the dog's muzzle steady, allowing the dog to swallow while the liquid is given. Large quantities can be administered relatively easily with this method.

MEDICATING IN "CHEEK POUCH"

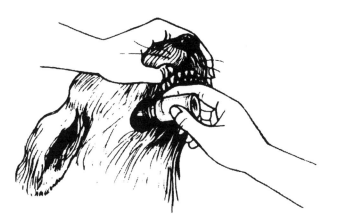

Force-feeding is sometimes necessary when nursing a sick dog. Blended foods and water can be force-fed in the same ways as liquid medication. Food balls can be given in the same manner as pills. Some special diets are indicated in this book; other times, if your dog needs special feeding, your veterinarian will recommend a specific diet.

EYE MEDICATION

Ophthalmic ointments are most easily applied into the conjunctival sac (see page 19). Use your thumb or forefinger to roll the lower eyelid gently downward and squeeze the ointment into the space

EYE DROPS

exposed. Eye drops should be instilled with the dog's nose tilted slightly upward. Use one hand to grasp the dog's muzzle and hold the lower lid open. Rest the base of the hand holding the dropper bottle above the eye to hold the upper lid open, then drop in the medication. Both techniques work best when you approach the eye so the medication container is not placed directly in the dog's line of sight. Avoid touching the end of the ointment tube or dropper bottle to the eye to prevent contamination of the solution and injury to the eye.

EAR TREATMENT

CLEANING EARS

When your dog's ears become inflamed (see page 145), a more thorough cleaning than you routinely give them is often necessary. In most cases, inflamed ears should be examined and cleaned by a veterinarian, who will have the necessary tools for observing the ear canal and eardrum during and after cleaning. Also, if the ears are painful, anesthesia is usually necessary to make most dogs hold still for a thorough and safe ear cleaning.

Veterinarians use several methods for cleaning ears. In one method a rubber bulb syringe filled with a warm water–antiseptic soap solution or a wax-dissolving solution is inserted into the ear canal and used to flush the fluid in and out of the ear. This is done several times and is followed by clear water or antiseptic rinses. The clean ear canal is dried with cotton swabs and appropriate ear medication is instilled. Another method relies on cotton-tipped swabs and the use of an instrument called an *ear loop*.

If you cannot take your dog to a veterinarian and your dog is very cooperative, you may be able to use the bulb syringe method for ear cleaning. It is very important not to wedge the syringe into the ear to form an airtight seal as the pressure that can build up in the ear canal can rupture the eardrum. Use a warm solution and flush the fluid in and out gently until all debris is removed. You can dry the vertical part of the canal with swabs, but it is probably not a good idea to try to dry the horizontal part without an otoscope. (If you are not familiar with the anatomy of the dog's ear, turn to page 20.)

(turn to page 20.)

After your dog's ears are cleaned you will usually have to instill medication in them at least once a day for one to two weeks. Most ear ointments have long nozzles that are placed into the ear canal. Liquids can be dropped into the canal. After the medicine is in the canal, grasp the lower part of the auricular cartilage through the skin and massage it up and down vigorously. If you are doing it properly, you will hear the medication squishing around inside. This will spread the medication down the length of the ear canal and is a very important part of nursing the ear properly.

MEDICATING EARS

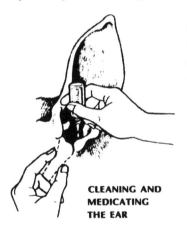

CLEANING AND
MEDICATING
THE EAR

It is a good idea to partially clean the ear daily while it is being medicated. One way is to use a cloth or facial tissue as described on page 55. Another, more effective way is to use a cotton swab. Although many veterinarians dislike this method of ear cleaning, it has been used successfully by others for many years. All that is necessary for a good result is caution and a gentle technique. Grasp the end of the pinna and hold it straight up over the dog's head.

Insert the swab into the ear canal parallel to the side of the head. You cannot damage the eardrum if you keep the swab vertical and parallel to the side of the head. However, you can if you angle both the ear and the swab perpendicular to the side of the dog's head once the swab is inserted. Use the swab to clean out old medication and debris before instilling the new. Turn the swab gently and try to lift out debris rather than compacting it.

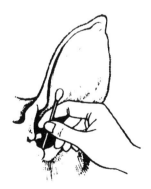

Wounds that require repeated cleansing at home are infected traumatic wounds and abscesses. These wounds are left open or partially open when treated to allow pus drainage and cleaning (see page 133). Other fresh wounds usually need only a simple disinfection and/or cleansing when they are physically contaminated with foreign material such as dirt, plant parts, or hair.

CLEANING OPEN WOUNDS

Solutions of povidone-iodine (0.001%–1%) or chlorhexidine (0.05%) can be made up at home from stronger antiseptic solutions purchased in a drugstore or directly from your veterinarian. (For information on hydrogen peroxide, see page 135.) If the opening of the wound is large enough, you can pour the disinfectant directly into it. A bulb syringe or turkey baster can be used to flush the solution into smaller wounds providing you are careful not to build up excessive pressure, which could force foreign material further into the surrounding soft tissue. The disinfectant can be applied to a gauze pad that can be inserted into very small wounds. As the solution is instilled, it may sting. Some dogs find this uncomfortable. Clean the wound until the visible tissue looks free of foreign debris and/or until the solution runs clear. Repeat the cleansing once or twice a day if there is a tendency for debris to reaccumulate. Since the stronger antiseptic concentrations also damage normal tissues, stop the daily application as soon as the wound has finished draining.

Simple wounds usually heal most rapidly when left uncovered. In cases where the wound is continually becoming contaminated or when the dog licks at the wound so much that it cannot heal or is made worse, it must be protected.

SOCK BANDAGE

A light foot bandage can be made by placing a sock over the foot and taping the sock to the leg with several wraps of adhesive tape applied to the top of the sock and leg. (Be sure the tape is loose enough to allow circulation to the foot.) For small- or medium-size dogs, a person's knee sock can be split at the top, the intact bottom slipped over the foot, and the tails brought up the dog's side and under the body, then tied together over the dog's back to hold it in place. These types of wraps leave most of the sock loose and allow some air circulation. They are best for covering the nails to prevent damage when a dog is scratching at a wound or to protect areas of the foot from licking. Ointments can be applied under such bandages, and the sock will keep the medication on the foot and off the carpet.

A more substantial bandage is made using roll or tubular gauze and adhesive tape. Pad the areas between the toes with small pieces of cotton and cover the wound with a gauze or nonstick pad. Wrap the foot firmly with gauze, applying several layers vertically as well as around the foot. Follow the gauze with adhesive tape. The long vertical strips not only form the end of the bandage, but help prevent it from wearing through. Try to apply even pressure from the toes to the top of the bandage to avoid dangerous swelling of the foot. A bandage applied improperly can cause impaired circulation, which can result in tissue death and the need for amputation.

TAPE BANDAGE

Flexible wire or electrical tape may be wrapped over the bandage to help prevent your dog from chewing at it. Bandages should be changed at least every third day unless your veterinarian directs you differently.

Many-tailed bandages can be made from any rectangular or square piece of clean cloth. These bandages are best used to try to prevent a dog from licking at a wound (e.g., an incision created during surgery). Gauze or cotton padding may be placed between the

ABDOMINAL, BACK, AND NECK BANDAGES

"MANY-TAILED" BANDAGE

wound and the bandage. A child's T-shirt can often be put on a dog in place of a many-tailed bandage. It is especially effective if a string or ribbon is run through the hem tunnel to provide a drawstring.

EAR BANDAGES Small wounds on the ear are often difficult to get to heal because of head shaking. In order to prevent ear damage due to head shaking,

the ear can be bandaged to the head. It can be placed over the head and held in position with a tube of nylon or other stocking that is taped to the skin at both ends. (Cut a hole in the stocking to allow the other ear to hang through, if you don't want both ears held up on the head.) Tape can also be applied to the ear edges to hold the ear up over the head by sticking it to the fur on the top of the head and neck, then wrapping under and around the chin and neck. Elastic tape is less likely to cause neck irritation, but regular adhesive tape can be used. If the tape seems too tight around the neck, a small cut made perpendicular to the long edge of the bandage under the chin will often relieve the irritation.

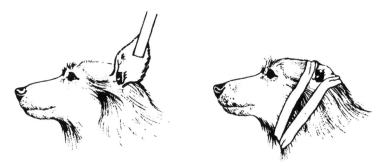

TAPING THE EAR UP

Some dogs will not leave wounds or other irritations alone no matter what bandaging method you try. They can prevent healing by continuing to lick or scratch at such areas. In these cases, muzzles, Elizabethan collars, or other means must be employed.

WIRE MUZZLES An appropriate muzzle can be purchased at a pet shop. Be sure the wire grid is small enough that your dog can't lick or chew through it. Also be sure to remove it frequently to provide supervised access to water.

ELIZABETHAN Readymade plastic or cardboard Elizabethan collars can be pur-
COLLARS chased at some pet stores or from some veterinarians, or you can

230

make one from heavy cardboard as illustrated. An alternative to an Elizabethan collar is a plastic wastebasket or bucket. Cut a hole in the bottom just large enough to slip the dog's head through. The cut edges can be covered with adhesive tape to make them more comfortable.

Both the Elizabethan collar and the bucket will prevent most dogs from disturbing wounds on their bodies. They are also effective against scratching of head wounds. However, some dogs cannot or will not eat or drink wearing an Elizabethan collar. Be sure you allow for this. Also, be sure you know the cause of your dog's illness. A collar will prevent your dog from scratching at his or her ears, but if otitis, for example, is present, it won't cure the problem.

CARDBOARD ELIZABETHAN COLLAR   **PLASTIC BUCKET**

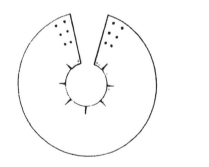

MAKING A MUZZLE

It is extremely important to know how to apply an effective muzzle when dealing with an uncooperative dog. A muzzle does not hurt the dog or interfere with breathing since dog noses are bony and the nasal passages cannot be compressed. A muzzle is for your protection and the protection of anyone helping you.

Use a long strip of rope, heavy cord, gauze, or handkerchief. Form a loop and slip it over the dog's nose as far as possible. Draw the loop tightly around the nose, then bring the ends under the chin and tie them tightly together. Now bring an end along each side of the dog's head and tie them together firmly at the nape of the neck. If the muzzle is properly applied, the dog's biting efforts will be ineffective. A single loop tied under the chin may be used, but is much less effective than the double-loop type. Many veterinarians, pet supply stores, and catalogs sell washable, slip-on nylon muzzles, which are easier to apply. Consider purchasing one to include in your first-aid kit.

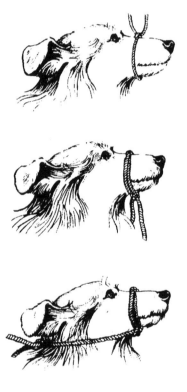

MUZZLE

DRUG INFORMATION

Drugs are identified by their formal *chemical name,* their *generic name,* and their *brand* (proprietary) *name.* The generic name is usually simpler and easier to remember than the formal chemical name. For example, *acetylsalicylic acid* is the formal chemical name for the drug generically called *aspirin.* If your veterinarian needs to write a prescription, request that he or she use the generic drug name rather than the brand name, if possible. This allows the pharmacist to give you the same drug, usually for less money than the brand-name drug would cost. However, keep in mind that some generic drugs have been shown to be badly formulated and it is not always possible to make a successful substitution. *If* you would like to comparison-shop, ask your veterinarian for a written prescription that you can take to various pharmacies. (In some cases there are no equivalent human drugs or appropriate dosage sizes available and you must purchase the drug in the veterinary clinic.)

In general, veterinary drugs are the same as human drugs but sometimes less expensive when they are sold under a veterinary name. Many veterinarians dispense the drugs you need instead of writing prescriptions for you to take to a pharmacy. Although veterinary hospitals make a profit with this practice, for the most part it is a convenience for you and may be less expensive than purchasing the equivalent medicine at a drugstore. Some companies (usually mail order) sell drugs directly to people who are not veterinarians. In some cases the drugs are the same ones veterinarians use. In other cases, however, they are less effective or more likely to be toxic than the drugs a veterinarian would choose. I believe that many of the companies that sell these drugs to the public are interested primarily in profit, not animal health. They usually make few attempts to be sure the drugs are used properly and sometimes fail to warn of possible side effects. Try to avoid such drugs unless they are recommended by a veterinarian you trust.

All drugs dispensed by a pharmacist or veterinarian should be labeled with the generic or brand name, expiration date, concentration, and clear directions for use. This avoids misunderstandings in treatment and helps others who may treat the case later. Since drugs are helpers, not magic potions, your veterinarian should not be secretive about what is being dispensed. Keep in mind that drugs are changing all the time. Although some generic drugs are mentioned in this book, better drugs may become available for use after this book is published, so keep this in mind.

ANTIBIOTICS

Technically, *antibiotics* are chemical substances produced by microscopic organisms that interfere with the growth of other microorganisms. In practice, antibiotics include a large number of substances, many synthetically made, that are used primarily in the treatment of bacterial infections. When properly used, antibiotics are miracle drugs. They enable us to cure infections that, in the past, would have certainly been fatal. They can, however, be easily misused.

Not all antibiotics are effective against all bacteria. A veterinarian's decision to use a particular antibiotic is based on the bacterium that is probably causing the disease and/or the results of laboratory tests in which the infective organisms are grown and tested for antibiotic sensitivity. If the wrong antibiotic is chosen, there is no beneficial effect. If the proper antibiotic is chosen and given at the correct dosage, growth of the bacteria is stopped or at least controlled sufficiently that the body's own natural defense systems can overcome the infection. If you fail to give the antibiotic as frequently as prescribed or if you discontinue the medication too soon, forms of bacteria resistant to the antibiotic may develop, or the infection may recur.

Antibiotics are not always effective alone. Other drugs and special nursing techniques must often be combined with their use. In cases of localized infection such as abscesses, antibiotic treatment must often be used with proper surgical intervention for success.

ANTIBIOTICS ARE NOT EFFECTIVE AGAINST VIRUSES Many people seem to believe that antibiotics are useful in combating any infectious or febrile disease. This is certainly untrue. A particularly common case in which antibiotics may be of no help at all is the viral infection. *Viruses* exist in body cells and depend on their metabolic processes for reproduction. Since the methods of viral metabolism are unlike those of bacteria, which, for the most part, survive outside of cells and multiply independently, drugs effective against bacteria are ineffective against viruses. When antibiotics are prescribed for use during a viral infection, it is to combat the bacteria that invade after the virus has weakened the animal *(secondary infection)*. There are very few drugs available for treatment of viral infections. Since viral reproduction is so intimately tied in with normal cellular function, most drugs that are found effective against viruses also destroy body cells.

DRUGS HAVE SIDE EFFECTS Like other drugs, most antibiotics have potential side effects. Since bacteria are single-celled organisms similar in many ways to the individual body cells, antibiotics can sometimes act against body cells in ways similar to the ways they adversely affect bacteria. Among the possible side effects are allergic reactions, toxic effects, alteration of metabolism, and alteration of normal (and beneficial) bacteria inhabiting the body. A good veterinarian will tell you if there are any side effects you should watch for when antibiotics are prescribed. Side effects can be made more likely by the use of outdated drugs, combining antibiotics with certain other drugs, and certain illnesses.

Indiscriminate use of antibiotics is to be avoided. Use with proper guidance will avoid toxic effects and stem the development of antibiotic-resistant bacteria. Be glad, not disappointed, if your veterinarian feels that the condition can be treated without antibiotics and sends you away empty-handed. And don't use "leftover" antibiotics unless directed to by your veterinarian. Antibiotics are available over the counter as ointments for *topical* (on-the-body-surface) use. Common effective ones contain *bacitracin, neomycin,* and/or *polymixin B.* These are suitable for applying to superficial wounds to achieve a local antibacterial effect. They should not be applied into deep wounds, as the carrier ointment for the drugs may interfere with healing.

ADRENOCORTICAL STEROIDS

Adrenocortical steroids (corticosteroids) include hormones produced by the adrenal glands and synthetic drugs similar to these natural substances. This group of drugs has a wide range of actions on the body, among them effects on fat, protein, and carbohydrate metabolism, water balance, salt balance, and cardiovascular, immune system, and kidney function. They are very important in the individual's ability to resist certain environmental changes and noxious stimuli.

Steroid drugs are commonly used in veterinary medicine for their effects against inflammation. (For example, to give relief from itching due to allergies or other skin diseases.) Because of the remarkable response following administration, some dog owners and some veterinarians may be inclined to misuse these drugs. Keep in mind that steroid drugs are only palliative, relieving but not curing disease, unless the condition is caused by a deficiency of the adrenal gland function. Also keep in mind the fact that steroids are not without side effects. Although they are safe, even lifesaving, when used properly, when misused they constitute a threat to your dog's health. Avoid preparations containing steroids sold in pet stores and rely on the advice of a good veterinarian regarding the use of steroids in maintaining the health of your dog. Some names of common steroid drugs are *prednisone, prednisolone, cortisone, hydrocortisone, triamcinolone, betamethasone, flumethasone,* and *dexamethasone.* Some have less wide-ranging effects than others.

DRUGS YOU MIGHT HAVE AROUND THE HOUSE

TRANQUILIZERS *Tranquilizers* are drugs that work on the brain in several different ways to achieve desirable behavior in dogs. Even the best-trained dogs sometimes need tranquilizers. These drugs have legitimate uses in relieving anxiety and producing sedation. (Some also affect the brain's "vomiting center," reducing nausea induced by motion; see page 166.) Veterinarians use tranquilizers to relieve the anxiety that makes some dogs uncooperative when they enter veterinary hospitals. Other common reasons for tranquilizing dogs include prolonged confinement (as when traveling), noisy situations (e.g., Fourth of July fireworks, thunderstorms), and sedation to prevent self-trauma (as in wound licking).

If you can anticipate the need for tranquilization, it is best to discuss the pros and cons with your veterinarian and get a prescription for tranquilizing drugs. If an unanticipated need arises, two human tranquilizers that are used for dogs are *diazepam* and *chlorpromazine*. In such situations call your veterinarian and ask about the advisability of using the drug you have, and ask what the correct dose for your dog should be. Over-the-counter pet tranquilizers contain *antihistamines* (such as *methapyrilene*) and other drugs (e.g., *scopolamine*), which normally produce sedation as a side effect of their medical use. In high doses these drugs may produce excitement, and their routine use is not recommended. *Do not* use tranquilizers merely for your own convenience; attempt to deal with recurrent problems by training. *Do not* use tranquilizers to sedate your dog following trauma that can cause severe injury (e.g., being hit by a car); they can have an undesirable effect on blood pressure in such situations and may contribute to shock.

ASPIRIN *Aspirin (acetylsalicylic acid)* is a common household drug that occasionally is useful in treating dogs. It relieves fever and mild pain and has some antiinflammatory effects, but is not a specific cure for any disease. Aspirin relieves fever by acting on the brain biochemistry to reset the body's "thermostat." It is believed to do this by inhibiting the production of *prostaglandins* in the preoptic region of the anterior hypothalamus. Prostaglandins are potent chemical mediators of inflammation formed in the body cells by metabolism of fatty acids. Aspirin also relieves local pain and blocks inflammation in tissues by interfering with the formation of prostaglandins.

Aspirin should be used to relieve fever in dogs only if the fever is

236

high enough (106°F [41.1°C]) and prolonged enough possibly to be damaging in itself. This rarely occurs. In many other cases of fever aspirin simply masks the signs and makes diagnosis more difficult. Aspirin's best use is probably to relieve pain associated with osteoarthritis in dogs. Of all the over-the-counter drugs available for relief of pain and inflammation associated with this condition, aspirin is the safest. It can, however, irritate dogs' stomachs and cause vomiting, stomach ulcers, and gastrointestinal bleeding. Aspirin combined with magnesium hydroxide antacid in a single tablet (Ascriptin) has been shown to be less irritating to dogs' stomachs than regular aspirin. Use aspirin only when necessary to relieve signs not treatable in other ways. Give it at the rate of about 11 milligrams per pound of body weight (25 mg/kg) with food no more frequently than every eight hours. Avoid enteric-coated aspirin. It is not effectively absorbed in dogs and is likely to cause vomiting.

ANTACIDS The use of antacids is discussed on page 165.

ANTI-DIARRHEALS The use of antidiarrheal drugs is discussed on page 167.

LAXATIVES The use of drugs with a laxative action is discussed on page 168.

POVIDONE-IODINE, CHLOR-HEXIDINE, HYDROGEN PEROXIDE See pages 228 and 135 for how to use povidone-iodine, chlorhexidine, or hydrogen peroxide to clean wounds.

ISOPROPYL ALCOHOL You can try isopropyl alcohol for treatment of inflamed ears; see page 146.

ANTIFUNGAL MEDICATIONS To use over-the-counter antifungal medicines such as miconazole or clotrimazole, see page 133.

5

BREEDING AND REPRODUCTION

PREVENTING PREGNANCY

BREEDING

CARE OF NEWBORNS

B oth male dogs and female dogs *(bitches)* usually reach puberty between six and twelve months of age. The actual onset of sexual maturity and the time of first breeding vary greatly with the individual dog because they are influenced by many factors, among them climate, nutrition, breed, and psychological maturity. Small breeds are usually capable of reproduction before one year; large or giant breeds often are not ready until eighteen to twenty-four months of age. A male dog may be able to produce sperm and copulate normally as early as four or five months of age, but the actual time breeding first occurs depends on many social factors not associated with physical maturity. A dog low in the social order may not have the confidence necessary to breed successfully.

Bitches undergo a cyclical rhythm of reproductive function called the *estrous cycle.* Each bitch has her own normal cycle that, once established, tends to repeat itself. Most breeds, however, show signs of heat approximately every six months and are considered *seasonally monocyclic* (having only one episode of ovulation at each reproductive season). The basenji breed is an exception; it ovulates only once a year, as is the case with many wild canids.

A bitch's reproductive cycle is divided into four stages: *anestrus, proestrus, estrus,* and *diestrus* (formerly called *metestrus*). Understanding the estrous cycle is as important to those who want to breed their dog as it is to those who don't.

During *anestrus* the ovaries are quiescent. This period lasts about two to four months. The anestrus state can be artificially induced by an *ovariohysterectomy* or "spaying" operation (see page 244).

Proestrus is the time during which a bloody discharge first appears at the vulva of a female. Many people commonly consider this the beginning of "heat." During this stage the follicles from which the ova are produced are growing. Proestrus usually lasts about nine days (the average is six to eleven days, but it may last up to twenty-eight days!). Its end is marked by a female's first acceptance of a male.

241

Estrus is the period during which a bitch is sexually receptive and breeding can occur. Many females continue the bleeding that is characteristic of proestrus throughout all or part of estrus. In these cases there is no external physical indicator of the onset of estrus except for the sexual receptivity of the bitch. In other females bleeding stops when estrus begins. Ovulation usually occurs about twenty-four hours after the first acceptance of a male (about ten to eleven days after the onset of bleeding). Ova survive and are capable of being fertilized for at least four days following ovulation. Therefore dog litters are capable of having more than one *sire* (father) if the female mates with more than one male after ovulation. Estrus lasts about five to nine days, or even longer in some females (up to twenty days may be considered normal).

Metestrus follows estrus. It is characterized by a physiological state of "pseudopregnancy" (see page 253), which is followed by a return of the uterus and ovaries to the anestrus, resting state, if a bitch did not become pregnant.

PREVENTING PREGNANCY

Because the estrous cycle shows so much individual variation, to prevent pregnancy in an unspayed female you must be constantly alert from the onset of bleeding (proestrus) until the end of receptivity (estrus), usually a total of about three weeks. Swelling of the vulva precedes the onset of heat often by as long as a month and sometimes longer. This can be used as a signal of the onset of heat, and is particularly helpful if your bitch does not bleed heavily.

ANESTRUS   **ESTRUS**

Do not let your female dog out of sight during heat unless she is confined in a dog-proof shelter. Dogs can perform remarkable feats to reach a female in heat. Even chain-link fences have been scaled, dug beneath, and torn down. Females who have gotten out of their owner's sight for only two or three minutes have been found "tied" with males. You must be *absolutely* sure your bitch is nonreceptive before you allow her to associate with males. At the end of estrus a female will be aggressively resistant to males, but a persistent dog will often be rewarded by final acceptance.

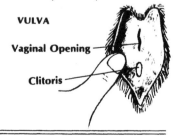

VULVA

Vaginal Opening

Clitoris

At this time there are no pills proven safe and effective for *long-term* birth control in dogs. A progesterone-like drug, *megestrol acetate* (sold in the United States under the name Ovaban) can be used to delay the onset of estrus providing it is not used prior to or during the first heat cycle. When it is used, it should not be administered for more than two consecutive treatments. It cannot be used in dogs with diseases of the reproductive organs or mammary growths of any kind or in females who may be pregnant. Side effects include temperament changes, breast enlargement possibly accompanied by milk production, increased appetite, and a possible predisposition to develop uterine infection (*pyometra;* see page 179) or diabetes mellitus.

In the past (and in countries other than the United States today), a progesteronelike compound, *medroxyprogesterone acetate* (Promone, Depo-Provera) was used by veterinarians to prevent estrus. Its use, however, was found to be related to undesirable behavioral changes and uterine infection, which sometimes appeared years after the last treatment. Its use has generally been discontinued. Other similar drugs of more recent manufacture are claimed not to be associated with such serious side effects (e.g., *proligestone*) but have not been used clinically in the United States.

Milbolerone is a powerful anabolic androgen-derived drug thought to block the secretion of the pituitary hormone LH *(luteinizing hormone),* which initiates ovulation. As a result estrus is prevented. This drug has many contraindications. It is not intended for use in females intended for future breeding; it is undesirable for use in immature females; it cannot be used in bitches suspected to have liver or kidney disease or tumors that depend on androgens for their growth. It is also recommended that bitches treated for longer than eight months undergo periodic liver function testing, and it is, therefore, not a significantly cost-effective means of birth control for pets.

Chlorophyll tablets, which can be purchased from some veterinarians or pet stores, were previously thought to help mask the attractive scent of the urine of a female in heat but are now generally considered ineffective. They are certainly *not* an effective birth control method. Bitches' "britches," panty-like devices containing absorbent pads to help prevent house soiling by the female's estrus discharges, can be purchased in pet stores or through mail-order pet-supply stores. Although they interfere with mating to some extent, they are not effective birth-control devices.

Plastic *intravaginal devices,* once promoted as a physical means of birth control, failed to fulfill their mission due to both dog and owner dissatisfaction. More recently an immunization to provide reversible birth control in bitches has been developed. It causes the formation of antibodies against the outer covering of the egg. Whether or not this method of birth control will be safe, convenient, and cost-effective in the long run remains to be seen.

The best method currently available for permanently preventing pregnancy in pets is the *ovariohysterectomy* or spaying operation.

Many misconceptions surround this operation. One of the most prevalent is that spaying will cause a female to become fat and lazy. Not so. As stated earlier, this surgery induces a permanent state comparable to natural anestrus. Dogs of either sex become fat only if they are using fewer calories than they are eating. Excess weight usually accompanies laziness. Obesity is sometimes caused by a metabolic abnormality (e.g., hypothyroidism), but it is usually caused by *overfeeding.* Any effect of spaying is small. Many bitches are spayed when they are young. Owners forget that all dogs need less food as they age, but they seem to remember when they find their pet overweight that she was lean when she was spayed and then draw the wrong conclusion. Although some breeds tend to remain extremely active as they age, most dogs mature into more quiet adults. Many people attribute this natural maturation to the spaying, since the surgery is often performed before the female has formed her adult personality. For breeds that do have a tendency to gain weight after spaying (e.g., beagles), proper diet and adequate exercise should be enough to prevent significant problems.

The best time to perform ovariohysterectomy is before the first heat but traditionally not earlier than five to six months of age. In any case, the surgery is easiest to perform when bitches are young and lean (it is therefore easier on the dog), and females who are spayed before their first heat have a lower incidence of mammary tumors (breast cancer) than females spayed later. Some people (but not most veterinarians) feel that it is better for a bitch to go through her first heat before spaying. In general, the heat has no beneficial effect. (Females may act differently during heat, while pregnant, and while nursing, but once the puppies are gone, most return to their usual anestrous personalities.)

Some veterinarians and humane organizations have experimented by performing ovariohysterectomy on puppies less than ten weeks of age. Although this practice has not yet been proven harmful, it does subject incompletely vaccinated and physiologically less mature dogs to the stress of a major surgical operation. Also, some females spayed before full maturation of their genitalia are plagued with dermatitis around their vulvas for the rest of their lives due to its abnormally recessed position. Pet owners should consider these facts when selecting the age at which to spay their females.

In most good veterinary hospitals the procedure for an ovariohysterectomy is similar to the following:

Veterinarians request that you withhold food from your dog for at least eight to twelve hours preceding surgery. This allows time for the stomach to empty, preventing vomiting and aspiration of the vomitus into the trachea and lungs during general anesthesia. Preanesthetic drugs are given to reduce apprehension before surgery and to prepare the body for general anesthesia. Anesthesia is usually induced with a short-acting drug given intravenously. Its effects last just long enough to allow the veterinary surgeon to place an *endotracheal tube* into the dog's windpipe *(trachea)*. This airway is the path via which gas anesthetic agents and oxygen are administered to maintain sleep during surgery; it also provides a ready means of resuscitation should an emergency arise.

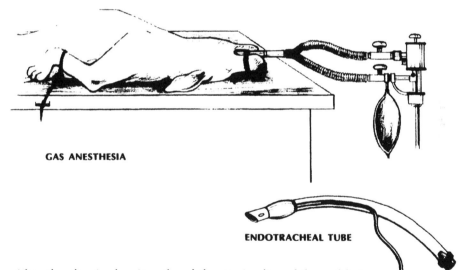

GAS ANESTHESIA

ENDOTRACHEAL TUBE

After the dog is sleeping, the abdomen is clipped free of hair, washed with surgical soap, and disinfected. The dog is then transferred to the surgery area and placed on the operating table belly up. An assistant stands by to monitor the anesthesia, breathing, and heart function. The veterinarian, who has been scrubbing his or her hands and donning sterile clothing, cap, mask, and gloves while the dog is prepared for surgery, steps in and places a sterile drape over the patient before surgery begins.

An incision into the abdomen is made at the midline. The length of the incision varies with the size of the dog and the difficulty of the surgery, but is usually one to four inches long. Most veterinarians use a special hooklike instrument to reach into the abdomen and pick up one horn of the uterus as it lies along the body wall. The uterine horn is brought out through the incision and followed to the ovary. Clamps are applied and the blood supply to the ovary is interrupted by *ligatures* (ties around blood vessels) or metal vascular clips. The ovary is cut away from its blood supply, which is allowed to return to the abdomen. The other uterine horn and ovary are brought to the incision and treated in the same manner. Then the uterine horns are followed to their point of attachment to the body of the uterus. Its blood supply is interrupted by ligatures or clips and the uterine body itself is ligated. A freeing incision is made through the uterus, and the horns and ovaries are removed. (Turn to pages 30–31 if you need to review the structure of the uterus and ovaries.) The inner part of the incision is closed with layers of absorbable suture material or stainless steel (which remains in place permanently); then the skin is *sutured* (stitched) closed. With modern anesthesia the dog begins to wake up shortly following the last stitches and is ready to go back to a kennel for final recovery. Most healthy dogs are completely themselves after one or two days following surgery. In fact, most feel so good that it is often a chore to try to restrict their exercise.

When you take your female home following the surgery, it's a good idea to take her temperature and examine the incision daily even if you are not given specific instructions to do so by your veterinarian. (These are good things to do following any surgery.) Fever and/or swelling, redness, or discharge at the incision site should alert you to call your veterinarian for advice. Normal feeding should resume twenty-four to forty-eight hours following surgery. Many veterinarians allow you to take your dog home before this time; if you do, provide small meals and water frequently but in small amounts at one time to avoid gastric irritation. Vomiting that occurs more than once or twice, especially if accompanied by inactivity, should prompt you to call the hospital where the surgery was performed for advice.

TUBAL LIGATION A few veterinarians and spay clinics perform *tubal ligations* (tying of the fallopian tubes so the ova cannot pass into the uterus). This involves the same type of abdominal entry as an ovariohysterectomy, and although it is effective in preventing pregnancy, it has definite disadvantages when compared to an ovariohysterectomy. It does not prevent *pyometra* (see page 179) or influence the development of mammary tumors. It does not prevent signs of heat. If you are *sure* you won't mind the signs associated with a female dog in heat—bloody drips, attracting males—you may choose a tubal ligation or, better in terms of health, a *hysterectomy* (removes the uterus but leaves one or both ovaries). Remember, however, that neither prevents the signs of heat or has an effect on the incidence of mammary tumors. People who choose a hysterectomy (or tubal ligation) often change their minds a year or two later and request additional surgery to remove the ovaries. Tubal ligation is not considered standard practice for female neutering in veterinary medicine.

ACCIDENTAL BREEDING

If your dog was bred accidentally, there are alternatives to having an unwanted litter. If you were planning to have your bitch spayed, your veterinarian can usually go ahead with the surgery. Particularly in the early stages, the surgery is not much more difficult than for a female in heat and the fee may be the same. In the later stages of pregnancy the surgery becomes more difficult and the fee increases accordingly. However, spaying is still probably the best solution to this difficult problem.

If you have not yet decided on the question of spaying and if you can get your dog to a veterinarian soon after breeding (ideally within the first twenty-four hours), an injection of an estrogen compound can be used to prevent pregnancy. The compounds used work by preventing implantation of the fertilized ova into their "beds" in the uterine wall. The signs of heat are prolonged following administration of these drugs, and sometimes extremely serious side effects leading to uterine infection or death of the bone marrow (followed by death of the patient) may accompany these treatments. Therefore your veterinarian will want to evaluate the situation thoroughly and will probably recommend other treatment.

Bitches that are more than thirty days pregnant can sometimes be induced to abort with several consecutive injections of prostaglandin, antiprogesterone, or antiprolactin drugs administered under veterinary supervision. These drugs and others have been used experimentally to terminate earlier pregnancies. An actual surgical abortion can be performed late in pregnancy if absolutely necessary. Methods similar to those used in humans have not generally been applied to dogs. Abortion in dogs, therefore, consists of *caesarian sections* in which the puppies are removed through uterine and abdominal incisions. This procedure usually results in blood loss, is stressful on the female, and is not encouraged by most veterinarians.

MALE BIRTH CONTROL

Castration is the surgical removal of the testes. A *vasectomy* is the surgical removal of a portion of the vas deferens (see page 29), which conducts the sperm from the testes to the urethra. Both of these operations will prevent a male dog from impregnating a female. (They are, however, inefficient methods of dog population control, since just one single unneutered male can impregnate many females.) If you live in an area where your male dog can roam unsupervised, a vasectomy (which has no effect on the ability or desire to breed) would be a good idea to prevent him from fathering unwanted litters and is socially responsible.

Castration is usually employed as a means of modifying undesirable behavior in male dogs such as territorial urination in the house and excessive aggression. Prepubertal castration prevents the development of sexual responsiveness in the male dog. Castration after puberty usually reduces aggressive behavior and sexual responsiveness. Some males, however, will continue to breed (but not impregnate) following castration, and some continue undesirable scent-marking behavior. In general, castration has no significant detrimental effects on dogs providing the neutered male receives adequate exercise and an appropriate diet. Castrated males *do* tend to gain weight if not managed carefully, and in some cases neutering is suspected to be associated with an increased incidence of *hypothyroidism* (low thyroid function) in adult male dogs.

Many animal population control advocates encourage the surgical neutering of male dogs by castration before six months of age. Although this effectively prevents breeding, males neutered at this age do not develop the characteristic secondary physical sex characteristics that distinguish mature male dogs (e.g., larger, better-defined muscles). Their behavior toward people is *not* adversely affected by early neutering. Should you desire normal male development and if you will be careful to prevent random impregnation of bitches by your pet, castration can be delayed until adulthood or avoided entirely.

Chemical castration induced by the injection of a sclerosing (scarring) agent directly into the testicle or epididymis (sperm storage area) has been used as a means of male neutering. This destroys the sperm-forming tubules and occludes the sperm exit. Ask your veterinarian if this technique should be considered for your dog.

CRYPTORCHIDISM

A *cryptorchid* ("hidden testicle") dog has only one *(unilateral crypt-orchidism)* or no testicles descended into the scrotum. If both testicles are not descended by six weeks of age, hormone injections given by a veterinarian may sometimes cause a delayed descent. Males with this condition should not be allowed to breed even if the treatment works, because the defect is inherited, as a genetic recessive. Breeding of the affected male's parents and siblings should also be discouraged. If both testes have not descended by six to eight months of age, you should assume that the condition is permanent. Retained testicles are more subject to tumor formation than normal ones, as well as to torsion (twisting around their blood supply, leading to strangulation of the testis); therefore it is advisable to have the retained testicle(s) removed. If the defect is unilateral, a vasectomy should be performed on the remaining testis to ensure that the defect will not be passed on.

BREEDING

DECIDING WHETHER TO BREED

Before you decide to breed your dog, ask yourself several questions. The first is, are you sure you will find good homes for the puppies? Even with purebred dogs, permanent *good* homes are difficult to find. There is an extraordinary excess of dogs (and cats) in this country. More than 27 *million* dogs and cats are impounded annually and more than 17 million are killed every year. Most animals entering animal shelters and pounds are killed. These are not just dogs who have strayed from home; many are pets who have been taken to the pound by owners who know that they will almost certainly be destroyed. They are unwanted gifts, cute Christmas puppies who because they have grown into adults have lost their cuddly charm, dogs bought on impulse from a pet shop window, unmanageable dogs who became so because no one took the time to train them properly, and others both purebred and mixed. If you are not *sure* your puppies won't end up in a pound or pet shop, and if you are not willing to provide a good home for puppies you can't find other homes for, do not allow your dog to reproduce.

Do you have a good place to keep the puppies and are you willing to care for them if the mother can't? Puppies aren't much trouble at all as long as their mother is taking care of them. If the female refuses to care for them or is unable to care for them, however, then you must assume the responsibility. Also, at about four weeks of age, when the puppies begin to eat solid food and can get around more easily, puppy rearing becomes more difficult. At this time the mother stops consuming the puppies' excreta and they are too young to housebreak, so you must be able to provide an adequate area in which to confine them when you can't be around picking up after them. This is one good reason to try to raise puppies in the spring and summer when, at least part of the time, they may be confined outside.

Why do you want to breed your dog? Almost everyone is awed by birth, and hardly anyone can ,esist the cuteness of a puppy, but the dog population cannot afford another litter bred solely so "the kids" or you can watch the birth. If this is the only reason for breeding, it might be better to make arrangements with a dairy, horse farm, or established kennel to watch a birth or to take advantage of films and books available on animal reproduction. If you are breeding for profit, you will find that it can be a full-time business to produce *quality* purebred dogs at a profit. Many purebred breeders have dogs as a hobby because they know they are likely only to break even or take a loss. If you are breeding so the female can "have the experience of being a mother," you are being too anthropomorphic. Dogs probably don't look forward expectantly to the experience of having puppies, and many (particularly those closely attached to humans) seem to prefer to neglect their puppies to be with their owners. Until the dog population reaches a more manageable size, our "best friends" will continue to experience mistreatment and neglect. Everyone, purebred breeders and pet owners alike, should think seriously before deciding to let their male or female breed and produce even a single litter.

BEFORE BREEDING   If you decide that it is reasonable to breed your dog, you need additional information. *Only outstanding individuals should be selected for breeding.* Both temperament and health should be given equal consideration, and if either is lacking, reproduction should not be permitted. Many physical abnormalities of dogs, including entropion, ectropion, cataracts, hip dysplasia, elbow dysplasia, retinal atrophy, idiopathic seizure disorders (epilepsy), tendency to *Demodex* infection and patellar luxation, are genetically influenced diseases and can be eliminated by appropriate selection of sires and dams. Diseases such as these cause unnecessary and extraordinary suffering for pets and expense for their owners. For more information, consult:

Foley, C. W., J. F. Lasley, and G. D. Osweiler, *Abnormalities of Companion Animals: Analysis of Heritability,* Iowa State University Press, Ames, Iowa 1979.

Clark, Ross D., and Joan R. Stainer, *Medical and Genetic Aspects of Purebred Dogs*, Veterinary Medicine Publishing Company, Edwardsville, Kansas, 1983.

In general terms, no animal affected with an inheritable disease or whose littermate or parent is affected should be allowed to reproduce. In some cases organizations such as the Orthopedic Foundation for Animals (OFA) and the Institute for Genetic Disease Control in Animals (GDC) can be used for screening of prospective dog parents. In any case, conformation should be considered carefully in regard to its effect on health right down to examining the mouth to be sure *both* parents have normal teeth and gums.

Plan far in advance of the female's anticipated heat to be sure all necessary treatments and screenings will be finished by the onset of proestrus. Live vaccines should not be given during pregnancy, but the female should be fully protected before breeding so she can pass on a protective level of antibodies to her puppies in the *colostrum* (first milk). Have a fecal sample examined by a veterinarian to be sure a female to be bred is free from intestinal parasites, which compete for nutrients. Blood tests are also desirable. The female should be found free from heartworms (see page 102). Both the male and the female should have a blood test for *canine brucellosis,* a serious bacterial disease of dogs that may cause spontaneous abortion and/or infertility and occasionally signs of illness not associated with the reproductive system. The causative organism, *Brucella canis,* is also capable of causing illness in humans.

It is generally best to avoid breeding a bitch on the first heat unless she is definitely full grown. By waiting until the second heat, she won't have to try to get enough nutrients to meet both requirements of growth and those of pregnancy. No special feeding is necessary before breeding, assuming your dog is already on a balanced diet, but avoid breeding obese females because they will have more difficulties at delivery. If your dog is over five years of age at the time you first consider breeding, definitely consider preventing pregnancy. Conception is less frequent and the incidence of difficult births is much higher in dogs who first whelp after the age of five.

BREEDING PROCEDURES

The ideal way to breed a female in order to ensure maximum litter size is to take her to the male's home and allow her to remain there during the whole estrus period—letting breeding occur at will. Emotional factors play an important part in determining whether or not a male dog breeds—a dog may not breed in unfamiliar surroundings or if he is fearful. Social factors also play a role; if the female does not "care for" the male, breeding often will not occur, so having

251

more than one male available increases the odds of success. If the male cannot be mated frequently with the female during estrus, then breeding should be allowed within twenty-four hours after the female first shows signs of estrus and, if possible, again forty-eight hours later.

ARTIFICIAL INSEMINATION Artifical insemination is used in special dog breeding situations (e.g., to avoid shipping dogs long distances). However, this technological means of reproduction eliminates the need for normal reproductive behavior and in the long run may be detrimental to natural means of reproduction if it is used indiscriminately.

SIGNS OF ESTRUS Female dogs in estrus often urinate more frequently than usual and may assume a partial leg-lifting posture. In the presence of a male, a normal female in true estrus will stand staunchly and wave her tail to one side to allow breeding to occur. You may also see a vertical lifting of the vulva *(winking* or *tipping)* in response to the presence of the male. If you don't have a male "teaser" dog, you can count the days from the beginning of bleeding and try breeding first on day ten or eleven, then every forty-eight hours afterward until two successful matings have occurred. This is probably the least reliable method. Your veterinarian can help you by examining a series of vaginal smears to give you an indication of when the female ovulates. Serial blood hormone measurements can also be of use in cases where the female's estrus cycle is atypical or the male dog is not readily available.

Play will often precede the time a female allows herself to be bred. The actual copulation may last five to thirty minutes, or slightly longer. The male mounts the female from behind, clasping her around the loin with his forepaws. During a series of rapid pelvic thrusts, intromission occurs; then the thrusts slow and a sperm-dense fluid is ejaculated. Engorgement of the bulbis glandis usually prevents the male from separating from the female at this time, which is called the *copulatory lock* or *tie.* During the tie the male will often rest on the hindquarters of the female or turn around so that the dogs are rump to rump. The tie is not necessary for fertil-

MOUNTED

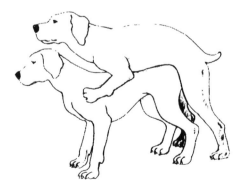

ization to occur since the sperm are ejaculated early in coition. Do not try to separate dogs found tied—it is painful for both male and female and will not prevent fertilization. Sperm survive about 30 hours in the female. Because ova survive about four days following ovulation, litters with several fathers are possible. So keep the female away from unwanted fathers after the breeding.

THE TIE

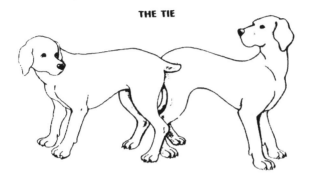

DETERMINING PREGNANCY

Between about three and five weeks following conception, it is often possible for a veterinarian to palpate (feel) the fetuses in the uterus through the abdominal wall. At this time they are distinct lumps in the uterus. This has been shown to be the most accurate aid to pregnancy diagnosis in the first month. Later it is often impossible to feel the pups. An ultrasound examination can detect pregnancies as early as day twenty, fetal heartbeats at day twenty-six. An X-ray film taken after about six and a half weeks of pregnancy (when the pups' bones are ossified) can be used for confirmation of pregnancy if ultrasound is unavailable. A blood test for pregnancy is also offered by some veterinarians. It is easy for a person unfamiliar with the reproductive cycle of the dog to think a dog is pregnant following estrus. Many dogs have an intensification of normal hormonal changes following estrus that results in a greater or lesser degree of false pregnancy *(pseudopregnancy)*.

FALSE PREGNANCY False pregnancy is characterized by deposition of abdominal fat, mammary gland development, and milk flow in varying degrees occurring about fifty to seventy days following estrus. Some dogs make a nest and go through pseudolabor. Some show a mothering instinct by adopting toys or other objects, and some are even capable of nursing puppies. Pseudopregnancy seems to occur most fre-

253

quently and intensely in females who have been bred. Hormones and/or *prolactin* (lactation stimulating hormone) inhibiting drugs can be administered by your veterinarian to relieve signs of severe pseudopregnancy. However, it is best to avoid hormone and/or drug treatment if possible. Females that become pseudopregnant once tend to have false pregnancies each time they come into heat. An ovariohysterectomy is indicated to prevent recurrent signs.

CARE DURING PREGNANCY

Pregnancy normally lasts fifty-eight to sixty-eight days. Most bitches whelp around sixty-three days. Pregnancies as short as fifty-seven and as long as seventy-two days have been recorded. The variation represents the discrepancy between the time of mating and the actual time of egg fertilization. Pregnancy increases the protein and calorie requirements of the mother, but no changes in caloric intake are necessary during the first six weeks. Throughout pregnancy it is extremely important not to overfeed and/or underexercise, in order to prevent obesity and poor muscle tone, which can cause a difficult delivery. High-quality proteins such as milk products (e.g., cottage cheese, yogurt), eggs, and muscle meat can be used to improve the protein quality of your dog's regular diet. However, the best diet to feed is a high-quality product that is complete and balanced without supplementation (see page 60). Later in pregnancy, as the dog's total caloric requirements increase (at around six weeks' gestation, caloric needs increase about 25%), high-quality proteins can be added to the regular diet. Commercial high-protein/high-energy or puppy rations are also suitable for use during the last weeks of pregnancy. Although food intake increases, caloric requirements on a *per pound* basis increase only slightly during pregnancy—to about 50 to 65 calories per pound per day. Increase the number of feedings per day as pregnancy progresses and continue multiple feedings throughout lactation. It is often impossible for a bitch to take in all the necessary food in one or two meals, particularly as the uterus enlarges and begins to compress the other abdominal organs. You can allow your female to self-feed as long as she is not becoming too fat. If food intake is poor, simply moistening a dry diet with water will often make it more palatable and increase food intake satisfactorily. Other supplements such as milk products, eggs, and muscle meat can be added as not more than 10% by volume to increase palatability further. If you are using a high-quality commercial ration as a basic diet, vitamin-mineral supplements are not necessary during pregnancy. If you are concerned about possible deficiencies, talk to a veterinarian, who can supply you with a balanced vitamin-mineral supplement.

Most dogs restrict their exercise sufficiently as the time of delivery approaches. In the last days before delivery, however, be sure not to encourage strenuous exercise (e.g., long hikes).

To minimize psychological stress, accustom your dog to a warm and draft-free whelping area well before the time of delivery. If you have provided your dog with a sleeping area from the time she was a puppy, there shouldn't be any trouble getting her adjusted to the whelping area. A whelping box should have sides high enough to keep the puppies from falling out, but low enough that the mother can get in and out easily. The best ones have a low shelf built around the inside perimeter that helps keep the bitch from accidentally crushing a pup between herself and the wall of the box. If you like, you can provide a completely enclosed whelping box with a door opening and removable top, but this is not usually necessary if you have only a single whelping female and she is going to have the pups indoors. The whelping box should be lined with several layers of clean newspaper at the time of delivery. You can use clean sheets or towels as well, but newspapers are easier to remove and discard during delivery.

WHELPING BOX

If you have a very long-haired dog, you may wish to gently clip (not shave) the hair away from the vulva and nipples before delivery. It makes delivery a little more tidy and makes it a little easier for the newborn pups to find the nipples, but is not a real necessity.

DELIVERY

About five days before the expected date of *parturition* (delivery) you may start taking your dog's temperature morning and evening. At the onset of the *first stage* of labor, the rectal temperature will drop transiently and markedly from the normal of 101–102.5°F (38.3–39.2°C) to as low as 98°F (36.7°C). At this time, or sometimes earlier, the female will lose her appetite and seek the nest box as labor usually follows in ten to twenty-four hours. Vomiting is a possibility. If you have failed to adjust her to the whelping area, your female may try to nest on your bed, in a closet, or in some other unsuitable spot. Take her back to the whelping box and stay with her until she becomes comfortable in the area. During the first stage of labor the female will shred and tear at the bedding, will often dig at the box floor, and may even pull hair from her own body in her attempt to make a nest. Panting and trembling are often seen, and her pulse rate will increase. Colostrum may drip from her nipples. Uterine contractions that move the pup from the uterine horn to the body of the uterus and cervix occur during this first stage, which may last twelve to twenty-four hours. A long first stage is particularly characteristic of a first pregnancy. If the signs last twenty-five hours or longer or your dog seems to pass into the second stage, then back to the first, or seems unusually uncomfortable, discuss the matter with your veterinarian before assuming everything is all right.

During the *second stage* of labor you will see forceful straining movements caused by the simultaneous contractions of the abdominal muscles and diaphragm. At the beginning of this stage you *may* see a small amount of straw-colored fluid passed at the vulva. This is due to the rupture of the *allantois chorion,* which covers the puppy as it passes into the vaginal canal. Although it may take as long as an hour or two for a pup to be delivered once the second stage begins, a veterinarian should be consulted if active straining continues without delivery of a pup in the first hour. The female may lie on her side or on her sternum. During the most vigorous portions of straining, some females stand and squat as if they were going to have a bowel movement. The *amnion* (membranous sac) enclosing the head of the puppy sometimes appears at the vulva. It may, however, rupture before the pup is delivered. Once the head and paws of the

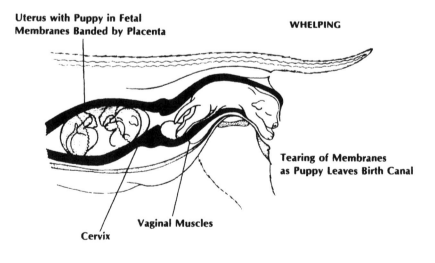

Uterus with Puppy in Fetal
Membranes Banded by Placenta

WHELPING

Tearing of Membranes
as Puppy Leaves Birth Canal

Vaginal Muscles

Cervix

puppy appear, complete delivery should be finished within fifteen minutes—if not, call your veterinarian. The nose and feet of the puppy should not appear and disappear each time the female strains. In the classic birth position the puppy is delivered with its sternum on the vaginal floor, nose first and front paws along the sides of his or her face. Thirty to forty percent of pups, however, are delivered rear legs first. This usually causes no problem.

As soon as the puppy is delivered, the amnionic sac (amnion) should be broken to allow the puppy to breathe. Inexperienced or nervous females may not do this. If this is the case, you must break the amnion by tearing it open with your fingers or the puppy will suffocate. If the umbilical cord is not broken during delivery, it is not necessary to break it immediately. Significant amounts of blood are found in the placenta, and by allowing the umbilical cord to remain unbroken, you give time for this blood to pass into the pup. Normally the mother nips the umbilical cord and breaks it as she cleans and licks the puppy following delivery. If she doesn't, a clean piece of thread or unwaxed dental floss should be tied around the cord about an inch from the puppy's body wall. Then cut or break the cord just beyond *(distal to)* the tie.

TIED UMBILICAL CORD

Normally the placenta (afterbirth) is delivered with or just after the puppy. It is a good idea to count the placentas as they are delivered to be sure all are passed. Retained placentas can cause uterine inflammation and infection (see page 179). It is normal, but unnecessary, for the female to eat the placenta following each delivery. It is best to let the bitch eat only one or two; the ingestion of too many can cause vomiting and diarrhea. The time of delivery of the placenta and the period of uterine rest that follows is the *third stage* of labor. During the rest period the bitch usually lies still and tends her pups. She may get up and take a drink of water. The rest period between puppies varies from ten to fifteen minutes to several hours. It is, however, not usually more than one or two hours. An average time for delivery of four or five pups would be six to eight hours, although normal parturitions may last up to twenty-four or even thirty-six hours. Consult your veterinarian if the interval between pups is more than four hours, especially if active straining occurs without prompt expulsion of a pup.

DIFFICULT DELIVERY (DYSTOCIA)

Difficult deliveries are usually caused by obstruction to delivery of the fetus or uterine inertia (see below). *Dystocia* must usually be treated with the help of a veterinarian. If any of the stages of labor seem abnormally long, if bloody, dark red, or black-colored fluid passes from the vaginal canal with no immediate live birth, or if your dog shows signs of excessive discomfort, call your veterinarian.

If you can see a puppy at the vulva but its delivery seems slow or it appears and disappears, you may be able to help deliver it. Wash your hands (a disinfecting soap is best) and lubricate a finger with a lubricant such as sterile petrolatum or sterile water-soluble jelly. Insert your finger into the vaginal canal and move it around the puppy, trying to determine where the head and front and rear legs are. You may be able to hook a front leg that is in an abnormal backward position and bring it forward. If the puppy seems fairly normally placed, grasp it with a sterile gauze pad, clean cloth, or your fingers, and gently pull with each contraction. It is best to try to grasp the pup around the shoulders to avoid excessive pressure on the head, and it is best to pull downward because the vagina is angled toward the ground. Do not pull on the amnionic sac surrounding the puppy. If the pup's head just seems too big to fit through the vulva, you can sometimes gently manipulate the edges of the vulva around the head. A veterinarian will sometimes make an incision at the upper part of the vulva to deliver a pup stuck at the bottom of the birth canal. This cut through the tissue *(episiotomy)* allows the vulvar opening to enlarge. It is not advisable to perform this procedure at home, unless it is impossible to get veterinary help.

If a retained placenta blocks delivery of a pup, you can often reach it. Grasp it with a gauze pad or cloth and gently but firmly pull until it passes out of the vaginal canal. Once an obstruction to delivery is relieved, a female will often have a prolonged rest period before the next puppy is delivered.

Failure of the uterus to contract efficiently *(uterine inertia)* may occur following prolonged straining to deliver a pup or may be primary as in the case of an obese, underexercised, or older dog. A form of uterine inertia can be caused by excessive excitement, or by other psychological stresses during delivery. This is why it is important to familiarize your dog with the whelping area well before delivery. It is also why strangers should not be present during delivery. A labor inhibited by psychogenic stresses can often be helped by having only one or two familiar people remain with the dog during delivery.

If no obstruction to delivery is found, your veterinarian may have to administer a drug called *oxytocin* to initiate new uterine contractions. Other drugs may be administered as well. If medical therapy does not initiate proper birth or there is some other problem that cannot be relieved with external manipulations, your veterinarian will want to perform a *cesarean section*—in which the puppies are removed through an incision in the abdomen. It is usually possible to spay your female at the time of such surgery. Unless the difficult birth is solely attributable to the puppies, it is probably best to have the spaying done. Dogs that have difficult births tend to repeat them. Most bitches are able to nurse and care for their puppies normally following cesarean section.

PUPPIES WHO WON'T BREATHE

If the bitch doesn't break the amnionic sac covering the puppy's head within a minute or two, you should. Then hold the puppy in your hands or wrap it in a towel. Support the head so it doesn't swing freely, then move the whole puppy vigorously in a wide arc from about chest to knee level. At the end of the arc the pup's nose should

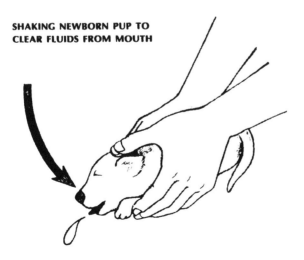

SHAKING NEWBORN PUP TO CLEAR FLUIDS FROM MOUTH

point toward the ground. This helps clear excess fluids from the nose and major airways. Other methods of removing excess fluids are to put your mouth over the puppy's nose and mouth and suck or to use an infant ear syringe to suck the fluid from the puppy's mouth and throat. After clearing the airways, rub the chest and body of the puppy with a rough towel. If the pup still does not start to breathe and cry, take in a breath of air, place your mouth over the pup's nose and mouth, and blow gently until you see the chest expand. Remove your mouth and let the puppy exhale, then repeat. Gentle, brief finger pressure on a pup's chest also helps stimulate respiration. (Using mouth-to-nose and -mouth resuscitation and/or airway clearing carries some small risk of infection for humans should the pup be contaminated with certain bacteria, so avoid it when possible.) Shaking and towel drying even healthy puppies is a good idea if the mother is not interested or is too slow.

CARE OF THE FEMALE FOLLOWING DELIVERY

Within twenty-four hours following parturition it is advisable to take the mother and pups to a veterinarian for examination or at least consult your veterinarian by telephone. During a veterinarian's exam the mother can be palpated to determine whether all the pups have been delivered. Some veterinarians administer an injection of oxytocin, which causes the uterus to contract, expelling excess fluids and any placenta that may remain. This also stimulates milk letdown. However, the need for this step is questionable as normal puppy nursing stimulates oxytocin release from the pituitary gland and achieves the same effect naturally. The veterinarian can also examine the pups for abnormalities. (If the pups are to have cosmetic surgery, page 266, wait to bring them in for examination until that time.)

A large amount of dark green, mucoid material called *lochia* is discharged from the vulva following the delivery. Within a week this discharge normally changes to a small amount of odorless brown or reddish material. Within another week, the discharge is usually clear mucus. If discharges persist beyond fourteen to twenty days, are accompanied by fever, are odorous or abnormal in amount, or look like pus or pure blood, do not wait further. Take your dog to a veterinarian for a thorough examination. (A rectal temperature of 102.5–103°F [38.3°–39.4°C] soon after whelping is not unusual and may persist for two or three days.)

Within twenty-four hours following delivery your dog should be normally interested in eating and drinking. For the first few days her diet can be the same as that preceding delivery. As lactation progresses, the rule of thumb is to feed the normal maintenance requirement *plus* 100 calories per day per pound of puppies. As in pregnancy, protein requirements for lactation are higher than normal maintenance levels and commercial foods designed for maintenance will not provide adequate nutrition. By the end of lactation a female may well be consuming three times as much food as she was before breeding. Again, however, the best guide is the appearance of the dog. If she looks thin and "worn out," her diet may need adjustment. Diarrhea in the nursing mother often indicates that a diet inadequate in energy is being fed. Poor-quality, high-fiber diets cause the mother to consume large volumes of food in an attempt to meet her nutritional requirements, and diarrhea soon follows. Avoid this problem by offering only good-quality high-protein/high-energy foods to nursing females. Balanced vitamin-mineral supplements are probably most beneficial when used during lactation.

PROBLEMS FOLLOWING PARTURITION

The common problems affecting the female following parturition are infection of the uterus *(acute metritis)*, inflammation of the mammary glands *(mastitis)*, and milk fever *(puerperal tetany)*. These problems are covered on pages 179, 141, and 209.

CARE OF NEWBORNS

ORPHAN PUPPIES

Many new mothers who need help with the first care of their newly delivered puppies care for them successfully later. So don't worry too much if your dog seems a clumsy mother to start. First-time mothers may not have much milk during the first twenty-four hours. This too is not cause for concern unless it continues. Bitches who ignore or actively reject their litters may be helped by tranquilizers, which your veterinarian can prescribe. In some of these cases, however, and in cases where the female dies, you must take the mother's place. A normal litter is quiet, and the puppies sleep most of the time when not nursing. Each puppy should gain 5–10% of his or her birth weight each day following birth. Normally the birth weight should double in ten to fourteen days. Puppies who fail to gain weight, cry, and squirm continually should alert you to look for signs of neglect or illness such as weakness, inability to nurse, diarrhea, or lowered body temperature (see page 262). If you find signs of illness, have the litter examined by a veterinarian, since treating very young puppies is difficult.

PUPPY'S AGE IN DAYS	NORMAL RECTAL TEMPERATURE (°F)	(°C)
1	92–97	33.3–36.1
2	95–98	35.0–36.7
5	96–98	35.6–36.7
7	96–98	35.6–36.7
14	97–98	36.1–36.7
21	98–99	36.7–37.2
28	99–101	37.2–38.3

If at all possible, the puppies should suckle the first milk or colostrum. It is rich in antibodies that can protect them against disease during the first weeks of life. Puppies are best able to absorb these special proteins through their intestine for twenty-four to thirty-six hours after birth. Should orphan puppies fail to suckle colostrum, contact your veterinarian for advice on immunization.

Puppies who must be separated from their mothers must be kept in a warm environment free from drafts because they have difficulty controlling their body temperature. From birth to about five days of age the room or box temperature should be 85–90°F (29.4–32.2°C); from five to twenty days, about 80°F (26.7°C). After twenty days the environmental temperature should be lowered gradually to somewhere between 70° (21.1°C) and 75°F (23.9°C) by the fourth week. The best way to provide the proper temperature for orphan puppies, if you don't have an incubator, is to use a heating pad. Water-circulating pads prevent burns, which may occur when electric pads are used. Hang the heating pad down one side of the box and onto about one fourth of the bottom. Then adjust the temperature control to maintain the proper air temperature. By covering only part of the floor, you allow the puppies to get away from the heat if necessary. For pups less than seven days of age, place the pad only on the side of the box, since their reflexes are not sufficiently developed to permit them to move if they are becoming overheated by the pad. The heating pad and box bottom should be covered with newspaper, cloth, or diapers that are changed each time they become soiled. Although newborns cannot stand or walk, they move with a swimming motion. The floor covering should provide firm footing to help them move and to avoid splaying of the legs, which can interfere with the normal development of walking (affected pups are called "swimmers"). Many authorities recommend that each puppy be kept in a separate compartment until two or three weeks of age to keep them from sucking each other's ears, tails, feet, and genitals, but if they are allowed to suckle sufficiently at each nursing period, you will probably find that this is not necessary and can thereby avoid this unnatural rearing practice.

Research indicates that puppies handled daily are more emotionally stable and resistant to stress. This does not mean, however, that children should handle them without direction or that they should be handled by strangers, who can carry disease. **NORMAL PUPPY DEVELOPMENT**

Expect the dried umbilical cord to fall off a normal puppy two to three days following birth. Although puppies are blind at birth, vision is present when the eyes open around ten to fifteen days of age. The eyes are normally blue-gray when they first open and change to the normal adult color by four to six weeks of age. Newborn pups can hear even though the ear canals are closed. The ear canals open at about two weeks of age. Puppies can normally support their weight on their front legs between one and two weeks of age and begin walking just after two weeks although they are not steady on their feet until they are three weeks old. Tail wagging and barking appear around this same time.

Orphan puppies should be fed a formula that most approaches the composition of normal bitches' milk. Although you can get by with home formulas made from cows' milk, improper formulas have been associated with cataract formation in pups fed them. Commercial formulas (e.g., Orphalac, Esbilac, Unilac, Veta-Lac, Havolac) are available in pet stores and from some veterinarians and come much closer to the real thing. These formulas can be used to supplement-feed large litters as well. The best way to determine how much formula each puppy needs is to weigh the puppy and use a table of caloric requirements. The required amount of formula is then divided into three or four portions fed at six- to eight-hour intervals. **FEEDING ORPHAN PUPPIES**

AGE IN WEEKS	CALORIES NEEDED DAILY/POUND (/KILOGRAM)
1	About 60 (130)
2	About 70 (150)
3	About 80–90 (180-200)
4+	Over 90 (over 200)

[Example: A ½-pound (225-gram) puppy needs ½ × 60 = 30 calories per day during the first week of life, or about 1 ounce (30 grams) of formula containing 1 calorie per gram.]

If you supply the proper caloric requirements, you do not need to feed a puppy more than three times a day. However, if the puppy cannot take in the required volume at three feedings, the number of feedings must be increased. At each feeding the puppy should eat until just comfortably full—not until the abdomen is tight and distended. A steady weight gain and a normal stool are indicators that the puppy is being properly fed. Expect a healthy puppy to gain one to two grams each day for each pound of expected adult weight (two to four grams per day per kilogram adult weight).

HOME FORMULAS FOR ORPHAN PUPPIES

8 fl oz (240 ml) fresh whole cow's milk	26.5 oz (795 ml) whole cow's milk
1 (15 g) egg yolk	6.5 oz (195 ml) cream (12% fat)
1 drop multiple infant vitamins	1 (15 g) egg yolk
1 tsp corn oil	1.5 tsp (6 g) bone meal
2–3 drops cod-liver oil	1 tsp 4 g) citric acid
	2,000 IU Vitamin A
	500 IU Vitamin D
About 30 calories per ounce	About 38 calories per ounce

All formula is best fed after warming to body temperature (about 100°F [37.8°C]). Keep all unused formula refrigerated and all equipment used scrupulously clean to avoid introducing infection. Formula can be administered with an eyedropper, syringe, nursing bottle, or stomach tube. A nursing bottle and anticolic nipple are usually easiest and safest in inexperienced hands. The holes in the nipple should be enlarged if the formula does not drip slowly from the nipple when the full bottle is inverted. Be sure the nipple size is suitable for the size of puppy you are trying to nurse. Tiny puppies need to be fed with a toy doll's bottle. Hold the puppy on its stomach. Gently separate the puppy's lips with your fingers and slip the nipple in. A healthy, hungry puppy will usually suck vigorously after tasting the milk. Use of a towel will give the puppy something to push and knead against as if nursing naturally.

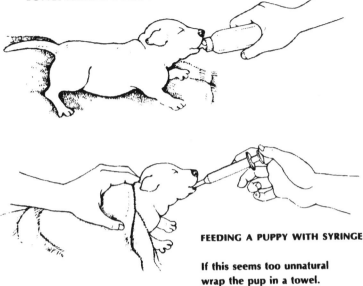

BOTTLE FEEDING A PUPPY

FEEDING A PUPPY WITH SYRINGE

**If this seems too unnatural
wrap the pup in a towel.**

Weak puppies may have to be held vertically and formula placed slowly in their mouths. *Do not* place a puppy on its back to feed it or squirt liquid rapidly into its mouth. These methods can cause aspiration of the fluid into the lungs, which will be followed by pneumonia. If you wish to use a stomach tube for feeding (the fastest method), ask your veterinarian for a demonstration.

After each feeding the puppies should be stimulated to urinate and defecate. Moisten a cotton swab, tissue, or soft cloth with warm water and gently, but vigorously, massage the ano-genital area. Nursing puppies' stools are normally firm (not hard) and yellow. If diarrhea develops, the first thing to do is dilute the formula by about half with the addition of boiled water. If this does not help within twenty-four hours, consult a veterinarian. Cows' milk often causes diarrhea because of its high lactose content.

WEANING

Between the ages of two and a half and three weeks you can start to wean most puppies, although the normal bitch doesn't begin this process naturally until the puppies are three to four weeks old. Place a shallow pan of formula on the floor of their pen. At first the puppies will step and fall into it and make a general mess, but soon they will be lapping at it. When this stage is reached, high-protein pablum, meat baby food, or puppy chow can be added to make a gruel. After the puppies begin eating the gruel, the amount of formula can be decreased until they are eating solid food and drinking water. Eggs, cottage cheese, yogurt, and meat may be added to their diet as they become adjusted to eating solid food. However, it is best to encourage the consumption of a complete, balanced commercial growth food instead of relying on human foods. All changes in feeding should be made gradually to avoid causing digestive upsets. Puppies with a natural mother should be allowed to continue nursing during the weaning process, until they are eating well-balanced meals of solid food on their own. During this time the mother may sometimes regurgitate food in front of her puppies. This is a normal part of the natural weaning process, similar to the behavior of wolves in the wild, and is no cause for worry.

By five weeks of age puppies have most of their baby teeth, so that the mother will usually become more and more reluctant to nurse. As the puppies increase their intake of solid food, you should decrease the mother's intake of food and gradually restrict the nursing time. Weaning may be achieved completely this way, but if there is an actual weaning day offer the bitch water but withhold food, or feed only a small portion of the maintenance diet on that day. Over the following five days gradually increase food back to the normal maintenance level. This procedure helps decrease her milk production.

If milk production does not seem to decrease rapidly enough and the female seems uncomfortable, *do not* remove milk from the glands. This will only prolong the problem. Cold packs applied to the mammary glands may help relieve discomfort. If the problem is severe, consult a veterinarian for help.

COSMETIC SURGERY

DEWCLAW REMOVAL, TAIL DOCKING, EAR CROPPING Removal of the dewclaws, part of the tail *(docking),* and part of the ear *(cropping)* are surgical procedures performed mainly for cosmetic reasons. Dewclaws are often loosely attached and tend to become caught and torn. This is a particular problem of hunting dogs and dogs that roam in the country. Removal of dewclaws and tail docking should be done by your veterinarian during the first week of life (three days of age is best), when anesthesia is not necessary and the surgery is the least traumatic. Which claws are to be removed and how much of the tail to remove varies with breed standards. If you have mixed-breed puppies or do not plan to sell your purebred puppies for show purposes, you may choose not to have the tails docked but just to have the dewclaws removed if they are particularly loose.

The optimal time for ear cropping varies with the breed, but is usually around nine weeks of age. This is purely a cosmetic procedure. It should be done only if the puppy is going to be shown in countries where natural ears are prohibited. (People who raise breeds required to have cropped ears can eliminate this old-fashioned requirement by lobbying the appropriate kennel clubs to change breed standards to accept the natural ear.) Although some puppies seem to experience little discomfort following ear cropping, many are extremely uncomfortable. In order to get many types of ears to stand, you must work seriously for weeks with various types of taping and supporting materials—an ordeal for both you and your puppy. In Canada and England dogs are shown without cropped ears, and tail docking is discouraged as well. If veterinarians and owners in the United States would refuse these surgeries, the breed standards could be changed and unnecessary surgical procedures could be abandoned.

UMBILICAL HERNIAS AND OTHER CONGENITAL DEFECTS

Serious birth defects are uncommon in mixed-breed puppies, but each member of the litter, purebred or not, should be examined soon after birth and watched as he or she develops to detect any defects that may be present. Problems to look for soon after birth include cleft palate (hole in the hard palate, which interferes with normal nursing), imperforate anus (anus sealed closed by skin, preventing stool passage), and umbilical hernia. A *hernia* is a protrusion of a part of the body or an organ through an abnormal opening of the surrounding tissues. A common hernia occurring in dogs is the umbilical hernia, in which a portion of fat or internal organs protrudes through an incompletely closed umbilical ring. Most umbilical hernias are present at birth, but some may be acquired if the mother chews the umbilical cord too short or as a result of other careless handling of the cord. Umbilical hernias in dogs are usually small, often get smaller as the puppy ages, and usually do not require surgical repair. If your puppies have large umbilical hernias or hernias that you can push into the abdomen with your finger, consult your veterinarian about the necessity of repair.

Heart defects are sometimes present at birth and are sometimes the cause of *runt* pups (smaller-than-average-size pups). Pups with such defects who survive until weaning are usually diagnosed abnormal by a veterinarian at their first physical exam.

INFANTILE PUSTULAR DERMATITIS

Pustular dermatitis is a skin condition of young puppies, usually less than three weeks of age. You may first notice crusts or scabs that stick the hairs together or a wet, sticky area of skin. These areas are often on the head or neck, but may be anywhere on the body. If you look closely over the puppy's body, you may see small red or pus-filled bumps. If you don't notice these early skin changes, you may first see a large swelling in the *ventral* (under-the-neck) region, or sometimes one or more swellings occur unaccompanied by changes on the skin surface. This is usually a sign of infection and of abscessation of lymph nodes in the areas, and it needs immediate veterinary attention. In this stage the syndrome is often called "puppy strangles." Abscesses must usually be opened and drained (see page 135). Daily gentle cleansing of the affected areas with antiseptic soap such as povidone-iodine (Betadine) shampoo followed by *thorough* rinsing may be sufficient to control localized skin infections. Although many scientists believe this condition is not due to bacterial infection, staphylococcal or streptococcal bacteria are sometimes isolated from the affected areas, and usually washing should be combined with antibiotic treatment prescribed by your veterinarian. Puppies that are severely affected are treated with corticosteroid drugs, which must be administered cautiously under a veterinarian's care.

If you need more information on breeding and reproduction, the following book may be helpful:

Joshua, D. Edward, and Joan O. Joshua, *Reproductive Clinical Problems in the Dog,* 2nd ed., Butterworth-Heinemann, Stoneham, Mass., 1988.

HOW TO SEX PUPPIES

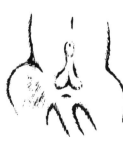

Male

Female

6

YOU, YOUR DOG, AND YOUR VETERINARIAN

HOW TO FIND A "GOOD" VETERINARIAN

Choosing a veterinarian is one of the most important decisions you will have to make concerning your dog's health. Just as in any profession, there are bad veterinarians as well as good ones. There are no specific rules for finding the best one for your dog. However, considering some of the following points may help you in your search.

Find a veterinarian with whom you feel comfortable. No matter how skilled the veterinarian, you cannot make the best use of the services of someone you dislike personally or feel uncomfortable being around.

A good veterinarian explains things thoroughly and in a manner you can understand. However, veterinary medicine is a career that puts great demands on an individual's time, and your veterinarian may sometimes seem rushed or fail to explain things thoroughly to you. This is understandable, but if it happens routinely and you are disturbed about it, let your veterinarian know. There is no need for your veterinarian to give explanations in totally technical terms. Medical terminology is more exact but can be confusing, so most matters should be explained in general terms that you can understand. Veterinarians who continually rely on technical language when discussing your dog's health may be on an "ego trip" or trying to "snow" you, but because they are so familiar with medical terms, sometimes the reason is simply that they forget that you aren't. Let your veterinarian know if you are having trouble understanding, and request a simpler explanation.

Good and bad veterinarians exist in all age groups. Don't fall into the trap of believing that an older veterinarian knows more and a younger one less, or vice versa. In general, veterinarians who have been in practice for a while have more experience, but remember, not everyone learns from experience. A recent graduate often has better knowledge of new techniques, but may seem clumsy or insecure. Keep these things in mind, and try to evaluate your veterinarian on the quality of care your pet receives. The best veterinarians are always improving their skills through continuing education acquired through courses, videos, and journals. The demand to update medical skills continually will sometimes call your veterinarian away from practice when you wish he or she were in. However, a good veterinarian will always provide a referral or a replacement veterinarian for you at those times.

One way to evaluate a new veterinarian is through your first office call. You should see the veterinarian personally, not be required to leave your dog and "check back later," or have veterinary assistants take care of the whole problem. The people who handle your pet, both the assistants and the veterinarian, should seem capable and use a minimum of restraint on nervous animals unless they have made an attempt to "make friends" without success. A thorough physical examination should be performed and questions regarding your dog's medical history should be asked. Unless your dog sees the veterinarian extremely frequently (more than once a week), a general physical should always be performed at each visit. (Since dogs can't tell us their problems, we have to look for them, and new problems can easily arise from one visit to the next.)

A clean office and new equipment are often indicative of good veterinary care. But don't be misled by a fancy "front room." Most good veterinarians will allow you to see the whole hospital *at a convenient time.* One who won't may have something to hide. Some veterinarians have fancy equipment but don't use it or use it improperly. Veterinarians in small towns or rural areas may not have enough demand to necessitate expensive specialized equipment in their offices, but even a simple veterinary clinic should be clean and orderly. Again, try to judge your veterinarian on the kind of medicine practiced, not entirely on appearances.

FEES It is as difficult to judge a veterinarian by his or her fees as it is according to the kind of equipment in the office. What is a reasonable fee varies between geographical areas and types of practices. In general, it is fair to expect to pay more for veterinary services at hospitals, where the latest equipment and specialized services are available, since it costs the veterinarian more to maintain such services. (Remember, most veterinarians, unlike physicians, don't have large central hospitals for patients who need special care and so must maintain their own.) *If you are concerned about the fee,* be sure to ask your veterinarian about it if he or she doesn't bring up the matter first. Most veterinarians assume it is their responsibility to practice medicine, the client's responsibility to inquire about the costs. A better rapport is established if you tell your veterinarian at the outset whether there will be monetary limitations. If so, a thorough discussion of what limitations this will place on achieving a diagnosis or a successful treatment can take place before proceeding with a medical plan. (In some states third-party payment, i.e., pet health insurance, or pet health maintenance plans may be available. Medical costs are spread among pet owners and can result in lower individual costs for veterinary care. However, many veterinarians believe that the traditional fee-for-service in veterinary medicine has actually helped keep overall veterinary costs for pet owners lower since the individual pet owner remains conscious of the actual costs of services, unlike in our human medical system, where patients are covered by medical insurance.) Should there be a fee or treatment dispute you cannot resolve with your veterinarian, contact the ethics committee of your local or state veterinary association and/or the American Veterinary Medical Association Judicial Council in writing. Serious issues of medical competence should also be referred to your state's veterinary medical licensing agency.

REFERRALS

Veterinarians who don't maintain specialized equipment and expertise must refer some cases. A good veterinarian recognizes his or her limitations. Veterinarians who won't make referrals when requested may be trying to hide their own inadequacies.

EMERGENCY CARE

Choose a veterinary clinic that provides emergency service or will be able to refer you to emergency care when necessary. Some communities have central emergency services that work closely with the local veterinarians; others do not. Find out what your veterinarian or the community provides while your dog is healthy so you won't waste precious time when a true emergency arises.

HOW TO BE A "GOOD" CLIENT

Since veterinarians are people and as such aren't infallible or tireless, they appreciate consideration on your part. If you keep a few simple courtesies in mind and try to practice them, these signs of appreciation will make most veterinarians respond with their best efforts.

If your veterinarian makes appointments, try to be on time. This keeps the veterinarian on schedule and helps prevent a long wait for others. Avoid "dropping in" with your dog without an appointment; call ahead if you have a sick pet and cannot wait another day. Never drop in for routine preventive care such as vaccination or deworming unless your veterinarian chooses not to use an appointment system. When you make appointments, your pet can be scheduled at the best time for a thorough and efficient evaluation of the problem and you can be saved a long wait. And when you do come in, be sure to bring your dog on a leash or in your arms to prevent mishaps and disturbances in the waiting room.

Avoid dropping your dog off for care unless your veterinarian specifically directs you to. Most people would never consider dropping their child off at the pediatrician's, but many seem to expect that veterinarians should provide "one hour, one stop" service. Your dog usually receives better care if you discuss the problem with your veterinarian as the examination is performed. If your animal is very sick and it is impossible for you to wait during an office visit, call ahead and discuss the problem with the veterinarian first. He or she may be able to advise you on home treatment, may be able to make an appropriate drop-off arrangement once the history of the problem is clear, or at least may be able to deal with the problem more calmly than if you show up in a rush hoping to leave your pet.

Do not disturb your veterinarian for nonemergency matters at night, on holidays, or during his or her other time off. If you have any doubts about the emergency nature of an illness, call, but don't call just for general information.

Don't expect your veterinarian to make a diagnosis over the phone or solely on the basis of a physical examination. And don't expect the veterinary clinic to be a drugstore, supplying drugs on demand. Competent veterinarians interested in your dog's health want to examine your pet and may require laboratory tests before prescribing drugs or making a diagnosis, no matter how sure you are of what the problem is. They do this not "to hassle" you, but to protect your dog as well as themselves. *If* you think the doctor may be performing "unnecessary" diagnostic tests, clarify the situation with a thorough discussion of the information expected to be gained by performing them. Though most veterinarians won't diagnose over the phone, don't feel that you can't even call your veterinarian for advice. Just be prepared with some solid facts. If you can tell your veterinarian whether or not your dog has a fever, what the basic signs of illness or injury are, and how long they have been present, he or she will probably be willing to give you some help over the telephone in spite of a busy schedule. If you can't supply such information, though, don't be surprised if you are told that it is impossible to help you over the telephone.

Don't let signs persist for several days without or in spite of home care before consulting a veterinarian. It is extremely frustrating for a veterinarian to see an animal die of an illness that could have been treated successfully if professional care had begun sooner. And once you have consulted a veterinarian, *follow directions.* It is quite irritating to a veterinarian to have someone complain that a treatment didn't work only to find out later that the medication was not used, or was used improperly. If you are having trouble, notify your veterinarian, but don't stop treatment without his or her advice.

A long-term relationship with an individual veterinarian is ideally developed over the years of a dog's life starting in puppyhood. The veterinarian becomes the dog's "best friend" in the veterinary clinic and has an excellent opportunity to become familiar with the dog's normal health and behavior as well as with any medical problems. The dog owner and the veterinarian have the opportunity to develop mutual understanding and respect, which are difficult to establish if you first meet over a serious medical problem. Learn to use your veterinarian as a resource for your animal's health. Know that help is there when you need it, but use this book, your patience, your common sense, and your intuition to take most of the responsibility for your dog's health. This book is intended as a tool to help you determine the limits of your responsibility and when you should draw on the veterinarian's resources. By using it in this way you will be practicing preventive medicine and may forestall illness and extra medical costs before they develop. Remember, your relationship to your dog, your moods, and your attitude toward his or her health and well-being are vital factors in the health of your pet and the effectiveness of your veterinarian. If you can temper your concern for your animal with an objectivity acquired through the knowledge you have gained about health care, you will avoid needless emotional upset and promote the growth of the three-way relationship of health among you, your dog, and your veterinarian.

INDEX OF SIGNS

diarrhea (*cont.*)
  194, 195, 196, 197, 198, 199, 200,
    201, 205
  bloody, 88, 90, 94, 167
  in newborn puppies, 261, 265
  in nursing mother, 261
  with vomiting, 165, 167
dilated pupils, 187, 193, 195, 196, 197
  and nonresponsiveness to light, 187
discharge:
  from any body opening, 214
  from ear, 20, 116, 145, 146
  from eye, 86, 101, 142, 143, 150
  from nose, 32, 86, 130, 147, 150–51,
    152
  from penis, 175, 176
  from prepuce, 175, 176
  from vagina, 176, 177
  from vulva, 175, 179
  from wound, 134
discoloration:
  of hair, 129, 142
  of milk, 141
  of skin, 141, 153, 214
  of teeth, 24, 58, 149
  of urine, 175, 178, 185, 187
drinking, increased, 89, 126–27, 175, 179,
    195, 216
drooling, 85, 110, 148, 166, 195, 196,
    197, 201, 204
dryness:
  of coat, 65, 140
  of eyes, 128, 143–44
  of mouth, 128
  of skin, 140

emaciation, 99

fainting, 215
fever, 86, 88, 89, 90, 115, 127, 150–51,
    165, 167, 178, 179, 209
  see also temperature, lowered
flatulence (intestinal gas), 95, 169–70

gagging, 148, 150, 215
gait, abnormal, 158, 161
gastrointestinal disturbances: *see* flatulence
grass eating, 164–65
growth, poor, 95

hair loss, 17, 109, 116, 118, 129, 139,
    214
  circular area of, 132
  irregular, 132
head:
  shaking, 116, 145
  tilting, 147
heart sounds:
  absence of, 186, 187
  irregularities in, 115, 204
  murmurs, 215
  rapid, 182, 193, 215
  slowed, 208
hemorrhage, 194
hiccups, continuous, 172
hives, 205
hunched-up abdominal appearance, 168

inability to nurse, puppies, 261
incoordination, 191, 198

inflammation:
  of eye, 115
  of kidney, 115
irritation:
  of eye, 101
  of skin, 200

lameness, 131, 137, 153–54, 156, 160,
    162, 214
  foreleg, 160, 161, 163
  hindleg, 158, 163
  of joints, 213
licking:
  at anus, 171
  at feet, 129, 131
  at prepuce, 176
  at vulva, 176, 177
light intolerance, 88
limping, 137, 138
listlessness, 86, 90, 162, 167, 178,
    179
lowered body temperature: *see*
  temperature, lowered
lumps: *see* bumps and lumps

manure eating, 170
motor control, loss of, 190
mucous membranes:
  congested, 207
  dryness of, in mouth and eyes, 128
  gray, blue, or white, 187
  pale, 194
muscle tremors, 86, 93, 110, 191, 193,
    194, 195, 196, 197

nesting, 255–56
neurological abnormalities, 115

obesity, 172–75
oozing:
  deformed toenails, 132
  from skin, 118, 129

pain, 124, 153, 193, 194
  abdominal, 88, 165, 175, 178, 186–87,
    194, 195, 196, 197, 199, 200
  ear, 145
  eye, 142, 143, 144
  in joints, 158, 160–61, 213
  in mammary glands, 141
  in mouth, 148
  in neck region, 163
  kidney, 195
pale:
  gums, 206, 215
  mucous membranes, 187, 194
  skin, 208
  tongue, 187, 206, 215
panting, 207
paralysis, 85, 155, 164, 185, 194, 195,
    196, 197
  hindlimb, 93, 163
  sudden, 180
  tongue, 201
pawing:
  at ear, 147
  at eye, 144
  at mouth, 148
pneumonia, 86, 93, 98, 101
potbellies, 98

pulse:
  absence of, 187, 208
  rapid, 182, 207
  weak, 182, 208
pupils, dilated, 187
  and nonresponsiveness to light,
    187
pus: *see* discharge

raw areas:
  on footpads, 137
  on nose, 147
  on skin, 109
redness:
  of ears, 20, 145
  of eyes, 101, 130, 143, 144
  of feet, 118, 131
  of gums, 23, 59, 149, 207
  of neck skin, 109
  of penis, 176
  of pulp area in tooth, 149
  of skin, 109, 118, 129
  of vulva, 176
  of wound, 134
respiratory distress: *see* breathing
restlessness, 191, 193, 194, 195, 196,
    197, 209
restriction of motion, 158, 161, 163
retching, 102
  unproductively, 165
  see also gagging; vomiting
rigid body, 137, 163, 191
  see also stiffness

scabs:
  on nose, 147
  on puppies, 268
  on skin, 101, 117, 118, 129, 132
scaly skin, 65, 118, 132, 140
scooting on anal area, 171
scratching, 99, 101, 116, 117, 118, 119,
    129, 140
  at ears, 116, 145, 147
shedding: *see* hair loss
shivering, 127, 208
shock, 128, 180, 182, 193, 205
slowed response to commands, 212
smell, abnormal:
  at anus, 15, 172
  from ears, 20, 145
  from mouth, 58, 149
  of skin, 140, 214
  at vulva, 179
sneezing, 130, 151–52
  with discharge, 152
  reverse, 152
  violent, 151
snorting, loud, 152
squinting, 144
stamina, loss of, 214
stiffness, 137, 158, 209, 214
  see also rigid body
stool:
  abnormal, 28
  bloody, 88, 90, 94, 100, 167
  eating, 170–71
  mucus in, 100
  voluminous, 72
  see also bowel control; constipation;
    diarrhea

straining:
  to defecate, 169
  to urinate, 177
stupor, 207
  see also coma, unconsciousness
sunken eyes, 128
swallowing, difficulty in, 137, 186,
    214
swelling, 153, 214
  in skin, 141
  of breast, 141, 214
  of ears, 141, 145
  on face, 136, 148, 205
  of feet, 118, 131
  of joints, 161
  of lips, 201
  lymph nodes, 26–27, 94,
    115
  prostate, 214
  of testicles, 178, 214
  of throat, 201
  of tongue, 201
  under neck of puppies, 268
  of vulva, 178
  of wound, 134, 135

tearing, 130, 142–43, 144
teeth:
  abnormal placement of, 23–24
  discolored, 24, 58, 86, 149
  marks on skin, small, 203
temperature, lowered, 127, 182, 208,
    255
  in newborn puppies, 261
testes, undescended, 249
thickened skin, 86, 129, 139
  of footpads, 86
  of nose, 86, 147
thirst, excessive: *see* drinking, increased
tiring easily, 102
tissue death in wound, 134

unconsciousness, 180, 182, 190,
    207
  with absence of heartbeat,
    187
  see also coma, stupor
urination:
  absence of, 187
  bloody, 175, 178, 185, 187
  decreased, 175
  difficult, 175, 177, 178, 187, 214
  followed by shock and collapse,
    205
  frequent, 175, 177, 195
  in house, 48–50, 216
  increased, 89, 175, 179, 216
  loss of control of, 175, 190

vomiting, 86, 88, 89, 90, 95, 98, 101,
    110, 130, 164–66, 178, 179, 180,
    186, 191, 193, 194, 195, 196, 197,
    198, 199, 200, 201, 205, 207, 216,
    255
  blood, 88, 165
  clear, frothy white or yellow fluid, 164,
    165–66
  with constipation, 168
  with diarrhea, 165, 167
  forcefully, 165

GENERAL INDEX

abdomen:
　bumps and lumps on, 14, 139, 142
　examination of, 21–22, 31
　pain in, 88, 165, 175, 178, 186–87,
　　194, 195, 196, 197, 199, 200
abortion, 247
abrasions, 153
abscesses, 135–36
　foreign body, 136
　of anal sac, 172
　of mammary glands, 141
　see also wounds
acne, puppy, 139
acupuncture, 159, 213
adrenocortical steroids, 235
age:
　equivalence (chart), 210
　indicated by teeth (chart), 27
　and life expectancy, 210
alcohol, isopropyl, 146, 237
allergic dermatitis, 129–131
allergy, 129–131, 140, 143, 205
American Boarding Kennels Association
　　(ABKA), 81
anal sacs:
　abscess of, 172
　anatomy of, 15
　expressing, 171–72
　inflammation of (anal sacculitis), 171–72
anatomy, 7, 8–38
　see also individual systems
anemia, 99, 104
anestrus, 241
antacids, 165
antibiotics, 233–35
antibodies, 35, 83
antidiarrheal drugs, 167
antifungal medications, 133
anus, 28
appetite, changes in, 126–27
　see also index of signs
arthritis, 115, 213
artificial respiration, 187–88
　for newborn puppies, 260
ascarids (roundworms), 97–99
aspirin, 159, 213, 236–37

balanoposthitis, 175–76
bandages:
　abdominal, back and neck, 229
　ear, 230
　foot, 228–229
　pressure, 183–84

bathing, 52–53, 107–108
bee stings, 205
behavior, 41–43
　changes in, 126
　see also index of signs
birth control, female, 242–49
　drugs, 243
　hysterectomy, 247
　with intravaginal devices, 244
　spaying, 244–46
　tubal ligation, 246–47
birth control, male, 248–49
bladder:
　control, loss of, 163
　examination of, 30–31
　inflammation of (cystitis), 176–77
　rupture of, 186–87
bladder infection: see cystitis
bladderworms: see tapeworms
blood:
　composition of, 34
　count (CBC), 34
　external loss of, 183–84, 185
　internal loss of, 185
　see also index of signs
"blue eye", 88–89
boarding your dog, 80–82
bones:
　anatomy of, 9–13
　feeding of, 50–51
　fractures of, 154–56
bowel:
　control, loss of, 163
　obstruction in, 98
　see also stool
breasts: see mammary glands
breathing:
　rate, 32
　see also respiratory system; index of
　　signs
breeding, 249–61
　accidental, 247
　before, 250–51
　deciding to, 249–50
　and determining pregnancy, 253–54
　procedures, 251–52
　and signs of estrus, 252–53
　see also parturition; pregnancy
bruises, 153
burns, 205–206
　chemical, 193, 206
　electrical, 206
　heat, 205–206

ABOUT THE AUTHOR

DR. TERRI MCGINNIS has loved and has had a rapport with animals from the time she was a child living in Southern California. Although, or perhaps because, she had few pets while growing up, her ambition was to become a veterinarian. She attained this goal in 1971, when she was awarded her Doctor of Veterinary Medicine degree from the University of California at Davis.

Since that time she has practiced in the San Francisco Bay area and has gradually limited her veterinary practice to care of companion animals. She began writing books for dog and cat owners in 1973. All have been popular, and *The Well Dog Book* and/or *The Well Cat Book* have been published in Great Britain, France, Australia, Germany, Holland, and Japan as well as in the United States. In addition to books, Dr. McGinnis has written articles about pet care for magazines, for an encyclopedia, and as a monthly columnist. She has served on the boards of her local veterinary association and the Oakland Society for Prevention of Cruelty to Animals. She has also made numerous television and radio appearances, hosting her own radio show in San Francisco for three years.